THE LAWS OF THE STATE OF NEW YORK AFFECTING CHURCH PROPERTY

THE CATHOLIC UNIVERSITY OF AMERICA
CANON LAW STUDIES
No. 388

The Laws of the State of New York Affecting Church Property

A DISSERTATION

*Submitted to the Faculty of the School of Canon Law
of the Catholic University of America in Partial
Fulfillment of the Requirements for the
Degree of Doctor of Canon Law*

BY

REVEREND JOSEPH P. MURPHY, A.B., J.C.L.
Priest of the Archdiocese of New York

THE CATHOLIC UNIVERSITY OF AMERICA PRESS
WASHINGTON, D. C.
1957

Nihil Obstat:

> Thomas O. Martin, Ph.D., S.T.D., J.C.D.,
> > *Censor Deputatus.*

Imprimatur:

> ✠ Francis Cardinal Spellman,
> > *Archbishop of New York.*

New York, May 3, 1957.

Printed by

THE PAULIST PRESS

401 WEST 59TH STREET

NEW YORK 19, N. Y.

51

TABLE OF CONTENTS

CHAPTER II

CHAPTER III

CHAPTER IV

FOREWORD

EVERY society of men has need of some form of property to attain the end for which it was established. Since the Catholic Church is a visible society of human beings with bodies as well as souls, it is evident that the Church must have temporal possessions for the fulfillment of its mission. The exercise of external worship, the support of its ministers, as well as the care of orphans, of the sick and of the aged, the education of youth—all involve the need of temporal possessions. Hence, the Church has always asserted its native right to acquire, hold and administer temporal goods for the attainment of the purpose for which it was founded, and that freely and independently of the civil authority. In the course of history, temporal society has accepted this claim of the Church in varying degrees. The basic purpose of this work is to see the degree to which this claim has been accepted in its laws by the State of New York.

Certainly, there are different ways in which this question can be approached. If one keep in mind the tremendous importance that the law of New York places on corporate personality as the basis of rights, one approach seems especially ideal. The first part of this work, therefore, will concern itself with an exposition of the Church's claim to juridical personality and the consequences which result from that claim. It must be kept in mind that, in the determination of the temporal rights and obligations of the Church before the law, it is of extreme importance to understand the status and forms of ecclesiastical legal personality. More particularly, the problem reduces itself to this: What view does the Church take of canonical personality, and how does that idea compare with the recognition actually accorded this juridical personality in the laws of the State of New York? This implies a statement of the legal standing which the Church is justly entitled to enjoy, and the extent to which it has obtained such a status under the present laws of New York.

The purpose of the second part of this work is to present the provisions of Church law regarding property dedicated by its owner's will to pious causes, and to indicate how these provisions may or may not be given effect in the New York courts. Special emphasis will be given here to the development of the present New York doctrine on charitable trusts.

The writer wishes to express his thanks to His Eminence Francis Cardinal Spellman, Archbishop of New York, for the opportunity to undertake graduate studies in Canon Law, and to the members of the Faculty of the School of Canon Law of the Catholic University of America for their kind assistance during the course of these studies and in the preparation of this work.

CHAPTER I

MORAL PERSONALITIES IN THE CHURCH

ARTICLE 1. NATURE OF MORAL PERSONALITY IN THE CHURCH

Section I. Historical Background

IN determining the temporal rights and obligations of the Church before the civil law, it is most important to understand the nature of the ecclesiastical legal personality. The fully developed doctrine on moral personality, as it can be found in the Code, is the result of a long historical process. A very brief examination of some of this history will prove helpful.

The notion of moral personality is not to be found in earlier Roman Law. The power to possess rights was in the beginning extended only to individual, natural persons.[1] While the Roman State, as a perfect juridical personality, had its own juridical power and its own patrimonial goods, nevertheless, it could not be said to be a juridical personality in the strict sense, since the State was looked upon as something transcendant so far as the private law was concerned, and private law recognized only private property. The patrimony possessed by the state was classified as *aerarium populi romani* in opposition to *res privatae*. The former was considered *res extra commercium*.[2]

In the time of the Republic certain groups known as *societates, collegia, sodalitates* did exist. Individuals were, therefore, capable of maintaining certain legal relations with each other and with society in general; but the ownership of any goods was not con-

---

[1] Brown, *The Canonical Juristic Personality with Special Reference to Its Status in the United States of America,* The Catholic University of America Canon Law Studies, n. 39 (Washington, D. C.: The Catholic University of America, 1927), p. 8 (hereafter cited Brown).

[2] Michiels, *Principia Generalia de Personis in Ecclesia* (2. ed. Parisiis-Tornaci-Romae: Desclée, 1955), 349 (hereafter cited Michiels); Brown, p. 10.

sidered as being vested in the association itself, as distinct from the individuals who made up such an entity.[3]

In the classical law of the Roman Empire not only the concept of moral personality,[4] but also the rights and specific types of such moral personalities can be found.[5] The principal reason for this legal recognition of such entities can be found in the substantial change which took place in the understanding of the purpose of the Republic in the political organization of the Roman people.[6] The evolution by which public property, *res publicae*, became a subject of private law was due at this time to the growth of the municipal government. These municipalities began to enjoy in some measure the status which persons had in private law. This was accomplished by means of an application to them of the principles regulating the acts and duties of individuals, which is just another way of saying that they were looked upon as moral personalities.[7]

The theory was further developed when it was made allowable for lawful societies such as communities of priests and vestal virgins,[8] military societies,[9] mutual benefit societies (*collegia tenuiorum*),[10] political societies,[11] etc., to have a certain proprietary capacity, and when there was acknowledged for them a status of legal persons in the realm of private law. For all such associations the law specified:

> quibus permissum est corpus habere collegii societatis sive cuiusque alterius nomine, proprium est ad exemplum reipublicae habere res communes, arcam communem et actorem sive syndicum, per quem tanquam in re publica, quod communiter agi fierique oporteat, agatur fiat.[12]

[3] Michiels, p. 349.

[4] It must be kept in mind that nowhere in the Roman Law will the distinction between physical and moral person be found. Yet, as will be seen, certainly the concept of "personality" can be found at this time.

[5] Cf. Brown, pp. 10-23.

[6] Michiels, p. 350.

[7] Brown, p. 10.

[8] D (32.38) 6.

[9] D (28.3) 6 & 7; C (6.62) 2.

[10] D (47.22) 1 pr.

[11] D (47.22) 1.

[12] D (3.4) (1.1).

So far reference has been made to what would now be called "collegiate moral personalities" or "corporations." In Roman Law Sources the technical name for such an entity was *universitas personarum*.[13] Concerning the "non-collegiate" moral personality [14] of the Code of Canon Law, it seems certain that such an entity was unknown not only in ancient but also in classical Roman Law.[15] Before the time of Justinian (527-565) all juristic personalities were known as corporations.[16]

At the time of Justinian, however, the "institution" [17] appeared in three forms: [18]

1. The institution was thought of as a fund administered by an individual person. Here the connection between the individual and the fund was necessary.[19]

2. The institution could have its *persona* in a corporation. Property was left to a corporation which administered it, but the property itself was not thought of as capable of standing alone.[20]

3. The institution could stand alone as an independent personality. Such a conception cannot be clearly found even in the law of Justinian. It was at this time, however, that juridical persons were gaining fuller legal recognition.

As has just been seen, at the time of Justinian there were institutions similar to the non-collegiate moral personalities contemplated in the present Code of Canon Law. Yet such an institution could not be called a juridical personality, for the patrimony of such an institution was always considered as belonging to a physical person or a corporation. Non-collegiate moral personalities in the

[13] D (46.47) 49; D (2.4) (10.4), cf. Brown p. 13.

[14] Authors often refer to such an entity with the technical term *universitas bonorum*. Cf. Brown, p. 19; Michiels, p. 351.

[15] Michiels, p. 351.

[16] Brown, p. 19.

[17] This term is used in opposition to the term "corporation." The latter term refers to those juridical persons which were constituted from a collectivity of physical persons; the term "institution" is used to designate the result of a collection of goods, or property, i.e. *universitas bonorum*.

[18] Cf. Brown, pp. 19-20.

[19] Cf. D (33.1) 6.

[20] D (31.30).

strict sense that they are the distinct subjects of rights and obligations began to be recognized only after the Christian religion became the State religion and the Church itself was recognized as a moral personality.[21] In fact it was actually Canon Law which developed the theory of the *universitas bonorum,* personifying the common ideal end to which masses of property, money and land had been dedicated.[22]

By way of summation, it may be said that with respect to the outward form of juristic personality, Canon Law borrowed the idea of the *universitas personarum* from the Roman Law, and in turn stimulated the legal conception of the institution, also the product of Roman Law, but not extensively developed by the latter juristic scheme.[23]

One final historical note on the nature of ecclesiastical juristic personality may be added. It was only in the last century that the division into *universitas personarum* and *universitas bonorum* was admitted by the law of any civil authority.[24] Ecclesiastical institutes, established under the influence of Christianity and recognized in law, were not considered as distinct juridical entities in themselves, but as entities depending on the Church, that is, the community of the faithful. The concept of an institute, as a moral personality in its own right and intrinsically distinct from what would now be called a collegiate moral personality, for many centuries was to be found in Church law alone.[25]

Section II. Juridical Personality in the Code

A personality in the juridical order is a subject of rights—a subject in which rights inhere inviolably.[26] Every man is a subject

---

[21] Michiels, p. 351.

[22] Brown, p. 21.

[23] Brown, p. 28. Brown in this same place gives the reason for such a development when he points out that "Christianity introduced a social consciousness into the individualistic Roman law."

[24] Michiels, p. 355.

[25] *Loc. cit.*

[26] Vermeersch-Creusen, *Epitome Juris Canonici* (3 vols., Vol. I, 7. ed., 1949, Mechliniae-Romae: H. Dessain), I, n. 206, p. 185 (hereafter cited *Epitome*).

of rights in the natural order.[27] In society, positive rights are added to the rights which are man's by nature. These positive rights attach to men who have membership in the society. Men are constituted members of the Church, *personae in Ecclesia,* by the reception of baptism.[28]

In the Church there are also moral personalities, constituted as such by public authority.[29] Although the Code gives no definition of a moral personality, it may be defined as "quidquid praeter personas physicas in Ecclesia iuris possidendi et exercendi capax in ss. canonibus habetur."[30] It is certainly manifest from the Code that ecclesiastical personality, that is, the power or capacity to acquire and exercise rights in the Church, which arises from the reception of baptism in the case of human beings, may also be conferred upon corporate bodies and institutions by public ecclesiastical authority.[31]

A basic division of moral personalities in the Church is made according to their structure. They are distinguished as those which are "collegiate" and those which are "non-collegiate."[32] A collegiate moral personality in the Church is a juridical entity materially consisting of a number of physical persons,[33] having a charitable or religious purpose. Such an entity is considered as a single subject of rights and duties—that subject being made distinct from the member persons, taken severally or collectively.[34] Some of these collegiate moral personalities carry on their activities "collegiately,"[35] while others act through appointed or elected admin-

---

[27] *Loc. cit.*

[28] Can. 87.

[29] Can. 99.

[30] Blat, *Commentarium Textus Codicis Iuris Canonici* (5 vols. in 7, Vol. II, Pars 1, 2. ed., 1921, Romae: Collegio Angelico), II, 36.

[31] Brown, p. 88.

[32] Can. 99.

[33] For the constituting of such an entity there must be at least three such physical persons. Cf. can. 100, § 2.

[34] Michiels, pp. 356-357.

[35] Chapters of canons, for example. Cf. cans. 391 ff. On collegiate procedure, cf. can. 101.

istrators and representatives.[36] The "non-collegiate" ecclesiastical moral personality is a juristic subject of rights, established by public authority, upon the basis of a sum of goods, either spiritual or material.[37] Of course, such an entity must also have a charitable or a religious purpose.[38]

Section III.   Juridical Capacity of Moral Personalities in the Church

Whatever be the juridical capacity of moral personalities according to modern civil laws, it may be given as a general rule that in the law of the Code such juridical entities necessarily can possess and acquire all the rights that are given to physical persons. The only exception to such a general rule are such rights as are from the nature of the case or from the positive regulation of the Code proper to physical persons alone.[39] Such an exception would be, for example, the right to enter matrimony.[40] Certainly the Code of Canon Law does not propose to give an exhaustive list of what these rights of ecclesiastical moral personalities are. An examination of the Code, however, will reveal many of these rights.[41]

A. *Rights Pertaining to Their Personal Status*

Moral personalities in the Church have rights of personal status. They may enjoy appropriate and distinctive names and titles,[42] and they may use distinctive seals.[43] Moral personalities have their legal "seats," which are analogous to the domicile and quasi-domicile of physical persons.[44] It must be kept in mind, however,

---

[36] Religious orders, for example. Cf. cans. 499 ff.

[37] Cf. Michiels, p. 357.

[38] Cf. Can. 1489 § 1.

[39] Michiels, p. 455.

[40] *Loc. cit.*

[41] Cf. Michiels, pp. 455-466, where the duties and rights of ecclesiastical moral personalities are divided into three groups: (1) rights pertaining to their personal status; (2) patrimonial rights, and (3) extra-patrimonial rights.

[42] Cf. cans. 492, § 3; 688; 689, § 1; 1490.

[43] Cf. cans. 381, § 2; 470, § 4; 450, § 1.

[44] Cf. cans. 1560, nn. 2, 3; 92; 93; 94.

that the rights just noted are not distinctive of moral personality as such, since these rights belong also to associations and private institutions which have not been established as ecclesiastical moral personalities.[45]

B. *Patrimonial Rights*

By the divine authority which constituted them, the Catholic Church and the Apostolic See have the right, freely and independently of any civil power, to acquire, hold and administer temporal goods as a means of achieving their proper purposes.[46] Moral personalities in the Church have the power to acquire, hold and administer property, within the limits of Church law.[47] From these fundamental principles it follows that the Church, and all moral personalities in the Church, have the right to acquire property by all just means, under natural or positive law, by which others may do so.[48] The canons legislate upon various modes of acquiring property.[49] The property of all ecclesiastical moral persons is referred to with the technical term, "ecclesiastical property," [50] and is consequently subject to the canonical rules which govern acquisition, administration, use and disposition of such property.[51]

It must also be kept in mind that ecclesiastical property in the strict sense is not subject to taxation by the civil authority. The

[45] Michiels, p. 456.

[46] Can. 1495, § 1.

[47] Can. 1495, § 2. Cf. can. 531, by which this right is explicitly given to religious congregations, their provinces and their houses; can. 676, § 1, concerning societies of the common life, their provinces and houses; can. 717, concerning certain confraternities and pious unions; can. 691, concerning canonically established associations; can. 1355, concerning diocesan seminaries; cans. 1409 and 1410, concerning ecclesiastical benefices; can. 1489, § 2, concerning ecclesiastical institutes; can. 1209, regarding the various moral persons which may have their own cemeteries.

[48] Can. 1499 § 1. Cf. can. 1498.

[49] Gift, can. 1536; last wills and testaments, cans. 1513-1517; adverse possession, can. 1508; tithes and first fruits, can. 1502; free offerings, can. 1182, §§ 2, 3; taxes, cans. 1504-1507.

[50] Can. 1497, § 1.

[51] For example: administrative vigilance, cans. 1519 to 1522; alienation of goods, cans. 1530-1543; contracts, cans. 536; 1527, § 2; 1529; 1533.

Code itself does not treat this particular point. Yet such an immunity does seem to be of divine law in the sense that the civil power, without the consent of the Church, cannot impose such burdens on ecclesiastical property.[52] Since the Church was constituted a perfect society by its Divine Founder, it follows that it is exempt from all civil jurisdiction. To impose a tax by law is a sign of jurisdiction and of true power over the subject in question. The State does not possess such a power with regard to the Church and ecclesiastical property.[53] The Council of Trent itself argued from the divine law also to prove the immunity of the Universal Church and the Apostolic See from any burdens placed upon them by the civil authority.[54] The immunity of lesser moral personalities in the Church is said by many authors to be granted by the positive law of the Church. The Church for prudent reasons can renounce this immunity and *de facto* has done so at times.[55]

C. *Extra-patrimonial Rights*

Moral personalities in the Church may acquire and exercise "extra-patrimonial rights." Among these are various spiritual rights,[56] and the exercise of true jurisdiction.[57] They may make statutes for their governance.[58] They may sue and be sued.[59] Their civil responsibility is a corollary of their contractual capacity.[60]

[52] Vromant, *De Bonis Ecclesiae Temporalibus* (3. ed., Bruges-Paris: Desclée de Brouwer, 1953), n. 9, p. 14; cf. Conc. Trident., sess. XXV, *de ref.*, c. 20.

[53] In the *Syllabus of Errors* Proposition 30 as condemned by Pope Pius IX reads as follows: "Ecclesiae et personarum ecclesiasticarum immunitas a iure civili ortum habuit."—Denzinger-Umberg, *Enchiridion Symbolorum Definitionum et Declarationum de Rebus Fide et Morum* (editio vigesima sexta, emendata et aucta, Friburgi Brisgoviae: Herder, 1947), n. 1730.

[54] Conc. Trident., sess. XXV, *de ref.*, c. 20.

[55] Vromant, *op. cit.*, n. 9, p. 14, footnote 2.

[56] Rescripts, can. 36, § 1; privileges, can. 72. §§ 3, 4; indulgences, can. 708.

[57] To rule a diocese *sede vacante,* can. 431, § 1; to rule a parish, can. 451, § 1.

[58] Cf. cans. 410; 689, § 1; 715, § 1.

[59] Cf. cans. 1552, § 2, n. 1; 1649 ff.

[60] Cf., e.g., cans. 1527; 536.

Ecclesiastical moral personalities enjoy the favorable legal status of minors.[61] This "favor of law" seems to be rooted in the analogy between moral personalities which must act through representatives, and minors who must act through guardians.[62] Both are similarly liable to damage through lack of care on the part of those who act for them. For that reason the law gives them special protection.[63] This principle was accepted in Roman Law,[64] and in the Decretals,[65] and was consecrated in later canonical doctrine.[66] At present, the principle is a true "rule of law," to be applied, therefore, not only in the cases expressly stated by law, but in cases to which the principle may be extended by proper analogy.[67] Many specific applications of the principle are found in the Code of Canon Law. For example, there is the right to *restitutio in integrum,* i.e., the extraordinary remedy of the law by which a person who has been gravely damaged by a valid but recissable act or transaction may, because of natural equity, be returned, through the ministry of a competent judge, to that status in which he was before being damaged.[68] Another example is to be seen in the extraordinary

[61] Can. 100, § 3.

[62] Cf. Wernz, *Ius Decretalium* (6 vols., Vol. III, 1901, Romae: S. C. de Propaganda Fidei), III, n. 149, pp. 183-184. Wernz here stated: "Cum subiecta dominii bonorum ecclesiasticorum sint personae iuridicae, quae per se agere non possunt, universa administratio illorum est penes personas physicas in Ecclesia constitutas. Quare personae illae iuridicae, quibus dominium proprietatis bonorum ecclesiasticorum competit, sese habent ad instar pupillorum, administratores autem ecclesiastici aequiparantur curatoribus vel tutoribus; illis enim administratio dominii pupillorum ad quam isti inhabiles sunt, ex legitima commissione est data magnaque diligentia et absque culpa exercendi."

[63] Michiels, p. 467.

[64] Cf. e.g., D (14.5) 5; D (11.29) 3; D (50.4) 9.

[65] Cc. 1, 3, X, *de in integrum restitutione,* I, 41; Jaffé, *Regesta Pontificum Romanorum ab condita Ecclesia ad annum post Christum natum MCXCVIII* (2 ed., correctam et auctam auspiciis G. Wattenbach, curaverunt F. Kaltenbrunner, P. Ewald, S. Loewenfeld, 2 vols., Lipsiae, 1885-1888), n. 13737; Potthast, *Regesta Pontificum Romanorum, inde ab anno post Christum natum MCXCVIII ad annum MCCCIV* (2 vols., Berolini, 1874-1875), n. 2681.

[66] Gillet, *La Personalité Juridique en Droit Ecclésiastique* (Molines: Godenne, 1927), pp. 92-94; 129.

[67] Michiels, p. 467.

[68] Feeney, *Restitutio in Integrum,* The Catholic University of America

obligation of judges to declare *ex officio* the nullity of certain acts of a moral personality or of its administrators,[69] and to summon witnesses *ex officio*.[70] Then, too, there is the obligation of representatives of moral personalities to obtain advice or even authorization before suing or contesting a suit in the name of the moral personality.[71]

ARTICLE 2. CREATION OF MORAL PERSONALITIES IN THE CHURCH

Section I. Natural Law

The right to form associations or societies whose purpose is legitimate and whose means are honest flows from the basic right of human liberty and from the necessities of human nature. It is a natural right.[72]

> The experience of his own weakness urges man to call in help from without. . . . It is this natural impulse which unites men in civil society; and it is this also which makes them band themselves together in associations of citizen with citizen; associations which, it is true, cannot be called societies in the complete sense of the word, but which are societies nevertheless. . . . Particular societies, then, although they exist within the State, and are each a part of the State, nevertheless cannot be prohibited by the State absolutely and as such. For to enter into a "society" of this kind is the natural right of man; and the State must protect natural rights, not destroy them; and if it forbids its citizens to form associations, it contradicts the very principle of its own existence; for both they and it exist in virtue of the same principle, *viz.*, the natural propensity of man to live in society.[73]

Canon Law Studies, n. 129 (Washington, D. C.: The Catholic University of America Press, 1941), p. 49; cf. cans. 1687, § 1; 1688. It must be kept in mind, however, that ecclesiastical moral personalities usually will make use of other safeguards given them by the canons of the Code (Cf. cans. 1526; 1527; 1530-1534; 1536; etc.).

[69] Can. 1682.

[70] Can. 1759, § 3.

[71] Cans. 1526; 1653.

[72] Goodwine, *The Right of the Church to Acquire Temporal Goods,* The Catholic University of America Canon Law Studies, n. 131 (Washington, D. C.: The Catholic University of America Press, 1941), p. 30.

[73] *Five Great Encyclicals* (New York: Paulist Press, 1939), nn. 37 & 38, p. 24; litt. encyl., *Rerum novarum,* 15 maii 1891—*Fontes,* n. 611, p. 373.

From these basic principles stated by Leo XIII in *Rerum nova-rum,* it follows that such private associations can be formed without the need of any permission from the State, and their existence and operations can be said to consist at least in the sum total of the rights that each member possesses, although each of these associa-tions (*personae collectivae*) might not be said to possess rights proper to itself and distinct from the rights of the individuals that go to make it up.[74]

Once there has been established the natural right of men to form such association, some very basic questions are now to be answered. Can these associations, as based upon the natural law itself, be classified as *distinct juridical personalities?* That is to say, can there now be found not merely a plurality of persons banded together, but rather a new and distinct subject of rights separate from the individual members? On the contrary, can this juridical personality be granted to such entities only by the determinate act of a superior authority?

As has been said, associations are used by man to attain those things which cannot be achieved by individual endeavor. It can now be said that such entities can truly be called moral person-alities, not from the concession of any public authority, but from the very natural law itself.[75] The freedom to associate with others for some legitimate purpose is, then, natural to man. Not every association of individuals, however, is a society, unless there exist some moral bond which makes a unit of the many individuals. This bond makes a united body, a living organism. If this were not present, the members would be only isolated individual persons grouped together for some purpose (e.g., a mob). If it is present, they form a society with rights, collective interests, and social needs. This moral bond, which is so important, arises from the very nature of things. It can exist without the help of the civil authority. If not, how explain the civil authority itself? It is this moral bond which gives the society its personality. Its juridical personality follows necessarily. Thus societies formed as a result

[74] Michiels, p. 388.
[75] Michiels, pp. 391-392.

of the impulses of human nature possess juridical personality independently of the civil law.[76]

It must be kept in mind, however, that such juridical entities are not entirely independent of the civil power. They are rather to be integrated in the civil society, which was established as such by God Himself in order to achieve the common good of the whole of society.[77] It follows, then, that these lesser associations and institutes are always established for a purpose which is subordinate to the general temporal welfare. The means used by such entities are naturally under the control and surveillance of the public authority; and thus the legislator, the public authority, is the judge of their usefulness or their danger to the general welfare. Hence the public authority is the judge of the licitness of such societies. It can even destroy them in certain circumstances, in order to safeguard the more important interest in the public order.[78]

So far no reference has been made to religious societies as such. Definite distinctions must be made with regard to what has just been said, when the relations of such entities with the public authority are discussed. It must also be kept in mind that all that will now be said will be restricted to the natural law. No reference, as yet, will be made to the positive divine law.[79]

The relations of the public authority with the religious society are quite different from those with other societies. The object of the civil society is the temporal welfare of its citizens. The end of the religious society, however, is the spiritual welfare of its members. A very important conclusion follows from this basic difference. Civil governments, therefore, were not formed for religion, or for the administration of sacred things. The affairs of religion are beyond the realm of the civil authority.[80] Considered then purely as a natural society, the Church has an object that is not

---

[76] Goodwine, *op. cit.*, pp. 31-32; cf. Ottaviani, *Institutiones Iuris Publici Ecclesiastici* (2 vols., Vol. I, 3. ed., 1947, Romae: Typis Polyglottis Vaticanis), I, n. 27, p. 62.

[77] Michiels, p. 392.

[78] Goodwine, *op. cit.*, p. 34; Michiels, pp. 392-393.

[79] Cf. *infra*, pp. 17-18.

[80] Goodwine, *op. cit.*, p. 34.

directly subject to that of the civil society. It follows, then, that
the purpose of the religious society, the spiritual welfare of men,
cannot be made subordinate to that of the civil authority, the purely
temporal welfare of men.[81]

To sum up this whole argumentation from the natual law:

> . . . the Catholic Church, the same as any religious society, has
> within itself sufficient reason for its existence. The individuals
> who compose the Church have the right to associate in order to
> obtain by the use of common means an end that is legitimate
> and not detrimental or harmful. Their society draws its rights
> from the will of its members, and is limited by only one law—
> the duty and obligation of not impeding other societies in the
> exercise of their rights.[82]

Section II. Civil Law

With regard to the attitude of various civil authorities concerning the necessary elements in the constitution of juridical personalities, it can definitely be said that there is no unanimity. The
variant answers to this basic question can be summarized under
three theories that have been followed by different civil authorities: [83]

1. The theory of liberty (*theoria libertatis*), according to which
the very will of the members of a society to form an association, or
the will of a founder to establish an institute, can be said to constitute by that very fact a juridical personality. Of course such a
society must pursue honest ends, and such an institute must be of
some benefit to the public. The intervention of a civil authority
would only be declarative of the personality already existing.—2.
The theory of the necessary constitution of juridical personality
(*theoria necessariae constitutionis seu concessionis personalitatis*).
In this case, although the association or foundation is entirely legiti-

---

[81] *Loc. cit.*

[82] *Loc. cit.* To avoid misunderstanding here, the reader is to keep in mind
that reference is here made to the Catholic Church, viewed as a natural religious society and in abstraction from its divine establishment. Certainly, the
Church, as a divine institution, cannot be said to draw its rights from the will
of its members.

[83] Michiels, p. 389.

mate and, therefore, capable of acquiring personality, nevertheless ,such personality is considered not to be granted *de facto* without an express and positive act of the public authority granting such personality to the entity in question.—3. The intermediate or normative theory (*theoria intermedia seu normativa*), which, as the name indicates, is midway between the two theories just seen. Thus for different types of associations or foundations, the authoritative recognition of the public authority can establish juridical personality which was not there before (*per recognitionem creativam*), or simply declare such personality to be already existing (*per recognitionem confirmativam*). A brief historical survey will ,help to bring out in practice the full meaning of these three theories.

In Roman Law, in the different periods of its history, there was a variation in doctrine as to the need of public recognition in order to have juridical personality. To complicate matters a bit more, a distinction must be made concerning what would now be called collegiate moral personalities [84] and non-collegiate moral personalities.[85]

As to collegiate moral personalities, at first there was no governmental supervision. Individuals were allowed a free hand in the formation of such organizations.[86] Such liberty can be deduced from a law of the Twelve Tables which only demanded that the statutes of such societies be not against public laws.[87] In 64 B. C., during the latter days of the Republic, a decree of the Senate (*senatusconsultus*) dissolved many *collegia* which were felt to be a threat to the existence of the State.[88] In general, during the period

[84] In Roman Law Sources such a term did not exist. Instead one finds such terms as *collegium, corpus, universitas, sodalitas*. Cf. Michiels, p. 365.

[85] Again, such a term did not exist in Roman Law Sources. In fact, there is doubt whether such an entity with its present meaning actually existed at all in Roman Law. Cf. *supra*, pp. 3-4. Certainly there were entities similar to the present non-collegiate moral personalities. There was no technical term for designating such entities. Instead, the reference was always to their proper names, e.g., *noscomia* (hospitals), *gerontocomia* (old age homes), *orphanotrophia* (orphan asylums). Cf. Michiels, pp. 351 & 365. The term "foundation" will be used here in designation of such entities.

[86] Brown, p. 65; Michiels, p. 390.

[87] D (47. 22) 4.

[88] Brown, pp. 65-66.

of the Empire *collegia* were to be formed only with the sanction of the Senate.[89] Under Augustus (30 B. C.-A. D. 14) an attempt was made for the improvement of the corporate system by way of constructive legislation. Certain ancient corporations were recognized, .e.g., *collegia sacerdotalia, corpora artificum*, as were also certain recent corporations, e.g., *collegia funeraticia*. Others explicitly were declared illicit and prohibited; any corporations that would arise in the future were also declared to be illicit, unless a previous authorization from the public authority was obtained. This was to be obtained from either the Senate or the Emperor.[90]

Whether the State's permission under the Roman Law constituted the creative act without which the corporation could not exist is greatly disputed.[91] Romanists do agree, however, that corporations not in harmony with the State could be disbanded. Divergent opinions still exist as to whether or not the State's sanction actually gave life to the corporation.[92]

As to "institutions," [93] which were the forerunners of present-day non-collegiate moral personalities, some authorities think that the confirmation of the State was needed before such entities could achieve a juridical existence. Many, however, pointing to a law in the Code of Justinian,[94] deny this and affirm that the destination of property within limits recognized once and for all by the law was sufficient. Such property had to have a charitable or religious destination.[95]

In modern civil law it may be said that there are three types of juridical persons: [96]

1. The Franco-Italian Type (*typus gallicus-italicus*).—Aside from France and Italy, this type of juridical personality is found also in Belgium, Holland, Portugal, and to a certain extent in

---

89 *Ibid.*, p. 66; cf. D (47. 22) 1 to 3.
90 Michiels, p. 390.
91 Cf. Brown, pp. 66-69.
92 *Loc. cit.*
93 Cf. *supra*, p. 3.
94 C (1. 3) 46.
95 Michiels, p. 390.
96 *Ibid.*, pp. 390-391.

Spain. In general these countries adhere to the *normative theory.*[97] Accordingly, the legislative authority approves by a general law all those corporations which it considers not harmful to the State. With regard to certain other corporations it demands special recognition on its part before such entities can legitimately function. Whether the recognition of the civil authority has only confirmatory force or actually creates such corporations is disputed by authors.[98]

2. The Germanic Type (*typus germanicus*).—This second type of juridical person is to be found in Germany, Austria and Switzerland. In this type there does not seem to be a clear distinction between the notion of "corporation" (a juridical personality) and the notion of "society" (a collection of physical persons joined together). In general it may be said that approbation by statute is required for foundations (which are parallel to the canonical non-collegiate moral personality). A distinction must be made with regard to private corporations. If they have a religious, scientific, artistic, or similar purpose (*ad scopum idealem*), they are only to be inscribed in the proper registers in certain jurisdictions, or the will alone of the members constituting themselves as the corporation is all that is required in other jurisdictions.[99] If, however, a corporation has a pecuniary purpose (*ad scopum oeconomicum*), inscription by the public authority is required in some places, or approbation each time by the proper authority is demanded in others.[100]

3. The Anglo-American Type.—This third type of juridical personality recognizes only one kind of moral personality, viz., the corporation (collegiate moral personality). This type can be either a corporation sole or a corporation aggregate. In either case the approbation of the proper civil authority is always required in order that such corporations may come into existence. That is to say, the approbation of the proper civil authority is regarded as

---

[97] Cf. *supra,* p. 14.

[98] Cf. Michiels, p. 391.

[99] Cf. Michiels, *loc. cit.,* for references to particular jurisdictions.

[100] Cf. again Michiels, *loc. cit.,* for specific references.

having creative and not merely confirmatory force with regard to any corporation. In New York only the corporation aggregate is recognized.[101]

Section III. Canon Law

A. *Origin of Ecclesiastical Moral Personality—General Concepts*

There are two moral personalities that exist by divine institution. They are the Catholic Church and the Apostolic See.[102] The distinction between these two moral personalities is a real and non-commensurate distinction; one is part of the other.[103] Apostolic See does not here refer to the Roman Congregations, Tribunals, or Offices.[104]

The Church Universal is a moral personality by divine right. It has the inalienable right to establish subordinate moral personalities[105] as efficient mediums for the fulfillment of its divine mission, as effective instruments, therefore, for the accomplishment of all those ends, whether spiritual or temporal, which help to contribute to the fulfillment of the purpose divinely ordained.[106] This is a fundamental consideration. At the Church's inception, its Divine Founder conferred upon the Church all the requisites of moral personality. In proof of this statement it must be kept in mind that, since the Church Universal is of divine foundation, it is impossible to reduce the character of the personality of the Church, as such, or even of its subordinate moral personalities to a merely natural plane. The discussion must assume theological aspects, which is beyond the scope of this study.[107] If this be kept in mind, it can definitely be proved that it was the intention of Christ to constitute the Church and the Holy See a moral personality, perpetual and transcendent.[108] Christ created a truly perfect

101 Cf. *infra*, p. 34.

102 Can. 100, § 1.

103 Bouscaren-Ellis, *Canon Law* (Milwaukee: Bruce, 1946), pp. 86-87.

104 *Loc. cit.* Cf. also can. 7.

105 Cf. can. 100, § 1.

106 Brown, p. 24.

107 Cf. Nicolau-Salaverri, *Sacrae Theologiae Summa* (4 vols., Vol. 1, 3. ed. 1955, Matriti: Biblioteca de Auctores Cristianos), I, 511-527.

108 Brown, p. 58.

society, sovereign and independent, for the purpose of realizing a definite end, with all the means necessary for its achievement, including therefore moral personality.[109] From this basic principle consequences follow. Since the Catholic Church and the Apostolic See are moral personalities,[110] it follows that they possess the right to utilize the medium of moral personality in the fullest sense, without any interference on the part of the State.[111]

The creation of subordinate moral personalities in the Church is the result of ecclesiastical authority. The words *"ceterae inferiores personae morales in Ecclesia eam sortiuntur . . .,"*[112] are indicative that these minor juridical personalities are dependent upon the Church and must be supported by it in the fulfillment of their ends and in the choice of means. They have a share in the divine commission, though they themselves were not divinely founded. There is thus implied the incompetency of the civil power in the creation of any ecclesiastical moral personality. According to the law of the Code, it is certain that competent authority, namely, the authority of Church, is needed. No canonical moral personality can exist which does not derive its authority from the Church.[113]

Moral personality in the Church is granted to certain associations or institutions in two ways, viz., by provision of the law itself

[109] Cf. Cappello, *Summa Iuris Publici Ecclesiastici* (5. ed., Romae: Apud Aedes Universitatis Gregorianae, 1943), nn. 95-103.

[110] Cf. Brown, pp. 90-91. This author makes a distinction between these two entities and other subordinate moral personalities in the Church. He states that the Catholic Church and the Apostolic See have the nature (*rationem*) of moral personalities but are not strictly such, as are other moral personalities in the Church. Such a distinction seems unfounded, since can. 100, § 1, uses the clause, *"rationem habent,"* in reference to the Catholic Church and the Apostolic See, and then the clause *"eam* (i.e. *rationem*) *sortiuntur"* with reference to subordinate ecclesiastical moral personalities. Can. 100, § 1, therefore, states that both classes of entities referred to in this canon have moral personality, which, however, they derive from different titles.

[111] Michiels, pp. 371-372. Cf. Ottaviani, *op. cit.,* I, n. 27. pp. 60-64.

[112] Can. 100, § 1.

[113] Brown, p. 91.

or by formal decree of the proper ecclesiastical superior.[114] Leaving aside for the moment the precise method by which such moral personality is obtained, one must keep in mind that a positive act on the part of the proper ecclesiastical authority is absolutely necessary for establishing such a personality.[115] This is a most important point, for there are associations approved by ecclesiastical authority which at the same time may not be considered ecclesiastical moral personalities.[116] Coronata[117] refers to such associations and calls them "private juridical personalities." This notion does not seem to be correct. As Coronata himself points out, there is lacking to such entities the recognition of ecclesiastical authority which would constitute them as "public juridical personalities" in the Church. Such a distinction does not seem to exist in the Code. In the Church there is recognized only one moral personality in the full and proper sense. It comes into being not simply through the recognition of the competent ecclesiastical authority, but rather through the act whereby this same authority actually constitutes an ecclesiastical moral personality in one or the other of the two ways mentioned in canon 100, § 1.[118] Referring to associations which Coronata would classify as "private juridical personalities," Gillet[119] points out that in the eyes of ecclesiastical authority their juridical personality is non-existent. They are not, as perhaps one would be tempted to believe, moral personalities simply lacking the character of ecclesiastical institutions, and hence they would not enjoy the privileges and would not be subject to the laws proper to those institutions. It is the moral personality itself which they lack.

[114] Can. 100, § 1.

[115] Michiels, p. 394.

[116] E.g., pious unions and sodalities. These are subject to the vigilance of the Church by reason of their purpose; cf. can. 336, § 2; also Michiels, pp. 396-397.

[117] *Institutiones Iuris Canonici* (5 vols., Vol. I, 4. ed., 1950, Romae: Marietti) I, n. 138, ad 4, p. 162.

[118] Michiels, p. 395, footnote 1.

[119] *La Personalité Juridique*, p. 258.

B. *Particular Ways in which Moral Personality Is Granted in the Church*

Having established the absolute necessity of a positive act on the part of the proper ecclesiastical authority for the constituting of a subordinate ecclesiastical moral personality, Church law specifies how this may in two ways be accomplished. This positive act constituting the moral personality is evinced either in the law itself (*a iure*) or in a special decree emanating from a competent ecclesiastical authority (*ab homine*).[120] It must be kept in mind, however, that this twofold method for the obtaining of juridical personality in the Church is not to be understood in a *conjunctive* sense, viz., in the sense that one and the same entity can achieve juridical personality in the Church in either of these two ways. Accordingly this twofold method is to be understood *disjunctively*, so that certain entities always can be classified as moral personalities created by the law itself, while others can obtain their ecclesiastical juridical personality only from the proper ecclesiastical authority by means of a special formal decree to that effect.[121]

The reason that vindicates this disjunctive meaning is to be found in the nature and the purpose of the juridical personalities which result from the application of this twofold method. Those ecclesiastical moral personalities which spring into being by the very operation of the law itself are those entities which are either absolutely or relatively necessary to the social-public life of the Church for its well-ordered operation and existence.[122] Those ecclesiastical moral personalities which are brought into being by means of a special decree of a competent ecclesiastical superior have as their object some charitable or religious purpose, and ordinarily are established or founded by private members of the faithful with the approbation of the public ecclesiastical authority. At times it is useful for the furtherance of pious undertakings that there be constituted such ecclesiastical moral personalities. This

---

[120] Can. 100, § 1.

[121] Michiels, pp. 398-399.

[122] Cf. Preti, "Il Riconoscimento delle Persone Morali in Diritto Canonico," *Archivo di Diritto Ecclesiastico*, II (1940), 321-331.

can be achieved by means of a special concession from a competent ecclesiastical superior through a formal decree.[123]

A more detailed discussion of the twofold method of constituting ecclesiastical moral personalities is now in order.

I. *A iure*

When the law declares that entities of a given sort enjoy juristic personality, every entity of that sort is a moral personality by the very fact that it is created. No special decree granting moral personality is needed, because personality is conferred by the law itself when the entity begins to exist. The law attributes juristic personality to some ecclesiastical entities explicitly; to other entities the law's attribution of juristic personality is implicit. There is implicit attribution of personality when the law attributes to a moral entity some capacity which can exist only in a moral personality.[124]

Canon Law explicitly denominates as moral personalities the following classes of ecclesiastical entities: dioceses; [125] by analogy to dioceses, abbacies and prelacies *nullius*,[126] i.e., of independent territorial status; parishes; [127] churches; [128] seminaries; [129] universities of studies; [130] ecclesiastical benefices.[131] The following collegiate bodies are so denominated: the College of Cardinals; [132]

---

[123] Michiels, p. 400.

[124] Cf. Michiels, pp. 420-421. He sums up this implicit attribution with these words, "*ex facto* quod legislator in aliqua lege enti collegiali aut non collegiali *specifice determinato qua tali,* seu qua entitati in se uni et per se stanti, *explicite agnoscit unam alteramve capacitatem juridicam* quae ex ipsa rei natura vel ex positivo juris canonici statuto *solis personis physicis* et entibus personalitate morali gaudentibus *specifice propria est iisve exclusive reservata,* . . ." The italics are those of Michiels himself.

[125] Can. 1557, § 2, n. 2.

[126] Can. 215, § 2.

[127] Cans. 1208, § 3; 1209, § 1.

[128] Cans. 99; 1423, § 2; 1495, § 2.

[129] Can. 99; 1354.

[130] Can. 2332.

[131] Cans. 99; 1409.

[132] Can. 2332.

religious orders and congregations, their provinces and houses; [133] monasteries; [134] monastic congregations.[135]

The capacity for ownership of property, and the capacity to sue and be sued are two distinctive characteristics of moral personalities. Whenever the law attributes either of these attributes to a class of ecclesiastical entities, it implicitly declares the entities of that class to be moral personalities by the very operation of the law. Ownership of property is attributed by the canons to the following entities: dioceses, vicariates apostolic, and prefectures apostolic; [136] parishes; [137] churches; [138] public oratories; [139] pious places; [140] seminaries [141] and ecclesiastical benefices.[142] The capacity of owning property is attributed to the following collegiate bodies: chapters, cathedral or collegiate; [143] the diocesan curia; [144] the Roman Curia.[145] The capacity for lodging or responding to suit is attributed, for example, to cathedral and collegiate chapters [146] cathedral churches; [147] ecclesiastical benefices; [148] and religious communities.[149]

It should be noted, however, that capacity for ownership is not essential to the constitution or existence of a moral personality in the Church. The law admits of moral personalities which are without that capacity.[150] Still less is actual ownership of goods

[133] Can. 536, § 1.
[134] Can. 1423, § 2.
[135] Can. 1557, § 2, n. 2.
[136] Can. 628, n. 1.
[137] Cans. 216, §§ 1 and 3; 1208, § 1.
[138] Cans. 485; 1182, § 1; 1183, § 1.
[139] Cc. 1188, § 2, n. 1; 1191; 1298, § 1.
[140] Can. 1298, § 1.
[141] Cans. 1475, § 2; 1355; 1356.
[142] Can. 1410.
[143] Cans. 391, § 1; 395, § 3.
[144] Cans. 363, § 2; 1572, § 2.
[145] Can. 427.
[146] Can. 1653, § 3.
[147] Can. 1653, § 1.
[148] Can. 1653, § 2.
[149] Can. 1653, § 6.
[150] Cans. 531; 582, n. 2.

essential to the existence of an ecclesiastical moral personality. The Catholic Church, for example, is a moral personality by divine right,[151] and has full capacity for ownership,[152] yet it actually possesses no property.[153] Also any non-collegiate moral personality in the Church retains its existence for a hundred years after the property, which was the substratum upon which the entity was erected, has perished.[154] Attribution of jurisdiction to a collegiate body does not indicate that the subject of such attribution is a moral personality. The chapters of exempt religious communities enjoy true jurisdiction, yet it is not the chapters which are the moral personalities.[155]

II. *Ab homine*

Other types of ecclesiastical entities do not, immediately and directly upon their constitution, receive juristic personality by the operation of the law. If they are to be moral personalities, they must be so constituted, by means of a special concession from a competent ecclesiastical superior through his issuance of a formal decree.[156] Many authors hold this this concession may be given at the time the entity is established, that it may be given later, or that it needs never to be given at all. The thing that these authors emphasize is that this concession is quite distinct from the act by which the entity is established.[157] They go on to point out that this grant of personality may be equivalent and indirect. An example of equivalent or indirect concession would be the attribution in the decree of some characteristic of moral personality, e.g., ownership of property or capacity to sue.

---

151 Can. 100, § 1. Cf. *supra,* p. 17.

152 Cans. 1495, § 1; 1499, § 1.

153 Cf. can. 1499, § 2: "Dominium bonorum, sub suprema auctoritate Sedis Apostolicae, ad eam pertinet moralem personam, quae eadem bona legitime acquisiverit."

154 Can. 102, § 1.

155 Cf. can. 501.

156 Can. 100, § 1.

157 Cf. Michiels, *Principia Generalia de Personis in Ecclesia* (1. ed., Lublin, 1932), pp. 353-355; Brown, pp. 93-94; Coronata, *Institutiones,* I, n. 138, ad 4; Jone, *Commentarium in Codicem Canonici* (3 vols., Vol. I, 1950, Paderborn: Schöningh), I, 111.

There is, however, a second group of authors who hold that the very decree of establishment of such ecclesiastical entities, of itself and apart from any further action of the ecclesiastical superior, grants moral personality to the entity in question.[158] It is interesting to note that Michiels, in his later edition of *Principia Generalia de Personis in Ecclesia*,[159] has changed his opinion. He now holds that when collegiate or non-collegiate entities are established by means of the formal decree of an ecclesiastical superior, such entities are by that very fact also given moral personality, as long as the ecclesiastical superior, in establishing such entities, has not expressly denied them such personality.[160]

By means of a formal decree of establishment from a competent superior, moral personality is conferred upon lay associations in the Church.[161] Canon 687 does seem to favor the view that moral personality in the Church can result from the very decree of establishment issued by the proper ecclesiastical superior. Nothing else seems to be required on his part. The sufficiency of the formal decree of establishment is confirmed by canon 708.[162] This canon states that confraternities can be constituted only by means of a formal decree of establishment, while the mere approbation of the ordinary suffices for pious unions.[163] It goes on to deny moral personality to a pious union, which needs only the ordinary's approbation, as if to say that a confraternity, when established by means

[158] Gillet, *La Personalité Juridique*, p. 249; Beste, *Introductio in Codicem* (Collegeville: St. John's Abbey Press, 1946), p. 154; Preti, "art. cit.," *Archivo di Diritto Ecclesiastico*, II (1940), 324-326.

[159] See p. 410 of this work. It appeared as a second edition in 1955. It is to this edition that the future references are made, unless the earlier (1932) edition is designated.

[160] *Loc. cit.* See pp. 405-413 for the detailed arguments presented in support of the opposing opinions on this question.

[161] Can. 687.—Ad normam can. 100, tunc tantum fidelium associationes iuridicam in Ecclesia personam acquirunt, cum a legitimo Superiore ecclesiastico formale obtinuerunt erectionis decretum.

[162] "Confraternitates nonnisi per formale erectionis decretum constitui possunt; pro piis autem unionibus sufficit Ordinarii approbatio, qua obtenta, ipsae, licet morales personae non sint, capaces tamen sunt obtinendi gratias spirituales ac praesertim indulgentias."

[163] Cf. can. 707 for the difference between a pious union and a confraternity.

of a formal decree, by that very fact is a moral personality and becomes certainly entitled to spiritual favors. There is at least one writer who claims that this is the certain meaning of this canon.[164] This seems to be saying too much, since this canon can be given the meaning that moral personality is not needed for spiritual favors, and that the approbation mentioned in canon 686, § 1, is sufficient.[165]

Great care must attend one's use of the argument drawn from canon 687. This can be seen from the arguments adduced by Ciprotti.[166] He holds that canon 687 stands as an exception to the general rule of canon 100. The general rule, he says, is that moral personality is granted only by means of a formal decree that contains in itself the concession of personality made either equivalently or expressly. For lay associations to obtain moral personality, the simple decree of establishment suffices, under the exception made in canon 687. Ciprotti points out that these associations obtain their moral personality *"ex ipso iuris praescripto."* Here are his own words: ". . . cum ex ipso iuris praescripto personalitatem acquirant sine speciali competentis Superioris concessione, sed cum solo decreto erectionis."[167] But Ciprotti's statement must be denied. According to canon 687, moral personality is granted not by the law itself, but by the fact that a particular superior establishes the association. Michiels wrote:

> Personalitas moralis enim in casu non a legislatore supremo, vi canonis 687 praescripti, sed a Superiore associationem erigente conceditur, et concessione speciali quidem, associationi de qua agitur individuatim data "per formale decretum," videlicet per formale decretum erectionis, quod vi principii in can. 687 statuti non est tantum associationis canonice constitutivum, sed insimul personalitatis moralis concessivum.[168]

164 Preti, "art. cit.," *loc. cit.*

165 Michiels, p. 408.

166 "De Formali Decreto Quo Persona Juridica Constituitur," *Apollinaris*, X (1937), 270 and 272. Cf. also another article of the same author, "A Proposito delle Associazioni di Azione Cattolica," *Il Diritto Ecclesiastico*, XLVIII (1937), 358-365.

167 "Art. cit.," *Apollinaris*, X (1937), 270.

168 *Principia Generalia de Personis in Ecclesia*, p. 409.

There are two other canons of the Code which throw further light on the meaning of canon 687. Canon 691, § 1, states that, once an association is legitimately established, it can possess and administer temporal goods, unless there is some express provision to the contrary.[169] In other words, the very fact of a legitimate canonical establishment of itself and regularly brings with it the capacity of the association to possess its own temporal property. This right is just a particular application of the general principle contained in canon 1495, § 2, which states that individual churches and other moral personalities which by ecclesiastical authority have been constituted in the estate of juridic personality have the right to acquire, keep and administer temporal goods, according to the norm of the sacred canons.[170] Any entity, therefore, which possesses such a right is presupposed to be a moral personality. So, in the light of this canon along with canon 691, § 1, the fact that an association has been legitimately established brings with it, of itself and regularly, the concession of moral personality, unless there has been some express provision to the contrary.

Moral personality, by means of a decree of the proper ecclesiastical authority, may be granted to hospitals, orphanages, and other similar institutes which are destined for works of spiritual and temporal charity.[171] Considered here are non-collegiate ecclesiastical institutes. No argument can directly be drawn from canon 1489, § 1, or any other canon, for a definitive solution of the dispute as to what is required in the decree of the ecclesiastical superior for constituting such entities as moral personalities in the Church.[172] Certain important facts, however, can be pointed out. Canon 100, § 1, certainly seems to offer a general principle

---

[169] "Associatio legitime erecta, nisi aliud expresse cautum sit, bona temporalis possidere et administrare potest. . . ."

[170] "Etiam ecclesiis singularibus aliisque personis moralibus quae ab ecclesiastica auctoritate in iuridicam personam erectae sint, ius est, ad normam sacrorum canonum, bona temporalia acquirendi, retinendi et administrandi."

[171] Can. 1489, § 1.—Hospitalia, orphanotrophia aliaque similia instituta, ad opera religionis vel caritatis sive spiritualis sive temporalis destinata, possunt ab Ordinario loci erigi et per eius decretum persona iuridica in Ecclesia constitui.

[172] Michiels, p. 412.

concerning the acquisition of ecclesiastical moral personality *ab homine*—a general principle which is to be understood *in the same sense* concerning collegiate and non-collegiate entities. In the light of the interpretational principle stated in canon 18,[173] it is through an application of the general principle enunciated in canon 100, § 1, with reference to non-collegiate ecclesiastical institutes that the doubtful sense of canon 1489, § 1, can receive the closer specification that harmonizes it with the established sense of the special application of this general principle in canon 687 concerning associations of the faithful.[174] Consequently, with a view to a juridical uniformity in the granting of moral personality *ab homine*, it seems that it can be concluded that non-collegiate ecclesiastical institutes, no less than associations of the faithful, are constituted as moral personalities in the Church by the very fact that they are formally established by ecclesiastical authority. This is true as long as nothing expressly to the contrary is stated by the superior who has power to establish such entities.

With regard to these non-collegiate ecclesiastical institutes, it must be kept in mind that they need not, in every case, be constituted as autonomous moral personalities. They may simply be approved,[175] or they may be established without autonomy, as subject to and dependent on some other moral personality in the Church.[176] In the class of "similar institutes, destined for works of religion or of spiritual or temporal charity"[177] are included, by reason of their pious and charitable destination, schools of any status or rank,[178] and other undertakings which are directed to religious and moral formation.[179] Certainly, homes for the aged,

---

[173] "Leges ecclesiaticae intelligendae sunt secundum propriam verborum significationem in textu et contextu consideratam; quae si dubia et obscura manserit, ad locos Codicis parallelos, si qui sint, ad legis finem ac circumstantias et ad mentem legislatoris est recurrendum."

[174] Cf. *supra*, pp.24-25.

[175] Cf. can. 1489, § 2.

[176] Can. 1491, § 2.

[177] Can. 1489, § 1.

[178] Can. 1375.

[179] Can. 1382.

dispensaries, recreation and vacation centers, and other social welfare services, come within the class of "similar institutes etc," as contemplated in canon 1489.

ARTICLE 3. EXTINCTION OF MORAL PERSONALITIES IN THE CHURCH

The existence of a moral personality in the Church is legally terminated either through suppression by legitimate authority, or through the juridical fact that the substratum of the moral personality has ceased to exist for the space of one hundred years.[180]

Section I. Extrinsic Extinction

Generally, the authority competent for suppressing a moral personality is the authority empowered by law to establish the moral personality in question.[181] There are, however, some notable exceptions to this rule.[182]

Regarding the extrinsic extinction of moral persons in the Church, it follows first of all that this must be accomplished by legitimate authority. As has been said, this would be the authority by which it was established, or some higher authority.[183] Non-ecclesiastical power would always be ineffectual, and thus lay or civil authority could not operate effectively.[184] From the canons of the Code concerning the extrinsic extinction of ecclesiastical moral personalities, it is possible to compile a list of the principal cases reserved to various ecclesiastical authorities. The following are reserved to the Holy See:

(1) the suppression of an ecclesiastical province or diocese;[185]

(2) the suppression of an episcopal see;[186]

---

[180] Can. 102, § 1.

[181] Cf. cans. 699, §§ 1 and 2; 1187. "Omnis res, per quascumque causas nascitur, per easdem dissolvitur."—c. 1, *de regulis iuris,* V, 41.

[182] Cf. can. 493, concerning religious congregations of diocesan approval; can. 1422, concerning ecclesiastical benefices; can. 1494, concerning non-collegiate ecclesiastical institutes. Cf. Michiels, pp. 538-539.

[183] Cf. *supra,* p. 18.

[184] Cappello, *Summa Iuris Publici Ecclesiastici,* n. 45, p. 47.

[185] Can. 215, § 1.

[186] Can. 2292.

(3) the suppression of any religious congregation, even one of diocesan approval, and even if there is only one house in such a congregation; [187]

(4) the suppression of a province of a pontifically approved religious institute; [188]

(5) the suppression of ecclesiastical benefices; [189]

(6) the suppression of a religious house belonging to an exempt religious congregation; [190]

(7) the suppression of religious societies living a common life without vows; [191]

(8) the suppression of non-collegiate ecclesiastical institutes established by the local ordinary, unless the agreement or charter drawn up at the time of their foundation provides otherwise; [192]

(9) the suppression of associations of the faithful established by the Holy See itself.[193]

With regard to the power of the local ordinary in this regard, it may be said that he has power to suppress all those moral personalities which were established by any of his predecessors or by himself, except those the suppression of which is reserved to the Holy See. In certain cases, however, the power of the local ordinary is further limited by definite conditions. From the canons of the Code, considered more in detail, one may say:

[187] Can. 493.

[188] Can. 494, § 1.

[189] Can. 1422.

[190] Can. 498.

[191] Cans. 674 and 493.

[192] Can. 1494. Such institutions would be, e.g., hospitals and orphanages.

[193] Can. 699, § 2.

(1) that he can suppress a parochial see, after he has sought the advice of the board of consultors; [194]

(2) that he can suppress not only those associations of the faithful which were established by himself or his predecessors, but also those associations which were established with his consent by religious in virtue of an apostolic indult. Recourse to the Holy See is open to the association against the bishop's decree; [195]

(3) that he can suppress the house of a diocesan religious congregation, after giving a hearing to the head of that congregation. [196]

Distinct from, yet in some respect similar to, suppression is an act of "modification," by which the juridical condition of a moral personality becomes changed. Such a change may affect the nature or the qualities of the moral personality. [197] The change may also affect the scope of the activity of the moral personality, as when a charitable association is made to serve the purposes of public worship; [198] or the autonomy of the moral personality, as when it becomes united with another moral personality; [199] or the substratum thereof, as when the goods or territory of a moral personality are

[194] Can. 2292. Cf. can. 427, which points out that the board of consultors takes the place of the cathedral chapter in the matters concerning the government of the diocese.

[195] Can. 699, § 1.

[196] Can. 498. As had been said, if such a congregation has only one house, then it can be suppressed only by the Holy See. Cf. can. 493.

[197] Cf. can. 492, § 2, where there is question of a religious congregation of diocesan approval becoming recognized as a congregation of pontifical approval; can. 1430, § 2, which adverts to the changes whereby simple benefices (*beneficia simplicia*) are converted into benefices that have the care of souls attached to them (*beneficia curata*). Cf. also cans. 391, § 2, and 1430, § 1.

[198] Cans. 497; 707.

[199] Can. 1419, §§ 2 and 3. The reference here is to the co-ordinative and subordinative unions of benefices.

divided or dismembered; [200] or the juridical seat of the same, as when there is a transfer of it to another place.[201] Such modifications sometimes require more authority than is needed for establishment of the person in question, since they involve a partial suppression which may be reserved to higher authority.[202]

Section II. Intrinsic Extinction

Intrinsic extinction of moral personalities in the Church results from the juridical fact that the personality's substratum has ceased to exist for one hundred years.[203] A substratum of goods ceases to exist when the property is entirely destroyed or when it is irrevocably removed from its owner's possession.[204] A substratum of persons ceases to exist upon the voluntary act of the group dissolving itself, or upon the resignation or death of every member of the group, when at the same time there is no replacement of membership. It must be remembered, however, that if but a single member of a collegiate moral personality survives, all its rights and powers become centered in that one survivor.[205] Another point to be kept in mind is that a dispersal of the group or a dissolution of it attempted by incompetent authority (e.g., by a persecuting civil power) does not effect a cessation of the moral personality's continued existence.[206]

[200] Can. 1421.

[201] Can. 1421.

[202] Cf. Michiels, pp. 541-542, where he furnishes a list that points to the various powers of the Holy See and of the local ordinaries in this regard.

[203] Can. 102, § 1.—*Persona moralis . . . extinguitur . . . si per centum annorum spatium esse desierit.*

[204] Cf. Michiels, pp. 542-543, where he gives the following examples: when a church is totally destroyed, or has deteriorated in such a way that divine services can no longer be conducted there; when the endowment of a benefice or the payment which is due to it ceases to exist; or when the patrimony, in virtue of which a charitable institute was established, ceases to exist.

[205] Can. 102, § 2.—*Si vel unum ex personae moralis collegialis membris supersit, ius omnium in illud recidit.* Cf. *Fontes,* n. 2827, p. 369; n. 4219, p. 566.

[206] Michiels, p. 544. A remark of Vermeersch is worth noting in this regard. He stated: ". . . illegitima potestas, quae personam moralem directe

The while the legal period runs, that is, from the time of the cessation of the substratum to the completion of the span of one hundred years, the rights of the moral personality are said to lie dormant (*quiescere, dormire*).[207] If at any time in the course of that period the lost property of a non-collegiate moral personality be recovered, or if some individual achieve the status of membership in the old collegiate body, the rights of the moral personality revive, and the prescription period for its dissolution ceases to run. The functions of the moral personality may, therefore, be resumed altogether apart from any new decree of the competent superior, though for the sake of assuring the full effects of its revival his assent is usually required.[208]

Section III. Destination of the Property of the Extinct Moral Personality in the Church

One further question remains to be treated. What is to be done with the property of a moral personality in the Church which has juridically become extinct? One thing is certain, it still remains ecclesiastical property in the strict sense,[209] and the State has no right over such goods.[210] In fact, the law of the Church has explicitly provided for such an eventuality. It points out that if a moral personality in the Church becomes extinct, its goods are to belong to the moral personality immediately superior to it, subject always to the will and the intentions of the founders and bene-

---

supprimere non poterat, causa indirecta exstinctionis esse possit." Cf. Vermeersch, "De Personae Moralis Extinctione et Resurrectione," *Periodica*, XX (1931), 86. From this pertinent observation it follows that if, for example, a persecuting civil power not only disperses, but actually kills, all the members of a particular moral personality in the Church, and there is no replacement of membership for a hundred years, then that moral personality would cease to exist juridically once the duration of the period of time postulated in the Church's law has actually elapsed.

[207] Cf. D'Angelo, "De Quiescentia in Codice Iuris Canonici," *Apollinaris*, I (1928), 502.

[208] Cf. Vermeersch, "art. cit.," *Periodica*, XX (1931), 87.

[209] Can. 1497, § 1.

[210] Michiels, p. 548.

factors, to the legally vested rights, and to the special laws which governed the extinct personality.[211] In pursuance of this general rule in practice, the property of any province of a religious institute should attach to the religious institute itself, the property of a religious congregation or diocese to the Holy See, the property of a parish to the diocese. The property of a non-collegiate ecclesiastical institute (e.g., a hospital) and that of an association of the faithful [212] would likewise attach to the diocese.[213]

[211] Can. 1501.

[212] Cf. cans. 687 and 691, § 1.

[213] Michiels, pp. 548-549. There were some, however, who contended that the property of an association of the faithful should attach to the parish, and not to the diocese. Cf. Couly, "Extinction des Personnes Morales," *Le Canoniste Contemporain*, XLIV (1921), 115.

CHAPTER II

RELIGIOUS AND CHARITABLE CORPORATIONS IN NEW YORK

Article 1. General Laws Concerning All Corporations

The Constitution of New York [1] provides that corporations are created only under general laws, except for municipal purposes and in cases where, in the judgment of the legislature, the objects of the corporation cannot be attained under general laws, in which case incorporation by special act is permitted. There are three general laws under which corporations for religious, charitable, and educational purposes may be formed: the Religious Corporations Law, the Membership Corporations Law, and the Education Law. Some corporations have been formed for charitable, religious, or educational purposes by special acts of the legislature. All corporations are subject to the provisions of the General Corporation Law, unless they are excepted by law in some matter.

A New York corporation must have a minimum of three incorporators, all of them natural persons of full age, and at least two-thirds of their number must be citizens of the United States, and at least one of their number must be a resident of New York State.[2] Thus, New York law contemplates the formation of only corporations aggregate, and does not provide for corporations sole or for "non-collegiate moral personalities." [3]

Every New York corporation as such has power, although not specified in the law under which it is incorporated:

(1) To have succession for the period specified in its certificate of incorporation or by statute, and perpetually when no period is specified. The succession may be specified as "perpetual." [4] Where

---

[1] *N. Y. Constitution,* Art. X, § 1.

[2] White, *New York Corporations* (2 vols. with cumulative supplement for 1955, Albany: Bender, 1947), I, 5.

[3] Cf. *supra,* p. 6.

[4] *McKinney's Consolidated Laws of New York, General Corporation Law* (Book 22 with 1956 Cumulative Annual Pocket Part, Brooklyn: Thompson, 1943, § 14, subd. 1 (hereafter cited *N. Y. General Corporations Law*).

succession is for a fixed term, this term may be extended before its expiration,[5] and in certain cases the corporation may be revived after expiration of the term.[6]

(2) To acquire property for the corporate purposes by grant, gift, purchase, devise or bequest, and to hold and to dispose of the same, subject to such limitations as may be prescribed by law.[7]

(3) To appoint such officers and agents as its business shall require.[8]

(4) To make by-laws, not inconsistent with the law, for the management of its business, the regulation of its affairs, the calling of meetings of its members, etc.[9]

Certain provisions of the General Corporation Law are not applicable to religious corporations and to educational corporations formed under the Regents, viz., the provision regarding judicial supervision of corporations and of officers and members thereof (art. 6), the provision regarding sequestration of property, action for dissolution, action for liability of individual members and directors, action to annul a corporation (art. 7), the provision regarding action to dissolve a corporation for insolvency or refusal to pay its debts for one year, or for suspension of ordinary and lawful business for at least one year (art. 8).[10] Membership corporations are not excepted from these provisions.

Non-stock corporations may take and hold property of the value of twenty million dollars or less, or the yearly income derived from which shall be two million dollars or less. In computing the value of such property no increase in value arising otherwise than from improvements made thereon shall be taken into account.[11] This

---

[5] *N. Y. General Corporations Law,* § 45.

[6] *Ibid.,* §§ 46; 49.

[7] *Ibid.,* § 14, subd. 3.

[8] *Ibid.,* subd. 4.

[9] *Ibid.,* subd. 5.

[10] *Ibid.,* § 130.

[11] *Ibid.,* § 15.

section has application to corporations formed under the Religious Corporations Law, the Membership Corporations Law, and the Education Law.

There is no law forbidding a corporation formed for religious, charitable or educational purposes to organize as a stock corporation. A diocesan purchasing corporation or holding corporation could be so organized.

Article 2. Membership Corporations

Section I. Their Creation

The term "membership corporation" means a corporation not organized for pecuniary profit, incorporated under the Membership Corporations Law, Chapter 36 of the Consolidated Laws of New York, or under any law repealed by this chapter.[12] Corporations may be formed under this chapter for any lawful purpose, or for several kindred or incidental purposes. No corporation, however, may be formed under this chapter for a purpose for which incorporation may be had under any other general law.[13] Therefore parish churches and dioceses, which may be incorporated under the Religious Corporation Law,[14] cannot be incorporated under this chapter. Institutions and organizations with purposes for which a corporation may be chartered by the Regents of the University of the State of New York may be incorporated under the present chapter, only if the consent of the Commissioner of Education is endorsed on the certificate of incorporation.[15]

The certificate of incorporation by which the membership corporation is to be formed shall state: the name of the proposed corporation, the purpose for which it is to be formed, the territory in which it shall operate, the town and county where it shall have

---

[12] *McKinney's Consolidated Laws of New York, Membership Corporations Law* (Book 36 with 1956 Cumulative Annual Pocket Part, Brooklyn: Thompson, 1943), § 2 (hereafter cited *N. Y. Membership Corporations Law*).

[13] *N. Y. Membership Corporations Law,* § 10.

[14] Cf. *infra,* pp.53-56.

[15] *N. Y. Membership Corporations Law,* § 11, subd. 2.

its office, the number of its directors (not fewer than three are required), the names and addresses of the directors to serve until the first annual meeting; that of the incorporators (who must sign the certificate) all are to be of full age, at least two-thirds of them are to be citizens of the United States, at least one of them is to be a resident of the State of New York, and of the named directors at least one is to be a citizen of the United States and a resident of the State of New York. The law requires at least five corporators.[16]

Certificates of incorporation are filed with the Secretary of State, and in some special cases with other officials of the State or County. To each certificate of incorporation shall be attached the approval of a Justice of the Supreme Court of the judicial district in which the office of the corporation is to be located. This Justice has to determine, from the certificate and other evidence, whether the objects and purposes are truly those that are set forth in the certificate, and whether the objects and purposes of the proposed corporation are in accord with public policy.[17] Also required in certain cases is the endorsement of the certificate by State officials who have competence regarding specified types of benevolent activities, viz., the State Board of Social Welfare, the Superintendent of Insurance, State Department of Social Welfare, the Board of Standards and Appeals, the Commissioner of Education.[18]

Existing unincorporated associations may be incorporated under this Chapter if all their purposes accord with the scope of the Chapter. There are special provisions regarding execution of their certificates of incorporation. When an existing association is so incorporated, all of its members are members of the corporation, all property owned by or held for it vests in the corporation.[19]

Creation of membership corporations is sometimes obtained by special law.[20] The legislature is permitted to enact such a special

---

[16] *Ibid.,* § 10.

[17] *Loc. cit.*

[18] *Ibid.,* § 11, subd. 1, 1b, 1a, and 2 respectively for the officials named above.

[19] *Ibid.,* § 12.

[20] *Ibid.,* § 2.

law only when the objects of the corporation cannot be attained under general laws.[21]

Section II. Their Operation

Any membership corporation, created by or under a general or a special law, may have a constitution, by-laws and rules, which shall be collectively known as by-laws and may provide methods for the amendment and repeal thereof. The provisions of the by-laws must be consistent with the law and with the certificate of incorporation. They may regulate the conduct of the affairs of the corporation, including the status of members, officers and directors, and conduct of its meetings. The by-laws may not establish for a meeting a quorum of less than one-third.[22]

This is a very important law. For it is through the by-laws of corporations representing juridical persons in the Church that the corporation's activities can be placed under the direction of ecclesiastical authority. Thus, for example, the bishop and his vicar general can be made members, directors and officers, *ex officio.* Management of corporate affairs between meetings, and the full power to invest and reinvest funds, can be reserved to an executive committee of three which includes the bishop and his vicar general. The bishop can be designated president *ex officio,* with power to name all committees, with membership *ex officio* in each committee, and with exclusive power to sign for the corporation all deeds and other instruments which bind the corporation. He can have the power to delegate such powers. All other officers would act under the authority of the executive committee, and no contract or obligation would bind the corporation unless made and approved by the executive committee. Similar restrictions could be placed on sale and lease of property. Provision could be made for an accounting of all the business in the annual meeting of the corporation, and even current accounts could be directed to be kept in the bishop's curia. There is no New York law forbidding any of these provisions. Religious superiors may be accorded, in the by-laws of corporations

[21] *N. Y. Constitution,* Art. X, § 1.
[22] *N. Y. Membership Corporations Law,* § 20.

representing their communities, powers here exemplified in reference to the bishop.

The law does require authorization by vote of at least two-thirds of the directors, or of a majority of them if they number twenty-one or more, for any purchase, sale, mortgage, or lease of realty by the corporation. For such sale or mortgage, and for a lease to run more than five years, leave must be had of the Supreme Court in a judicial district in which some of the property is located. The Court may grant leave to a membership corporation to convey real property, without consideration, to another corporation created not for pecuniary profit and for purposes similar to those of the grantor corporation.[23] This last provision would be applicable, for example, when a corporation represented a juridical personality in the Church, whose goods and territory were to be divided, or when a juridical personality was to be suppressed.

Membership corporations created either by general or by special law, and their books and vouchers, are subject to the visitation and inspection of a Justice of the Supreme Court or his appointee. No more than one accounting, however, may be required within one year, and no second accounting may be required while proceedings are pending for an account under this Section. Appeal from the final order of the Supreme Court may be taken to the Appellate Division and to the Court of Appeals.[24]

At the annual meeting of a membership corporation, its directors are required to present a verified report showing the following: the whole amount of real and personal property owned by it, where it is located, and where and how invested, the amount and nature of the property acquired during the year immediately preceding the date of the report, the amount and the purposes, objects or persons to or for which applications, appropriations or expenditures have been made, the names and addresses of persons admitted to membership during the year; which report is to be filed with the records of the corporation and an abstract thereof entered in the minutes of the proceedings of the annual meeting.[25]

---

23 *Ibid.,* § 21.
24 *Ibid.,* § 26.
25 *Ibid.,* § 46.

In the absence of fraud or bad faith, the directors of a membership corporation created under or by a general or special law shall not be personally liable for its debts, obligations or liabilities.[26] No director or other officer shall receive any emolument, unless authorized by the by-laws of the corporation, or by the vote of two-thirds of the directors. No director or other officer shall be interested in any contract relating to the operations of the corporation or for furnishing supplies thereto, unless authorized by vote of two-thirds of the directors.[27]

By a process similar to that of incorporation, an existing membership corporation may alter its purposes or powers, or other provision of its certificate of incorporation.[28] Similarly, it may consolidate with another membership corporation created for like purposes.[29] Any gift or grant made before or after such consolidation to either corporation shall inure to the benefit of the consolidated corporation and, so far as is necessary for that purpose, the existence of such constituent corporations shall be deemed to continue in and through the consolidated corporation. The rights and liabilities of the constituent corporations continue as if the consolidated corporation had itself acquired them.[30]

Section III. Their Dissolution

Membership corporations, except those formed under the Regents of the University of the State of New York,[31] are liable to dissolution by judicial process under Articles 6, 7 and 8 of the General Corporations Law.[32] All membership corporations are liable to dissolution by order of the Supreme Court.[33] All corporations having a fixed term of succession [34] are dissolved on expira-

---

[26] *Loc. cit.*

[27] *Ibid.,* § 47.

[28] *Ibid.,* § 30.

[29] *Ibid.,* § 50.

[30] *Ibid.,* § 51.

[31] Cf. *supra,* p. 36; *infra,* p. 43.

[32] *N. Y. General Corporations Law,* § 130; cf. *supra,* p. 35.

[33] *N. Y. Membership Corporations Law,* § 26.

[34] Cf. *supra,* pp. 34-35.

tion of that term; but they may obtain extension of corporated existence by filing a certificate as provided in the General Corporations Law, § 45.

Any membership corporation created under or by a general or a special law may obtain dissolution by filing in the office of the Secretary of State a certificate entitled and endorsed "Certificate for dissolution of . . . pursuant to article eight of the membership corporations law." That certificate of dissolution shall be either subscribed and acknowledged by every member entitled to vote, or subscribed and acknowledged by the president or a vice-president and the secretary, authorized by the votes of two-thirds of the members entitled to vote.[35] Such certificate shall have endorsed thereon or annexed thereto the approval of a Justice of the Supreme Court of the judicial district in which the office of the corporation is located. If the corporation is one which could be created under Chapter 36 of the Membership Corporations Law only on approval of a state or a local board or body,[36] the approval of such board or body must be endorsed on or attached to the certificate of dissolution.[37] Upon filing of such certificate, the Secretary of State shall certify that the corporation has complied with this Section and is dissolved.[38]

In the case of membership corporations dissolved in accordance with the requirements of Membership Corporations Law, or by expiration of their corporate existence, the Supreme Court upon proper petition, may, from time to time, take cognizance of certain matters arising out of such dissolution. On receiving such petition, the Court will give notice to such surviving directors as are not petitioners, and notice to such other interested parties as the Court may specify. Some of the matters to be ordered and adjudged by the Court are the following:

(1) Notice of the time and place for presentation of all claims and demands against the corporation.

(2) The payment or satisfaction in whole or in part of claims

---

[35] *N. Y. Membership Corporations Law*, § 55, subd. 1.

[36] Cf. *supra*, p. 37.

[37] *N. Y. Membership Corporations Law*, § 55, subd. 1.

[38] *Ibid.*, § 55, subd. 5.

and demands against the corporation, or retention of moneys for such purpose.

(3) The administration of any trust or the disposition of any property held in trust by or for the corporation.

(4) The sale and disposition of any remaining property of the corporation, and the distribution or division of such property or its proceeds, among the members or persons entitled thereto, except that in the case of a corporation formed for any of the purposes described in § 11, subd. 1,[39] the court must give a twenty-day personal notice to the Attorney General, and a four-week notice by publication to the members, creditors, and contributors to the funds of the corporation. Thereafter the court may make an order that such property or its proceeds shall be transferred to such other corporation or association as the court shall specify, to be administered or used in such a manner as in the judgment of the court will best accomplish the general purposes for which the corporation so dissolved was organized. This determination of the court shall be without regard to and free from any express or implied restriction, limitation or direction imposed upon such corporation.[40]

ARTICLE 3. CORPORATIONS FORMED FOR EDUCATIONAL PURPOSES

The Education Law provides that the Regents of the University of the State of New York may incorporate "any university, college, academy, library, museum, or other institution or association for the promotion of . . . knowledge or of education in any way . . . and other associations whose approved purposes are . . . of educational or cultural value deemed worthy of recognition and encouragement by the university."[41] Such incorporation is effected by an instrument under the seal of the Regents. The charter will set forth the name of the corporation, the number of its trustees or other

[39] That subdivision enumerates certain charitable purposes, and directs that corporations for such purposes shall not be formed without consent of the State Board of Welfare.

[40] *N. Y. Membership Corporations Law*, § 56.

[41] *McKinney's Consolidated Laws of New York, Education Law* (Book 16, Part 1 with 1956 Cumulative Annual Pocket Part, Brooklyn: Thompson, 1953), § 216 (hereafter cited *N. Y. Education Law*).

managers, and the powers, privileges and duties of such trustees, subject to such limitations as the Regents may prescribe in conformity with law.[42]

The legislature may incorporate educational institutions and associations by special act, when it appears that the objects of the corporation cannot be attained under the general laws.[43]

Educational institutions and associations may be incorporated under the general laws, e.g., under the Membership Corporations Law,[44] but such incorporation may not be affected without consent of the Regents, if the corporation to be formed is such that it might have been incorporated by the Regents.[45]

No corporation shall, under authority of any general act, extend its business to include establishing or carrying on any educational institution or work, without the consent of the Board of Regents.[46]

The Regents have power, at any time, for sufficient cause, by an instrument under their seal, to change the name, or alter, suspend or revoke the charter of incorporation of an educational institution. This power extends to any educational institution which they might incorporate, if the institution is subject to their visitation or chartered or incorporated by the Regents or under a general law.[47] The only institutions not subject to this power would be those that were created by special act and saved by that act from the Regents' power of visitation.

The Regents have special power with regard to gifts made to institutions incorporated by them. Notwithstanding any limitation by charter, by special law, or by general statute, such institutes may, with authorization by the Regents given within one year after the delivery or probate of the instrument of gift, take gifts of any value, whether given absolutely or in trust, for any of the corporate purposes of such institution. The gift shall be valid whether made in the corporate name or to the trustees of the corporation, and the

---

[42] *Loc. cit.*

[43] *N. Y. Constitution*, Art. X, § 1.

[44] *N. Y. Membership Corporations Law*, § 11, subd. 2.

[45] *N. Y. Education Law*, § 216.

[46] *Ibid.*, § 218.

[47] *Ibid.*, § 219.

powers given the trustees in relation to the gift shall be the powers of the corporation.[48]

The Regents exercise legislative functions concerning the educational system of the State, they determine its educational policies, and they establish rules for carrying into effect the laws and policies of the State relating to education. This legislative power is subject to and must conform to the Constitution and the Laws of the State. It is specifically provided that no enactment of the Regents shall modify in any degree the freedom of the governing body of any seminary for the training of priests or clergymen to determine and regulate the entire course of religious, doctrinal or theological instruction to be given in such institution.[49]

The Supreme Court may order dissolution of any educational corporation which is subject to the visitation of the Regents, whether the incorporation was effected through the charter of incorporation by the Regents or under a general law. The order may be issued upon application of the majority of the corporation's trustees, whenever such corporation will cease to act in its corporate capacity, or will have its charter revoked by the Regents. The court is empowered to decide whether dissolution is proper. Having ordered and decreed the dissolution, the court shall order the settlement of the corporation's property. After directing sale and conveyance of the property, and having directed determination and payment of debts and the expenses of the sale and proceedings for dissolution, the court may then dispose of the balance of the property, if any remain. That balance is to be devoted and applied to such educational, religious, benevolent, charitable, or other purposes, as the trustees of the corporation may indicate by their petition, and the court may approve.[50]

ARTICLE 4. RELIGIOUS CORPORATIONS

Section I. Historical Background

A brief resumé of the more significant historical facts regarding the development of the New York law on religious corporations will

---

[48] *Ibid.,* § 226, subd. 5.

[49] *Ibid.,* § 207.

[50] *Ibid.,* § 220, subd. 1 & 4.

be helpful. While the Toleration Act of 1689 had granted religious freedom to dissenting Protestants (the sects other than the Anglican) in colonial New York, this did not mean that these groups could secure incorporation of their church property. In 1696 the Dutch Reformed Church of New York City received such a charter, and other churches of this denomination received similar privileges in the following year.[51] On close examination, however, it will be found that incorporation was granted to no other dissenting group during the colonial period.[52] Catholics, during this time, fared much worse than did the dissenting Protestant sects.[53] In fact, no Catholic churches existed in the colony of New York. A few Catholic priests ministered there from time to time, but no parishes were established.

From the War of Independence until 1784, religious corporations could be organized in New York only by special legislative act. The Religious Incorporations Act of April 6, 1784, was a general law permitting creation of such corporations without recourse to the legislature in each case.[54] It was under this statute that the trustees of St. Peter's Church (first Catholic church in New York) were incorporated. It was in this board of trustees that the ownership of the church property was vested.

In 1813 there was passed in the Legislature of New York an *Act for the Incorporation of Religious Societies.* In it there are found separate provisions for the Episcopal and Dutch Reformed Churches. Then follows a general section which regulates other religious bodies, including, therefore, the Catholic Church.[55] In evaluating the implications of this act one may well refer to a state-

---

[51] Dignan, *A History of the Legal Incorporation of Catholic Church in the United States* (New York: Kenedy, 1935), p. 27.

[52] O'Callaghan, *Documentary History of New York* (New York: 1849), III, 489-494, 504, 508.

[53] Cobb, *The Rise of Religious Liberty in America* (New York: 1901), p. 336.

[54] *Laws of the State of New York,* I (edited by Jones and Varick, New York, 1789), pp. 104-109.

[55] *Laws of the State of New York, 1812-1813,* II (Albany, 1813), pp. 214-216.

ment as found in an important later judicial decision, which will presently be seen in more detail:

> The whole act (1813) shows that it was the intention of the legislature to place the control of the temporal affairs of these societies in the hands of the majority of the corporators, independent of priest or bishop, presbytery, synod or other ecclesiastical judicatory. This is the inevitable effect of the provision giving to the majority, without regard to their religious sentiments, the right to elect trustees, and to fix the salary of the minister. The courts cannot disfranchise any corporator, who possesses the qualifications prescribed by the statutes.[56]

Obviously the Acts of 1784 and 1813 concerning the incorporation of church property were framed by legislators who had Protestant types of Church discipline in mind. This fact was to be the root of much trouble in New York for the next fifty years. In the ensuing years the peace of the diocese depended on the very uncertain outcome of trustee elections.[57] From the conflict one thing emerged quite clearly, namely, the legal helplessness of the bishop against a body of trustees who were determined to resist to the bitter end. The only course left to the bishop was to try to secure, if possible, the election of a body of trustees who would obey him.[58]

In 1852 the so-called Taber Bill was introduced in the New York Legislature. In its purpose it sought to enable Roman Catholic bishops in New York State to hold, in their official capacity, church property in trust for religious and charitable purposes. It would have made the bishops corporations sole and would have eliminated the need of lay trustees, as well as the danger for church property to attach to heirs at law.[59] Know-Nothing protests, combined with protests from rebel trustees in Rochester and Buffalo, were responsible for the ultimate defeat of the bill in 1853.[60]

It was to members of this Know-Nothing party that the trustees

---

[56] Robertson *v.* Bullions, 11 N. Y. 243 (1854).

[57] McNamara, "Trusteeism in the Atlantic States, 1785-1863," *Catholic Historical Review,* XXX (1944), 135-154.

[58] Dignan, *op. cit.,* p. 96.

[59] *Ibid.,* p. 185.

[60] *Loc. cit.*

of St. Louis Church in Buffalo came with a request for the passage
of an act which provided that the Catholic Church *must* incorporate
in accordance with the trustee incorporation law of 1813, under
penalty of escheatment to the State of church property thenceforth
handed down in any other way.[61] The consequences of such a bill
certainly could be far-reaching. As one writer later summed it up:

> . . . it was more revolutionary in its character than any theory
> relative to the tenure of land advocated in modern times. It is
> the first enactment denying individual property in land, and
> asserting the right of the State not only to confiscate all land
> without compensation, but even to convey it at will. It made
> void any deed, lease, or devise of any Catholic bishop, and on
> his death vested the property in any incorporated congregation
> happening to use the same.[62]

This bill (the Putnam Bill) was passed on April 9, 1855, and
in effect gave lay corporations the power to overrule the bishop if
they felt so inclined. As has been said, it was made impossible for
the bishop to hold church property so as to be able to transmit it
to his successors in office. The reaction to this measure may be
summed up very simply. It was not applied in practice. No other
Catholic congregation (than that of St. Louis Church in Buffalo)
took advantage of it.[63]

Around this same time a very important change took place in
the whole legal theory of church corporations in the courts of New
York State. The result was the evolution of the corporation aggregate instead of the old trustee corporation, which meant that the
congregation, rather than its trustees, became the basis in fact of
the corporation. The law considered a church under three aspects
under a trustee corporation system: (1) the *spiritual organization,*
of which the law said nothing; 2. the *society,* of which the law took
cognizance; 3. the *trustee corporation,* which was the legal repre-
sentative of the society.[64]

[61] McNamara, "art. cit.," *Catholic Historical Review,* XX (1944), 150.

[62] Farley, *The Life of John Cardinal McCloskey* (New York, 1918),
p. 193.

[63] Dignan, *op. cit.,* p. 196.

[64] Zollman, *American Church Law* (St. Paul: West Publ. Co., 1933), p.
117; cf. Lawyer *v.* Cipperly, 7 Paige 211 (N. Y., 1838).

As far as the courts were concerned the trustee corporation gave rise to a twofold disadvantage. The first disadvantage was to be found in the fact that the courts were burdened with a multitude of disputes between the trustees and the church societies of the various sects, which disputes often turned upon the changing tenets of religious groups.[65] Zollman expressed the second disadvantage as follows:

> Another unexpected evil developed by the trustee corporation theory was that church property without any express exemption was held to be execution proof. If judgment was recovered against the corporation, an execution became useless, since it held only the legal title. The creditor, however good his claim, was without remedy, even if he was able to recover judgment. But even this slight consolation was denied him. It was held that the trustees had no power to contract debts. If they did, the creditor, unless he by some chance could hold the individual trustees, was helpless. The spectacle of a church, a moral agent, evading its just debts on a technicality, is certainly not very elevating.[66]

Now, in the case of Robertson *v.* Bullions,[67] which came before the New York Court of Appeals in June, 1854, the trust relation between the society and its trustees was removed. The case involved a Presbyterian minister who had been excommunicated by the presbytery and synod, but whom the trustees of the Associate Church of Cambridge, New York, wished to retain.

The result of this case was that thenceforth in the State of New York the trustee corporation gave way to the corporation aggregate, in which the congregation as such was held to be incorporated. The corporate franchise was extended to all the members of the society, and from exclusive corporators the trustees were reduced to mere officers of the corporation. The distinction between society and corporation was abolished, so that churches thenceforth presented only a twofold aspect (spiritual organization and corpora-

---

[65] Zollman, *op. cit.*, pp. 120-122.

[66] *Ibid.*, p. 122.

[67] 11, N. Y. 243 (1854).

tion) instead of a threefold aspect (spiritual organization, society, and corporation).[68] It followed that, since the trustees, though still called such, were in fact only officers, there was no trust relation between them and their associates. The entire theory of a trust arising out of this relation was thus entirely done away with.[69]

On May 29, 1857, a Memorial was presented to the New York Legislature which read, "Be it enacted . . . that male persons of any religious denomination or society may incorporate accordingly as may be most suitable to their discipline. . . ."[70] The request failed. In 1863, however, the Putnam Bill was repealed by the New York Senate. In that same year, Archbishop Hughes had Charles O'Conor, a New York lawyer, draft a church incorporation law, which on March 25, 1863, was passed in the New York Legislature as an *Act Supplementary to the Act entitled An Act to provide for the Incorporation of Religious Societies, passed April 5, 1813*.[71] This extremely important amendment reads in part as follows:

> It shall be lawful for any Roman Catholic church or congregation now or hereafter existing in this state to be incorporated according to the provisions of this act; the Roman Catholic archbishop or bishop of the diocese in which such church may be erected or intended so to be, the vicar-general of such diocese, and the pastor of such church for the time being, respectively or a majority of them, may select and appoint two lay men, sign a certificate, showing the name or title by which they and their successors shall be known and distinguished as a body corporate by virtue of this act, which certificate shall be duly acknowledged or proved, in the same manner as conveyances of real estate. . . .
>
> The trustees of every such church or congregation, and their successors shall have all the powers and authority granted to the trustees of any church, congregation or society, by the fourth section "Act to provide for the incorporation of Religious Societies," passed April fifth, eighteen hundred and thirteen. . . .[72]

[68] Cf. *supra*, p. 47.

[69] Petty *v.* Tooker, 21 N. Y. 267 (1860).

[70] Dignan, *op. cit.*, p. 207.

[71] *Loc. cit.*

[72] *Laws of the State of New York passed at the Eighty-sixth Session of the Legislature* (Albany, 1863), pp. 65-67.

Here for the first time the New York law removed the danger of lay interference with ecclesiastical jurisdiction by giving ecclesiastics a predominant place on the trustee board, and by granting to them the nomination of the lay trustees.

Until 1875 it was held, on the authority of Robertson *v.* Bullions,[73] that a religious corporation had the legal right to change its form of ecclesiastical government and its creed, without losing its hold upon the church property. Chapter 79 of the Laws of 1875 enacted that the property of religious corporations formed under the general law shall be applied by the trustees for the benefit of such corporation "according to the discipline, rules, and usages of the denomination to which the church members of the corporation belong."

In 1895 there was added a further amendment requiring the sanction of the Catholic bishop or administrator for the validity of the corporate acts of the board. It stated:

> No act or proceeding of the trustees of any such incorporated church shall be valid without the sanction of the archbishop or bishop of the diocese to which such church belongs, or, in the case of their absence or inability to act, without the sanction of the vicar-general or of the administrator of such diocese.[74]

A further amendment was enacted in 1902. It permitted the bishop to transfer without consideration the property of a divided parish to the parish newly established by the division, and to divide the receipts proportionately.[75]

On July 29, 1911, the Sacred Congregation of the Council sent a letter to the ordinaries of the United States. It serves as a definitive norm in any estimation of the relative values of the different systems of church tenure as existing in this country. It states in part:

---

[73] 11 N. Y. 243 (1854).

[74] *General Laws of New York,* I (Albany, 1895), 499.

[75] *Consolidated Laws of the State of New York,* II (Albany, 1909), art. 5, § 92.

Of the methods which now exist in the United States, for possessing and administering the possessions of the Church, that is to be preferred, which is popularly called the *Parish* Corporation, with, however, those conditions and precautions, which are in use in the State of New York. This method, therefore, Bishops will take care immediately to introduce, if the civil law allows, for the temporal possessions in their diocese.[76]

Until 1917, the New York law contemplated only the formation of "Roman Catholic" churches, which term referred only to parishes subject to a local ordinary of the Latin rite. The Laws of 1917, Chapter 353, § 2, added a section governing the formation and management of church corporations under the Ruthenian-Greek jurisdiction.[77]

Section II. Nature of Religious Corporations

A religious corporation in New York is defined as "a corporation created for religious purposes."[78] The New York Court of Appeals pointed out that one is not much wiser for this statutory definition. It furthermore indicated that the whole history of the law on this subject excluded from operation of the present Chapter (on religious corporations) all benevolent, charitable, missionary, philanthropic associations in which religion is an incidental purpose.[79] A lower court declared: "It seems that a religious corporation should be one formed primarily for religious purposes; exercising some ecclesiastical control over its members, having some distinct form of worship, and some method of discipline for violation thereof. . . ."[80] A decision of the Appellate Division declared that a religious corporation "must be either, first, an incorporated church created to enable its members to meet for divine worship or other

---

[76] *The Ecclesiastical Review*, XLV (1911), 585; cf. Bouscaren, *Canon Law Digest* (3 vols., Vol. I, 1934; Vol. II, 1943; Vol. III, 1953, Milwaukee: Bruce), II, 444-445.

[77] Cf. *N. Y. Religious Corporations Law*, §§ 100-103.

[78] *N. Y. Religious Corporations Law*, § 2.

[79] Matter of Watson, 171 N. Y. 256, 63 N. E. 1109, *reversing* 70 App. Div. 623, 75 N. Y. S. 1134, *affirming* 36 Misc. 504, 73 N. Y. S. 1058 (1902).

[80] Matter of Fay, 37 Misc. 532, 76 N. Y. S. 62 (1902).

religious observances, or, second, an incorporated congregation, society, or other assemblage, accustomed to meet for the same purpose." [81]

It is to be kept in mind that in the United States the Catholic Church as such is not recognized as a corporation. [82] In the United States its dioceses and other territorial areas will not be judicially noticed [83] or recognized as corporations. [84] Religious corporations created under New York law are not governmental corporations, but private ones. [85] "These incorporated societies are not to be regarded as ecclesiastical corporations, in the sense of the English Law, which were composed entirely of ecclesiastical persons, and subject to the ecclesiastical judicatories, but as belonging to the class of civil corporations to be controlled and managed according to the principles of the common law, as administered by the ordinary tribunals of justice." [86] It seems clear, therefore, that the law of New York, in principle, takes no cognizance of the divinely constituted social structure of the Church, or of the juridical character of "moral personalities" constituted by Canon Law. In practice, however, the general provisions of § 5 of N. Y. Religious Corporations Law on "denominational control," [87] and the special provisions for Catholic churches in §§ 90 to 92 and 100 to 102 give effect to a hierarchical rule [88] over Catholic religious corporations.

It has been said that it is the general scope and purpose of the Religious Corporations Law to authorize the creation of religious corporations as secular agencies to aid in the conduct of church

[81] Johnston *v.* Hughes, 112 App. Div. 524, 98 N. Y. S. 525 (1906), *reversed on other ground,* 187 N. Y. 446 (1907).

[82] The Catholic Church is recognized as a corporation in our island possessions by the Treaty of Paris, which concluded the Spanish American War. Cf. *Treaty of Paris,* art. 8, cited in Ponce *v.* Roman Catholic Apostolic Church in Puerto Rico, 210 U. S. 296, 310, 28 S. Ct. 737, 52 L. Ed. 1068 (1908).

[83] Baxter *v.* McDonnell, 155 N. Y. 83, 95, 49 N. E. 667 (1898).

[84] McCaughal, *v.* Ryan, 27 Barb. 376, 390 (N. Y., 1857).

[85] People *v.* Keese, 27 Hun 483 (N. Y., 1882).

[86] Robertson *v.* Bullions, 11 N. Y. 243 (1854).

[87] Cf. *supra,* p. 50.

[88] Cf. *supra,* pp. 49-50.

business and affairs, including the acquisition, the holding and the disposal of property.[89] The New York Law points out: "But this section does not give to the trustees of an incorporated church any control over the calling, settlement, dismissal or removal of its minister, or the fixing of his salary; or any power to fix or change the times, nature or order of the public or social worship of such church."[90] By definition, the term "clergymen" and the term "minister" include a "duly authorized pastor, rector, priest, rabbi, and a person having authority from, or in accordance with, the rules and regulations of the governing ecclesiastical body of the denomination . . . to which the church belongs . . . to preside over and direct the spiritual affairs of the church. . . ."[91] Accordingly, the courts of New York have held that it is the duty of trustees to receive a minister assigned by ecclesiastical authority, and that the minister so assigned has the remedy of a writ of mandamus to put him in possession of the church.[92] Further, trustees retaining a deposed minister are guilty of misusing the property of the corporation.[93] "A priest or minister of any church by assuming that relation necessarily subjects his conduct in that capacity to the laws and customs of the ecclesiastical body from which he derives his office and in whose name he exercises his functions; the decisions of the proper church judicatory on these matters is binding on him and will be respected by the civil courts. The decisions of the courts in this country are substantially in accordance with this view."[94]

Section III. Creation of Religious Corporations

A Roman Catholic diocese in New York may be organized as a "corporation with governing authority over, or advisory relations with, churches. . . ."[95]

[89] St. Nicholas Cathedral of Russian Orthodox Church of North America *v.* Kedroff, 276 App. Div. 309, 94 N. Y. S. 2d 453 (1950); cf. Walker Memorial Baptist Church *v.* Saunders, 285 N. Y. 462, 35 N. E. 2d 42 (1941).

[90] *N. Y. Religious Corporations Law,* § 5.

[91] *Ibid.,* § 2.

[92] People *v.* Conley, 42 Hun. 98, 2 N. Y. St. R. 372 (1886).

[93] Isham *v.* Tullager, 14 Abb. N. Cas. 363 (N. Y., 1881).

[94] *In re* Haebler *v.* N. Y. Produce Exchange, 149 N. Y. 414 (1896).

[95] *N. Y. Religious Corporations Law,* § 15.

This general statute, however, seems poorly adapted to the needs of Catholic dioceses. It states in part:

> An unincorporated diocesan . . . governing . . . board having jurisdiction over or relations with several or a number of churches . . . some or all of which are located in this state, may at a meeting duly held, determine to become incorporated by a designated name, and may, by a plurality vote, elect not less than three nor more than fifteen persons to be the first trustees of such corporation. . . . The trustees of every incorporated governing or advisory body and their successors shall hold their offices during the pleasure of such body, which may remove them and fill vacancies in accordance with its rules and regulations.[96]

There are particular provisions for the Episcopal, Orthodox, and Lutheran religions, but none for a Catholic diocese.[97] All the Catholic dioceses in New York, therefore, have been incorporated by special acts of the legislature. The provisions of such an act are exemplified in Chapter 238, Laws of 1941, by which The Roman Catholic Diocese of Albany, New York, was reincorporated. The corporation created by this act succeeds the corporation formed October 9, 1894, by certificate of incorporation under a provision of the general law which was analogous to the present Religious Corporations Law on this matter. This act designates the bishop, the vicar-general, and the chancellor of the diocese, and their successors in office, as *ex officio* accredited members of the body corporate. They are its only members. In addition to the powers given by law to membership corporations created by special act, this corporation is granted power to take real estate and personalty by purchase or devise, either absolutely or in trust, for any of its purposes, without limitation as to amount or value. Sale, lease or mortgage of its real property must be authorized by the bishop, or, in his absence or inability to act, by the vicar-general or the administrator of the diocese. If there is a vacancy in the see, all powers of the bishop under this act devolve upon the administrator

---

[96] *Loc. cit.*

[97] *Loc. cit.* The regulations for the Lutheran religion may be found in the annual pocket supplement for the year 1956 under § 15.

of the diocese. The diocesan corporation so organized is still subject to the provisions of law applicable thereto, unless those provisions are inconsistent with the special act.

The certificate of incorporation of a religious corporation is to be acknowledged or proved before an officer authorized to take such acknowledgment or proof.[98] If the corporation is to have an office or place of worship, the certificate is filed in the county where that office or place of worship is to be situated; otherwise the certificate is filed with the Secretary of State.[99] The incorporators, who execute the certificate, must be qualified according to the provisions of General Corporation Law, § 4.[100] The certificate of incorporation of a Catholic church in this State is to make mention of the name of the corporation, and also of the location where its principal place of worship is to be situated.[101]

The certificate of incorporation of a "Roman Catholic" church in this State is to be executed and acknowledged by the Roman Catholic archbishop or bishop and the vicar-general of the diocese within which the place of worship is or is to be located; and by the rector of the church, and by two laymen, members of the church to be incorporated, who are to be selected by the three church officials.[102]

The certificate of incorporation of a "Ruthenian Greek Catholic church" in this State is to be executed and acknowledged by the Ruthenian Catholic bishop, appointed by the pope of Rome to have supervision over Ruthenian Catholics of the Greek rite in the United States, or in case of a vacancy in the office of bishop, the Ruthenian administrator of the Ruthenian Catholic diocese duly appointed and recognized by the apostolic delegate in the United States, and by the chancellor of the diocese in which the place of worship is or is to be located, and by the pastor of the church and

---

[98] *Ibid.*, § 3. There are certain officers authorized to take acknowledgment or proof. Cf. *McKinney's Consolidated Laws of New York, Real Property Law* (Book 49, Part 2 with 1956 Cumulative Annual Pocket Part, Brooklyn: Thompson, 1945), § 298.

[99] *Loc. cit.*

[100] Cf. *supra*, p. 34.

[101] *N. Y. Religious Corporations Law*, §§ 90 and 100.

[102] *Ibid.*, § 90.

by two laymen, members of the church to be incorporated, elected by the three church officials.[103]

On filing such certificate, the church shall be a corporation known under the name stated in the certificate.[104]

Section IV. Regulation of Operations of Religious Corporations

A. *Categories of Corporations with Disinterested Purposes*

Anglo-Saxon jurists ordinarily put into three categories the corporations with disinterested purposes, depending on whether they are religious, scholastic, or charitable.[105] Religious corporations are conceived as having as their exclusive purpose the divine cult and everything pertaining to it. Scholastic corporations have as their purpose the inculcation of intellectual learning. Charitable corporations have as their purpose philanthropic works, such as the maintenance of hospitals, of foundling homes, of dispensaries, etc.[106] From this threefold division certain fundamental facts follow. On principle, charitable and educational activities do not enter into the sphere of religious purposes, and the funds that are directed toward them are not considered as ecclesiastical property.[107]

Looking more particularly at New York law, one will find that it defines the notion of ecclesiastical property by the purpose to which it is directed, and not by the quality of the person who possesses it.[108] This is completely contrary to the definition of ecclesiastical goods as given in canon 1497, § 1.

To follow out this arbitrary division would be to attack the rights of the Church, which has always considered the formation of youth and the exercise of charity as essential parts of its mission. Fortunately, the importance of this distinction is more theoretical

---

[103] *Ibid.*, § 100.

[104] *Ibid.*, §§ 90 and 100.

[105] Ghesquières, "La Corporation Paroissiale aux Etats-Unis," *Ephermerides Iuris Canonici*, VII, no. 3-4 (1951), 272-273.

[106] *Ibid.*, p. 273.

[107] *Loc. cit.*

[108] Cf. Matter of Watson, 171 N. Y. 256, 63 N. E. 1109, *reversing* 70 App. Div. 623, 75 N. Y. S. 1134, *affirming* 36 Misc. 504, 73 N. Y. S. 1058 (1902).

than practical, as can be seen from a close examination of New York law on this matter.

The highest court in the State has stated that "a church is more than merely an edifice affording the people the opportunity to worship God. Strictly religious uses and activities are more than prayer and sacrifice."[109] The same tribunal has stated that "accessory uses (viz., a parochial school in a parish) are within the scope of a church's activities."[110] Such statements are in line with one of the basic New York statutes on the formation of religious corporations. It states in part: "Any religious corporation may acquire property for associate houses, church buildings, chapels, mission-houses, school houses for Sunday or parochial schools, or dispensaries of medicine for the poor, or property for the residence of its ministers, teachers or employees, or property for a home for the aged. . . ."[111] The New York court has pointed out that "the fact that the legislature has seen fit to confer upon such a religious corporation power to administer to the temporal wants of those to whom it was organized to administer, would not change the general character of the corporation, the primary object being to provide churches and clergymen for the religious needs of those whom it was intended to benefit, and the additional power being subsidiary thereto. . . . The incidental charitable work in connection with a church does not make a church any less a religious corporation."[112]

B. *Adverse Possession*

Religious corporations can also acquire by adverse possession in the same manner as physical persons. In New York there was a famous case in which this rule was emphatically affirmed.[113] This case demands more extensive treatment because of three facts: (1) the immense value of the property under discussion; (2) the

[109] Matter of Community Synagogue *v.* Bates, 1 N. Y. 2d 445 (1956).

[110] Matter of the Diocese of Rochester *v.* Planning Board of Town of Brighton *et al.*, 7 N. Y. 2d 508 (1956).

[111] *N. Y. Religious Corporations Law*, § 6.

[112] Matter of Prall, 78 App. Div. 301, 79 N. Y. S. 971 (1903).

[113] Bogardus *v.* Trinity Church, 4 Paige 178 (N. Y., 1833).

thorough manner in which the matter was presented to the courts, and (3) the great care with which the case was decided.

One Annetje Jans appears to have been owner of the disputed property in 1663. Her devisees in 1671, with the exception of one or two, united in a "deed of transport" to Colonel Lovelace, the governor of New York. Under this deed the English government took possession. In 1705 the land was granted to Trinity Church by a patent which on its face conveyed the entire estate. The church here mentioned went into possession and remained undisturbed till about 1785, when one of the descendants of Annetje Jans caused trouble by entering certain parts of the land. He was finally persuaded to relinquish his claims in return for payment of seven hundred pounds. The right of the church remained undisputed until 1830, when one Bogardus, under claim that he was a descendant of one of the heirs to Annetje Jans who had not joined in the deed of transport commenced action, claiming a one-thirtieth interest in the land. He contended that the church, by the deed of 1705, had become a tenant in common with the Jans heir, under whom he claimed. The church as a defense set up adverse possession since 1705, which contention was upheld in 1833.[114] This ruling was again upheld upon appeal.[115]

The litigation still continued. Eventually there followed an important ruling in 1846. In this ruling the court, in holding that such possession was a proper and just defense in favor of the church, stated:

> The law on these claims is well settled, and it must be sustained in favor of religious corporations, as well as private individuals. Indeed, it would be monstrous, if, after a possession such as has been proved in this case, for a period of nearly a century and a half, open, notorious, within sight of the temple of justice, the successive claimants, save one, being men of full age, and the courts open to them all the time (except for seven years of war and revolution) the title to lands were to be litigated successfully upon a claim which has been suspended for five generations. Few titles in this country would be secure under such an ad-

114 *Ibid.*, at 203.

115 Bogardus *v.* Trinity Church, Wend. 111 (N. Y., 1835).

ministration of the law; and its adoption would lead to scenes of fraud, corruption, foul injustice, and legal rapine, far worse in their consequences upon the peace, good order and happiness of society, than external war or domestic insurrection.[116]

All attempts directed against the corporation through a suit brought by individuals having thus completely failed, an attempt was made in 1856 to divest the church of its property through an ejectment suit brought by the state. The plaintiff simply relied on a presumption that it was *prima facie* the owner of all land in the state and proved the possession of the defendant. A nonsuit, on the ground that the plaintiff had failed to establish its title and that, if it had established it, such title was barred by the statute of limitations, was granted at the trial and upheld on appeal.[117] With this case all attacks on the property of the church came to an end.

In surveying other cases in which church property has been protected through an application of the statute of limitations, one will find that they generally resemble the *Trinity Church Case,* not so much in the length of possession or the value of the property, but in the fact that there is generally some instrument giving color of title to the possession. It is elementary that such possession is more favored than mere naked possession. A person or corporation taking possession honestly under a void deed is entitled to more consideration than the mere squatter who simply appropriates the land.[118] Therefore deeds to a church organization void because no judicial sanction was obtained,[119] or because the grantee at the time was unincorporated,[120] have served as foundations for adverse possession by church corporations and have become important in the chain of title.

It is also to be noted that a church may by adverse possession acquire land of greater value than the law under which it exists per-

---

[116] Bogardus *v.* Trinity Church, 4 Sandf. Ch. 633, 762 (N. Y., 1846).

[117] People *v.* Rector of Trinity Church, 30 Barb. 537, *aff'd* 22 N. Y. 44 (1859).

[118] Zollman, *American Church Law,* p. 527.

[119] Reformed Church of Gallupville *v.* Schoolcraft, 65 N. Y. 134 (1875).

[120] Reformed Church of Gallupville *v.* Schoolcraft, *loc. cit., reversing* 5 Lans. 206 (1871).

mits.[121] The restriction imposed on the corporation is in no way the concern of any private individual, but rather a question of governmental policy, with which the individuals have nothing to do.[122] The title thus acquired is perfectly good before the whole world, the State alone excepted, and even before the State itself, it is not void but simply voidable at the State's option.[123]

While, however, a written instrument is important, it is not absolutely necessary. Title may be acquired without it. A church, like any other individual or corporation, may simply take possession of property, and if possession is maintained for the requisite time it will be protected by the statute of limitations, to the extent of the substantial and actual inclosure.[124] There is a very recent New York case which clearly illustrates this situation. When a Greek Catholic church to which title of certain church property had been given by members of a small organized church in return for pastoral service failed to give such service and the congregation of the latter thereafter adhered to Orthodox rites and practices, renovated their church property, paid off the mortgage, and continued to operate and maintain the church property through lay members for over twenty years, the Greek Catholic Church was deemed to have abandoned its trust in the property, and the latter church to have obtained title by adverse possession.[125]

New York law at present requires a period of fifteen years for adverse possession of real property. The present law states: "An action to recover real property or the possession thereof cannot be maintained by a party other than the people, unless the plaintiff, his ancestor, predecessor or grantor, was seized or possessed of the

---

[121] Bogardus *v.* Trinity Church, 4 Paige 178 (N. Y., 1833); Harpending *v.* Reformed Dutch Church of City of N. Y., 16 Pet. (41 U. S.) 455 (1842). Cf. *supra*, p. 35.

[122] Bogardus *v.* Trinity Church, 4 Sandf. Ch. 633, 758 (N. Y., 1846).

[123] Humbert *v.* Trinity Church, 24 Wend. 587, 630 (N. Y., 1840).

[124] Harpending *v.* Reformed Dutch Church of City of N. Y., 16 Pet. (41 U. S.) 455, 493 (1842).

[125] Saint Nicholas Ruthenian Ukrainian Greek Catholic Church of Rome *v.* Kapsho, 202 Misc. 893, 114 N. Y. S. 2d 27 (1952).

premises in question within fifteen years before the commencement of the action."[126]

C. *Zoning Laws*

In the matter here considered one may also inquire how zoning laws affect church property in the State of New York. It is interesting to note that it was not until 1926 that the United States Supreme Court expressed its plenary approval of zoning laws.[127] There was presented to this tribunal a case which put in issue the validity of a comprehensive use zoning plan encompassing an entire community. The court held that zoning legislation is a proper subject of police power, and that the ordinance in its *general scope* and *dominant* features was valid.[128] While giving this blanket approval to zoning laws generally, the court pointed out that the validity of a specific regulation must be determined by the facts of each case. The test for determining the validity of each regulation is its substantial relation to the public health, morals and general welfare of the community.[129] It is significant to note that the court in the *Ambler* case specifically omitted from its consideration the position of the zoning ordinance relating to churches. It states: "For the present purposes the provision of the ordinance in respect of [sic] these uses (churches and schools) may, therefore, be put aside as unnecessary to be considered."[130] The court thought it prudent not to pass upon this delicate aspect, since it was not absolutely necessary to the decision in the instant case. The holding relates solely to provisions restricting industrial and profit-making enterprises.

Looking at the New York law on the question, first of all, one will note that it is well established by the court that a zoning ordinance may not *wholly exclude* a church or synagogue from any residential district. Such a restriction is stricken out precisely on

[126] Civil Practice Act, § 34; Before 1938 a period of twenty years was required. Cf. Laws of 1938, c. 97.

[127] Village of Euclid *v.* Ambler Realty Co., 272 U. S. 365 (1926) (hereafter cited Ambler case).

[128] Ambler case, at 387.

[129] Ambler case, at 395.

[130] Ambler case, at 385.

the grounds that it bears no substantial relation to the public health, safety, morals, peace or general welfare of the community.[131] An ordinance will also be stricken out if it attempts to exclude private or parochial schools from any residential area where public schools are permitted.[132]

There have emanated from New York's highest tribunal two very recent decisions,[133] which shed great light on zoning restrictions concerning church property. The Court of Appeals in the two cases cleared the way for the construction of a synagogue in Sands Point and a Roman Catholic church and a parochial school in a Rochester suburb. In both decisions the court overruled lower courts, which had upheld local authorities in refusing to grant permits for the necessary construction and use. The Court of Appeals was divided six to one on each case.

Writing for the majority in the Sands Point case, Chief Judge Albert Conway said:

> . . . the board (i.e. the local authority who had denied authorization to build) determined that the requested use of the petitioner was for purposes other than a "church for public worship and other purely religious uses." We cannot agree. A church is more than merely an edifice affording the people the opportunity to worship God. Strictly religious uses and activities are more than prayer and sacrifice, and all churches recognize that the area of their responsibility is broader than leading the congregation in prayer. Churches have always developed social groups for adults and youth where the fellowship of the congregation is strengthened with the result that the parent church is strengthened. . . . It is a religious activity for the church to provide a place for . . . social groups to meet, since the church by doing so is developing into a stronger and closer knit religious

[131] North Shore Unitarian Society, Inc. *v.* Village of Plandome, 200 Misc. 524, 525, 109 N. Y. S. 2d 803, 804 (Sup. Ct. 1951).

[132] Long Island Univ. *v.* Tappan, 305 N. Y. 893 (1953), *aff'd* 281 App. Div. 771 (1953), *which aff'd* 202 Misc. 956 (1952); Matter of Property Owners Assn. *v.* Board of Zoning Appeals, 2 Misc. 2d 309 (1953).

[133] Matter of Community Synagogue *v.* Bates, 1 N. Y. 2d 445 (1956) (hereafter cited Sands Point case); Matter of the Diocese of Rochester *v* Planning Board of Brighton *et al.*, 1 N. Y. 2d 508 (1956) (hereafter cited Rochester case).

unit. To limit a church to being merely a house of prayer and sacrifice would, in a large degree, be depriving the church of the opportunity of enlarging, perpetuating and strengthening itself and the corporation. . . . [134]

One of the reasons given for the refusal of the necessary building permit by local authorities was that the proposed buildings would be used for other than "public worship and other strictly religious purposes," with reference here made to the planned meeting rooms for synagogue services. In answer to this charge, Judge Conway gave the answer just quoted.

In another section of his ruling the same judge pointed out:

The position of the Village, as stated clearly in its brief . . . is that the board of appeals, under the provisions of the ordinance here should have the power to deny an application for the location of a church at a "precise spot." This would not, of course, *prohibit* the use, erection, alteration or improvement of buildings or structures for churches and synagogues, in municipalities as the interventor says, but would *limit* them. While many may be tempted to think that the solution offered by the interventor is excellent, when one thinks it through one realizes that, if the municipality has the unfettered power to say that the "precise spot" selected is not the right one, the municipality has the power to say eventually which *is* the proper "precise spot." That, we all can see, is the wrong solution. . . . We think that we should accept the fact that we are the successors of "We the people" of the Preamble to the U. S. Constitution, and that we may not permit a municipal ordinance to be so construed that would appear in any manner to interfere with the "free exercise and enjoyment of religious profession and worship."[135]

Associate Judge Charles Froessel, in writing the majority opinion in the Rochester Case, referred to the right of the planning board to reject the so-called "package deal" offered in the case in question. He pointed out that the accessory uses proposed by the diocese are within the scope of a church's activities. He elaborated this point by quoting with approval the view which holds that any

[134] Sands Point case, at 453.
[135] Sands Point case, at 458.

Roman Catholic parochial church project is composed of four component parts, viz., church, rectory, convent and school. A parking lot and playground will also be considered as proper accessory uses to a church.[136] Here are the words of the decision itself:

> Thus church and school and accessory uses are, in themselves, clearly in furtherance of the public morals and general welfare. The church is the teacher and guardian of morals . . . and "an educational institution, whose curriculum complies with the state law, is considered an aid to the general welfare." . . . These proposed structures will not interfere with the public health, nor can they be said to be a danger to the public peace and safety. . . .[137]

D. *Powers and Duties of Trustees*

The trustees of any Roman Catholic[138] or Ruthenian Greek Catholic[139] incorporated church are the three church officials who subscribed the certificate of incorporation[140] and their successors in ecclesiastical office, together with two laymen of the incorporated church, elected by these three church officials or by a majority of these officials. The two laymen who signed the certificate are trustees of the church for one year, and they or other qualified laymen are elected trustees for terms of one year thereafter. When a vacancy occurs in the office of a lay trustee, the three church officials elect his successor. No act or proceeding of the trustees of any such incorporated church is valid without the sanction of the bishop of the diocese to which such church belongs. In case of his absence or inability to act, there is needed the approval of his vicar-general or of the administrator of such diocese. The section relating to Ruthenian Greek Catholic churches requires that this approval be in writing; the section relating to Roman Catholic churches does not incorporate this requirement.

Whatever be the extent of the power granted to religious cor-

---

136 Rochester case, at 525-526.

137 Rochester case, at 526.

138 *N. Y. Religious Corporations Law*, § 91.

139 *Ibid.*, § 101.

140 Cf. *supra*, p. 55.

porations, one point is certain. In New York these powers reside in the board of trustees. Only the members of the board have the power to buy, sell, mortgage, enter contracts in the name of the society. The faithful have nothing to say on this point, even though they are members of the corporation. If they have reason to believe that the administrators betray their interests and abuse the mandate which has been given them, they can have recourse to only one remedy, appeal to the competent tribunals.[141]

The faithful have not always accepted their purely passive rôle as set forth in the law of 1863.[142] They have tried to regain the influence which was formerly theirs. Such efforts did not have any success before the New York tribunals, for they always reaffirmed the exclusive right of the five directors to conduct the affairs of the society.[143] Nevertheless, in all this matter the exact function of the board of trustees must not be lost sight of. Since New York has an aggregate form of corporation, the title and corporation sovereignty vest in all the members of the congregation for whom the trustees act simply as agents or administrators.[144]

Now, what are the powers and duties of trustees of religious corporations? Their general powers and duties are stated in Religious Corporations Law, §5. The trustees have custody and control of all the property, real and personal, belonging to the corporation, and of the revenues of such property. Contributions taken in the church or in connection with other activities conducted by the corporation are the property of the corporation.[145] The trustees "shall administer the same in accordance with the discipline, rules and usages of the corporation and of the ecclesiastical governing body . . . to which the corporation is subject."[146]

---

141 Ghesquières, "La Corporation Paroissiale aux Etats-Unis," *Ephermerides Iuris Canonici*, VII (1951), 278.

142 Cf. *supra*, p. 49.

143 People's Bank of the City of N. Y. *v.* St. Anthony's R. C. Church, 109 N. Y. 512, 17 N. E. 408 (1888).

144 People *v.* Fulton, 11 (1 Kern) 94 (N. Y., 1854).

145 Buffalo First Church of Christ Scientist v. Schreck, 70 Misc. 645, 127 N. Y. S. 174 (1911).

146 *N. Y. Religious Corporations Law*, § 5.

The law clearly points out that these administrators are not to exercise their discretionary powers to their personal profit, for as is pointed out, "such property (is) to be held in trust and to be invested and reinvested in such manners as trust funds are allowed to be invested. . . ."[147] The primary purpose of the trustees' administration is the support and maintenance of the corporation. They may, however, use the property of the corporation for some religious, charitable, benevolent or educational object conducted by the corporation or in connection with it, or with the denomination with which the church is connected.[148]

They may not devote the property to other uses, nor may they divert the property from the uses indicated here. Hence, New York courts insist that the trustees of the parish corporation, if distinctly Catholic, shall not divert the property from Catholic uses, but shall act in accordance with the discipline and usages of the Catholic Church, and equity will enforce this principle.[149]

The trustees may make or amend by-laws governing their conduct of affairs, by a two-thirds majority vote of those present at a meeting. Such vote, however, may be taken only after notice, including the text of the by-laws or amendments proposed, has been given in writing at a previous meeting, and in addition upon notice of the meeting in which the by-laws or amendments are to be enacted.[150]

The trustees' powers as here enumerated do not belong to them individually, since the trustees must act as a body, and not simply as individuals for binding the corporation.[151] This supposes a double condition: (1) that the decision receive the number of votes required by law, and (2) that it be taken in the course of a regular session of the administrative council. An examination of each of these conditions is now in order.

---

[147] *Loc. cit.*

[148] *Loc. cit.*

[149] Brown, p. 142; cf. Cummings and Gilbert, *Membership and Religious Corporations of New York* (Albany: 1907), p. 271.

[150] *N. Y. Religious Corporations Law,* § 5.

[151] People's Bank *v.* St. Anthony's R. C. Church, 109 N. Y. 512, 17 N. E. 408 (1888).

The first of these conditions can easily be understood. A resolution can entail responsibility for a juridical personality only if it really expresses that personality's corporate will, and not when it reflects the will of but one of the other of its members. It is a recognized doctrine of the law on corporations that a corporation cannot be bound by the action of its directors unless they use their collective authority by acting as a body. Separately the directors of a corporation possess no authority to bind the society.[152]

This rule suffers no exception. The bishop himself, although he has the right of veto,[153] cannot in the administration of the affairs of a religious corporation decide on any positive course of action without the consent of his colleagues. Under these circumstances, he has but one vote in the council, and it is rigorously equal to that which each of the four other directors enjoys.[154]

With all the more reason is this true of the pastor. As far as the civil law is concerned, his title does not confer on him any privilege in this respect, and does not make him the agent for the corporation's affairs, unless it be by special delegation.[155] In passing, one may note that the special delegation is almost always granted to the pastor by the rule of the corporation. As agent of the corporation, the pastor can then deal with all current affairs. Under these circumstances he can still be bound to consult his colleagues and to obtain their consent in the cases that exceed the limits of ordinary administration.[156] Note, however, that the pastor cannot act simply in accord with his own initiative. He cannot authorize

[152] Parucki *v.* Polish N. C. Church, etc., 177 N. Y. S. 206 (1917).

[153] *N. Y. Religious Corporations Law,* § 5.

[154] Ghesquières, "art. cit.," *Ephermerides Iuris Canonici,* VII (1951), 279-280.

[155] Constant *v.* St. Alban's Church, 4 Daly 305, 308 (N. Y., 1872). This decision states in part: "A religious corporation, like any other, is bound by the acts of its authorized agents in matters that are within its corporate capacity, and may by the enactment of by-laws, or the distribution of the exercise of its powers among its various officers, or by conferring authority on special agents, so charge itself as to become amenable for the acts of individuals representing it, and acting by its authority."

[156] Ghesquières, *ibid.,* p. 280. Cf. Brown, p. 166.

the smallest repairs in his church, unless he has been previously authorized to do so by the board of trustees.[157]

The New York courts have singled out certain fundamental principles which must be kept in mind. "The presumptions of fact applicable to religious corporations are not in all cases the same as the presumptions of fact applicable to other corporations. There is no presumption that a treasurer of a religious corporation has power to borrow money, sign notes, and bind the corporation."[158] It is, therefore, absolutely necessary that trustees have express authority to execute such instruments in order to make them an obligation binding on the church. "An executory agreement of a religious corporation cannot be enforced, without proof of authority in the person executing the agreement to execute the same in the name of the corporation; or without showing ratification by the corporation with the knowledge of all the facts."[159] It has been definitely stated that the president of the church trustees has, as such, no power to make contracts.[160] The mere fact that a note purporting to be made by a religious corporation is signed by its president and secretary does not show that it is the note of the corporation without proof that it was made by its authority. The agency can neither be created nor proved by the acts or declarations of the assumed agents alone.[161]

If it happen, however, that the board of trustees knowingly permits one of its members to act in its name without making the slightest protest, this is equivalent to a tacit ratification of the operation which it did not prevent when it could have done so. It would be impossible, for example, for the administrators to claim ignorance when they have let the pastor make repairs on his church

---

[157] Malerba *v.* Friars Minor of Order of St. Francis, etc., 180 App. Div. 441, 167 N. Y. S. 1000 (1917); Kelly *v.* St. Michael's R. C. Church, 148 App. Div. 767, 133 N. Y. S. 328 (1912).

[158] Wilson *v.* Tabernacle Baptist Church, 28 Misc. 268, 59 N. Y. S. 148 (1899).

[159] Wilson *v.* Tabernacle Church, *loc. cit.*

[160] Hart *v.* Shearith Israel Congregation, 49 N. Y. Sup. Ct. 523 (1883).

[161] Columbia Bank *v.* Gospel Tabernacle Church, 127 N. Y. 361, 28 N. E. 29 (1891).

and build a school under their eyes, especially if, besides, they voted a mortgage to pay part of the construction expenses.[162]

A very practical question is now to be answered. How many votes are needed for a decision to become valid? As a general rule, it may be said that in the absence of any particular provision of the law, the absolute majority, e.g., three out of five votes, is necessary and suffices.[163] In such a case the ecclesiastical members of the board of trustees, not needing the support of the lay votes, can exercise an absolute control over the direction of affairs and reduce the other two members of the board to the rôle of consultors, whose advice can either be followed or relinquished.

In New York the financial decisions must evince at least a two-thirds majority of the votes [164] of the board of trustees. To constitute a quorum four members must be present. A Pastoral Letter of the Archbishop of New York clearly stresses this point:

The statutes of the diocese (Syn. V, Tit. XX, No. 249) make it suspension *ipso facto* to hold personally, in one's name for three months the property of the church, unless for special reasons, permission to do so has been obtained from the Ordinary.

No property can be bought or sold for the church corporation without the previous consent of the archbishop. This consent is only obtained after the matter has been submitted to the consultors, and after a meeting of the trustees of the corporation has been legally called, at which at least four of the members of the corporation being present, a resolution has been passed approving the proposed transaction. As the board of trustees in our church corporations consists of five members, . . . the law relating to business transactions by such board requires the presence of two-thirds of this body to form a quorum; two-thirds, therefore, of five calls for the presence of four members; so that a majority which would be only three does not constitute a quorum, as some have been led to believe.[165]

---

[162] Cf. Condon *v.* Church of St. Augustine, 112 App. Div. 168, 98 N. Y. S. 253 (1906).

[163] Ghesquières, *ibid.,* pp. 281-2.

[164] *N. Y. General Corporations Law,* § 50, subd. 5.

[165] *The Ecclesiastical Review,* XLV (1910), 598.

There is a second condition which calls for fulfillment if the board of trustees is to act validly. It is necessary that the consultation take place in circumstances which guarantee as much as possible that the decisions were taken freely and in full knowledge of the case. Accordingly, the tribunals of New York refuse to recognize acts which were not decided in regular session, even if all the directors, afterward, separately give their adherence.[166] To exercise their corporate functions the trustees must, therefore, "meet as a board so that they may hear each other's views, deliberate and then decide. . . . Their separate action, individually, without consultation, although a majority in number should agree upon a certain act, would not be the act of the constituted body of men clothed with corporate powers." [167] The trial of the case of People's Bank *v.* St. Anthony's [168] offers a good example of New York jurisprudence on this matter. The court here refused to recognize eight receipts which had been signed by the president of the corporation, i.e., the bishop, by the secretary, or by the treasurer outside a regular session, because none of the signers were personally authorized to borrow money in the name of the society.

From what has been said it follows logically that the members of the board cannot give their vote unless they are personally present at the deliberations. A vote by correspondence or by delegation is not admitted, unless it be expressly authorized by the law or by the articles of incorporation. This facility is extended to the bishop and to the vicar-general, whose functions do not permit them to participate at all the sessions.[169]

There are more specific functions of the trustees yet to be considered. The trustees may invest the property of the religious corporation by transferring all or any part of the funds or real estate to an authorized bank or trust company, or to a holding company of the same denomination organized under the laws of the

---

[166] Constant *v.* St. Alban's Church, 4 Daly 305 (N. Y., 1872).

[167] Commeyer *v.* United German Lutheran Churches, 2 Sand. Ch. 186, 229 (N. Y., 1844).

[168] 109 N. Y. 512, 17 N. E. 408 (1888).

[169] Philipps *v.* Wickham, 1 Paige 598 (N. Y. Eq. 1829).

State of New York,[170] or to a national banking association whose principal office is located in the state of New York.[171] Property so transferred is to be held in trust and invested in accordance with law. The income thereof is to be paid at the times agreed upon between the depositing corporation and the trustee corporation; and the depositor corporation may from time to time, designate other and different trustees similarly qualified and under similar regulation and restriction. No such transfer of the property of an incorporated Catholic church can be made without the consent of the bishop or archbishop of the diocese to which the church belongs. If the bishop be absent or unable to act, the consent must be obtained from his vicar-general or from the administrator of the diocese.[172]

The trustees of any religious corporation may invest its funds in securities, investments, or other property, according to their own judgment and without being restricted to those classes of securities which are lawful for the investment of trust funds under the laws of the State.[173] This power, however, of the trustees is subject to the discipline, rules, and usages of the ecclesiastical governing body, and to the limitations and conditions contained in any gift, devise or bequest.[174]

---

[170] *N. Y. Religious Corporations Law,* § 5. The holding company will not be a religious corporation, but a stock or membership corporation under denominational control, organized in conformity with the Banking Law.

[171] The latter clause was added to the law in 1955. Cf. Laws of 1955, c. 90.

[172] *N. Y. Religious Corporations Law,* § 5.

[173] *N. Y. Religious Corporations Law,* § 5-a. Cf. *N. Y. Decedent Estate Law,* § 111; *N. Y. Personal Property Law,* § 21; *N. Y. Banking Law,* § 35; *In re* Pessano's Estate, 180 Misc. 829, 45 N. Y. S. 2d 877 (1943). An examination of these sources will show some of the restrictions placed upon the investment of trust funds under the laws of New York. Such an examination is beyond the scope of this study.

[174] *N. Y. Religious Corporations Law,* § 5-a. Cf. *AAS,* XLIV (1952), 44, where the Sacred Congregation of the Council pointed out that the funds realized on the alienation of church property in accordance with the rules of canons 534, § 1, and 1532, § 1, n. 2, are to be invested only in realty. This does not apply to alienations by religious institutes which are exclusively under the jurisdiction of the Sacred Congregation of Religious. The practice of this

E. *Consolidation*

The law of New York permits the corporation of a parent church to rent or to convey to a corporation formed to represent a mission church or chapel the property used for the benefit of the people frequenting that mission church or chapel. The lease or conveyance may be made with or without consideration.[175]

New York also makes provisions for incorporated churches to consolidate, with the permission of the Supreme Court of the State. This law states in part:

> Two or more incorporated churches may enter into an agreement, under their respective corporate seals, for the consolidation of such corporations, setting forth the name of the proposed new corporation, the denomination . . . to which it is to belong . . . the number of such trustees, the names of the persons to be the first trustees of the new corporation, and the date of its first annual corporate meeting. . . . Such agreement shall not be valid unless approved . . . by the governing body of the denomination . . . to which each church belongs, having jurisdiction over such church. Each corporation shall thereupon make a separate petition to the supreme court for an order consolidating the corporations, setting forth the denomination . . . to which the church belongs, that the consent of the governing body of that denomination having jurisdiction over such church has been obtained, the agreement therefor, and a statement of all the property and liabilities and the amount and sources of the annual income of such petitioning corporation. . . . When such order [by the court] is made and duly entered, the persons constituting such corporations shall become an incorporated church by, and said petitioning churches shall become consolidated under, the name designated in the order, and the trustees therein named shall be the first trustees thereof, and the future trustees thereof shall be chosen by the method therein designated, and all the estate, rights, powers and property of whatsoever nature belonging to either corporation shall without further act or deed be vested in and transferred to the new corporation as effectually as they were vested in or belonging to the

Congregation still follows the general norms of canon 1531, § 3. Cf. Bouscaren, *Canon Law Digest,* III, 581.

[175] *N. Y. Religious Corporations Law,* § 6.

former corporations; and the said new corporation shall be liable for all the debts and liabilities of the former corporations in the same manner and as effectually as if said debts or liabilities had been contracted or incurred by the new corporation . . .[176]

One further note must be added with regard to consolidation. This section does not authorize the consolidation of a religious corporation with a membership corporation. It has been decided that when a membership corporation attempts to consolidate with a religious corporation the proceedings followed in the so-called consolidation are not authorized, even when the court approves them, and the title to real estate does not vest in this consolidated corporation.[177]

> The organic differences between the corporation of a church under denominational control and a charitable society organized under the free church act are so striking that the property of the latter should not be allowed to be diverted from the uses to which it was intended to be devoted by its donors, to the support of an organization so essentially distinct and different.[178]

The statement just noted crystallizes the reasoning that underlies the New York ruling.

F. *Division*

A Roman Catholic bishop who has jurisdiction over a parish has authority also to divide such a parish. When that is done, the existing corporation retains part of the parish and a new corporation is formed for the part separated. When real property is situated in the area now subject to the new corporation, which property belongs wholly or partially to the old corporation, the bishop may transfer title of such property to the new corporation. The transfer may be gratuitous, but if consideration is given, the bishop may hand over that consideration to the old corporation, or he may

---

[176] *Ibid.,* § 13.

[177] Selkir *v.* Klein, 50 Misc. 189, 100 N. Y. S. 449 (1906).

[178] Stokes *v.* Phelps Mission, 47 Hun. 570, 14 N. Y. St. R. 901 (N. Y., 1888).

divide the consideration between the two corporations. He must act in accordance with the Code of Civil Procedure, but his determination of the matter is independent of any action of the trustees or either corporation.[179] It is to be noted here that no similar provision obtains in New York law regarding the dividing of Ruthenian Greek Catholic parishes.

G. *Dissolution*

Religious corporations may not be dissolved by proceedings under Articles 6, 7, and 8 of the N. Y. General Corporations Law,[180] nor by proceedings under § 55 of the N. Y. Membership Corporations Law.[181] The absence, however, of a statutory procedure for the dissolution of a religious corporation does not preclude the State from seeking dissolution of a religious corporation for abuse of corporate powers and violation of State laws.[182]

Procedure for the dissolution of a religious corporation which shall cease to act in its corporate capacity and to keep up the religious services is provided in N. Y. Religious Corporations Law, § 18. Application for the dissolution of such a corporation may be made by a majority of the trustees; [183] or, if the church is subject to an ecclesiastical governing body, that body may apply, provided the trustees or officers or members of the corporation refuse to apply after request by the governing body.[184]

The petition by which application is made to the court is to be verified, and it is to state the particular reason or cause why dissolution is sought, the situation, condition and estimated value of the corporation's property, and the purposes to which it is proposed that the surplus proceeds of the sale of the property shall be de-

---

[179] *N. Y. Religious Corporations Law,* § 92.

[180] Cf. *N. Y. General Corporations Law,* § 130, and *supra,* p. 35.

[181] Cf. *supra,* p. 41.

[182] People *v.* Volunteer Rescue Army, 262 App. Div. 237, 28 N. Y. S. 2d 994 (1941).

[183] The acts of the trustees of incorporated Catholic churches always look to and need the consent of the diocesan authority. Cf. *N. Y. Religious Corporations Law,* §§ 91 & 101, and *supra,* pp. 50 & 64.

[184] *N. Y. Religious Corporations Law,* § 18.

voted. The petition must always be accompanied with proof that the intended application has been advertised in a newspaper published in the county where the corporation is located, once each week for at least the four successive weeks preceding the application.[185]

The application is directed to the Supreme Court of the State, and the court, according to its judgment, is to grant the application by giving an order and decree for the dissolution of the corporation, and by ordering and directing for that purpose a sale and conveyance of all property of the corporation. After providing for the payment of all debts of the corporation, and of the costs of the sale and proceedings for the dissolution, the court may order and direct devotion of any surplus remaining to any religious, benevolent, or charitable purposes as they are indicated in the application of the trustees and approved by the court. When the application was made by the ecclesiastical governing body, the proceeds are to be turned over to that body.[186]

H. *Alienation*

A religious corporation is not to sell or mortgage or lease for a term exceeding five years any of its real property without leave of the Supreme Court, obtained pursuant to Article 5 of the N. Y. General Corporations Law.[187] The trustees of an incorporated Catholic church may not make application for leave of the court without the consent of the archbishop, the bishop, the vicar-general, or the administrator, as set forth above.[188] Their petition to the court must state that such consent has been obtained.[189] It is permitted that such real property be transferred for a nominal con-

---

[185] *Loc. cit.*

[186] *Loc. cit.*

[187] *N. Y. Religious Corporations Law*, § 12, sub. 1. The requirement of the court's approval for a lease which runs for more than five years was put into the law in 1953. Cf. Laws of 1953, c. 722.

[188] Cf. *supra*, pp. 50 & 71; regarding Roman Catholic churches: *N. Y. Religious Corporations Law*, § 12, subd. 3; regarding Ruthenian Greek Catholic churches: *N. Y. Religious Corporations Law*, § 12, subd. 4.

[189] *N. Y. Religious Corporations Law*, § 12, subd. 6.

sideration to another religious corporation, and the court in granting its approval will not inquire into the benefits of the consideration to the grantor corporation, provided that it appears that religious or charitable objects generally are conserved by such conveyance, unless, however, the transaction tend to impair the claim or remedy of any creditor.[190] Special provision is also made concerning court orders confirming sale or mortgage made without authority of the court.[191] This provision which demands the assent of the court for certain types of transaction by the religious corporation is to be found only in the State of New York, and certainly demands further clarification.

The reason for this restriction in New York goes back to the happenings in the time of Queen Elizabeth. At that time and shortly afterwards several statutes were passed in restraint of the absolute power of religious corporations to alienate their property.[192] These statutes were considered as having been brought along by the colonists to the colony of New York.[193] This conception, together with the power which equity had over the real estate of church corporations under the trustee corporation theory, which flourished in the State of New York till 1850,[194] cast a doubt over the title conveyed by any such corporation.[195] It therefore became the practice to petition the legislature for leave to sell, so as to be able to convey clear title. This soon proved to be burdensome, both to the petitioners and to the legislature. Accordingly a statute was passed in 1806, and re-enacted in 1813 as part of the religious incorporation act, which statute made it lawful for the chancellor, on the application of any religious corporation, in case he should

---

[190] *Ibid.*, subd. 8.

[191] *Ibid.*, subd. 9.

[192] Zollman, "Powers of American Religious Corporations," *Michigan Law Review,* XIII (1915), 657.

[193] De Ruyter *v.* St. Peter's Church, 3 Barb. Ch. 119, 122 (N. Y., 1848), *cited with approval* in Wyatt *v.* Benson, 23 Barb. 327, 333 (N. Y., 1857); Madison Ave. Baptist Church *v.* Baptist Church of Oliver St., 46 N. Y. 131, 142 (1871); cf. Dudley *v.* Congregation of St. Francis, 138 N. Y. 451, 456 (1893).

[194] Robertson *v.* Bullions, 11 N. Y. 243 (1854); cf. *supra,* pp. 47-50.

[195] Dutch Church in Garden St. *v.* Mott, 7 Paige 77, 84 (N. Y., 1838).

deem it proper, to make an order for the sale of any real estate and to direct the application of the moneys therefrom to such uses as the corporation, with the consent and approbation of the chancellor, should conceive to be more for its interest.[196]

Though this act in terms was merely permissive, the courts, by judicial construction of it, soon were firmly committed to the doctrine that it operated to forbid sales of real estate by religious corporations without the court's consent.[197] The word "sale" was construed to include "mortgage," [198] though it was pointed out that a mortgage was a lien rather than a sale.[199] Investors were thus forced to insist on a judicial approval of every mortgage issued by a church corporation.[200] In 1953 religious corporations were required to secure judicial approval for leases that run for more than five years.[201]

This, however, is the extent to which the courts have extended the statute by judicial construction. In all regards the enactment is recognized as impairing what would otherwise be a common law right, and is, therefore, strictly construed.[202] The court's consent need be procured only for an actual sale of of real property by a religious corporation. A deed as a gift,[203] a purchase money mortgage,[204] an agreement to sell,[205] or a sale in a partition action [206]

196 *Laws of the State of New York, 1812-13*, II, 215; *In re* Brick Presbyterian Church, 3 Edw. Ch. 155, 166 (N. Y., 1837).

197 Dudley *v.* Congregation of St. Francis, 138 N. Y. 451, 456-57 (1893).

198 Dudley *v.* Congregation of St. Francis, *loc. cit.*

199 Manning *v.* Moscow Presbyterian Society, 27 Barb. 52 (N. Y., 1858).

200 *In re* St. Ann's Church, 23 How. Prac. 285, 14 Abb. Prac. 424 (N. Y., 1862); *In re* Church of Messiah, 25 Abb. N. C. 354, 12 N. Y. S. 489 (N. Y., 1890); cf. cases cited in Moore *v.* Rector, etc., of St. Thomas Church, 4 Abb. N. C. 51 (N. Y., 1873).

201 Cf. *supra,* p. 75, note 187.

202 Congregation Beth Elohim *v.* Central Presbyterian Church, 10 Abb. Pr. (N. S.) 484, 489 (N. Y., 1871).

203 Muck *v.* Hitchcock, 212 N. Y. 283, 106 N. E. 75 (1914).

204 South Baptist Society *v.* Clapp, 18 Barb. 35, 47 (N. Y., 1853). This was explicitly excluded by statute in 1954. Cf. Laws of 1954, c. 578, § 1.

205 Congregation Beth Elohim *v.* Central Presbyterian Church, 10 Abb. Pr. (N. S.) 484 (N. Y., 1871).

206 New York Home Missionary Society *v.* First Free Will Baptist Church, 73 Misc. 128, 130 N. Y. S. 879 (1911).

will not be regarded as a sale within the statute. The cases in which the courts may act are thus quite limited.

It is important to realize what this judicial approval entails. The courts have no original jurisdiction over the property. They cannot, therefore, originate any scheme either for the sale of the property or for the disposition of the proceeds.[207] They can only say yes or no in regard to any plan proposed by the corporation. They can only regulate and permit. The agreement of the corporation is indispensable, and the option to sell or not to sell, down to the moment when a valid contract for the sale is made, belongs entirely to the religious corporation.[208] The order of the court is simply an authority to the church to complete its voluntary undertaking, and gives the deed regularity of form. It does not make the sale a judicial one,[209] nor an adjudication between the parties.[210] A New York religious corporation, therefore, "has the title to its real property, may determine when it should be sold, and has the sole and exclusive power to enter into contracts for that purpose. The only distinction which exists between its power of alienation and that possessed by other corporations is that the assent of the court is necessary."[211]

While thus the jurisdiction of the courts is quite limited in more than one respect, when they do have jurisdiction their assent must be procured, or else the transaction will be void, though it consist only of a mortgage.[212] The courts will not even allow the statute to be frittered away by the application of the principles of estoppel.[213]

---

[207] Wheaton *v.* Gates, 18 N. Y. 395, 402 (1858).

[208] Bowen *v.* Irish Presbyterian Congregation, 19 N. Y. Super. Ct. 245, 266-67 (1860).

[209] Christie *v.* Gage, 71 N. Y. 189 (1877).

[210] St. James Church *v.* Redeemer Church, 45 Barb. 356, 31 How. Pr. 381 (N. Y., 1865).

[211] Congregation Beth Elohim *v.* Central Presbyterian Church, 10 Abb. Pr. (N. S.) 484, 488 (N. Y., 1871).

[212] Dudley *v.* Congregation of St. Francis, 138 N. Y. 451 (1893).

[213] Associate Presbyterian Congregation of Hebron *v.* Hanna, 113 App. Div. 12, 98 N. Y. S. 1082 (1906).

ARTICLE 5. SPECIAL PROBLEMS

Section I. Property Rights and Church Membership

Does church membership involve any property rights which will be recognized by the temporal court? This is the question that will now be considered. In New York the parishioners are members of the parochial corporation (corporation aggregate). At once certain questions arise. What are the rights of the parishioners (who are corporators) over the goods of the religious corporation? Do they have rights of pecuniary value? If the answer is in the affirmative, what will happen when the ordinary is forced to excommunicate a Catholic and bar him from the use of the corporate goods? What will happen when the bishop takes from a parish part of its patrimony to create a new parish? Will the local community to whom these goods belong legally, be able to complain before the civil tribunals? Will the simple parishioner have the right, as a corporator, to have recourse to the secular judge? These questions are complex, but of tremendous importance.

There is one point on which American jurisprudence is unanimous. It is that the faithful, taken individually, are neither proprietors nor beneficiaries of these goods, since they belong to a legal personality perfectly distinct from the members who compose it. If the civil law grants them some rights over these goods, it can only be as members of the corporation and only as long as they remain so. The faithful therefore automatically lose all their privileges at the very instant they leave the society, whether it be of their own free will, for example, when they move to another parish, or against their will, for example, in virtue of a decision of the ecclesiastical authority.[214]

It has been held in New York that, inasmuch as the religious corporations are essentially societies with distinterested purposes, the law will not allow them, under any pretext, to divide their capital or their revenue among the members.[215] This point is well ex-

---

[214] Ghesquières, "La Corporation Paroissiale aux Etats-Unis," *Ephermerides Iuris Canonici,* VIII (1952), 47.

[215] Wheaton *v.* Gates, 18 N. Y. 395 (1858); Application of Congregation

pressed in a judgment of the United States Supreme Court, which shows that it is not the parishioners, even taken as a whole, who are the beneficiaries of the trust, but the parish.[216]

With regard to the precise question whether church membership does involve any property rights which will be protected by the civil courts, the tribunals of the different states are not in agreement.[217] The New York courts treat the question of church membership as an entirely ecclesiastical one, involving no right which a civil court may recognize.[218] It is, therefore, recognized as a purely spiritual privilege. In particular cases New York courts have ruled that no property rights are involved in church membership because of the fact that the interests of their members touch only the general transactions of the church as a religious body.[219] The fact that church membership confers the right of burial in the church cemetery,[220] or involves the discontinuance of one of the chapels of a congregation,[221] has been held to be immaterial. In each of these cases church membership is shown not to confer any property rights. Consequently, just or unjust, an excommunication entails no loss of property, nor any damage, which can justify the intervention of a secular judge.[222]

It must be kept in mind that there are tribunals in other states which treat the question in a very different way. It has been held in some states that every parishioner possesses a "beneficiary

Beth David Anshey Roman of Roumania, 206 Misc. 600, 133 N. Y. S. 2d 589 (1954).

[216] Mason *v.* Muncaster, 22 U. S. 445, 6 L. Ed. 131 (1824).

[217] Zollman, *American Church Law,* pp. 306-7.

[218] Walker *v.* Howell, 20 Misc. 236, 45 N. Y. S. 790 (1897); Fairchild *v.* Tillotson, 118 Misc. 639, 195 N. Y. S. 39 (1922).

[219] People *v.* German United Evangelical St. Stephen's Church of Buffalo, 3 Lans. 434, 442 (N. Y., 1871).

[220] McGuire *v.* St. Patrick's Cathedral, 54 Hun. 207, 7 N. Y. S. 345 (N. Y., 1889).

[221] Burke *v.* Rector, etc., of Trinity Church, 63 Misc. 43, 117 N. Y. S. 255, *aff'd* 132 App. Div. 930, 117 N. Y. S. 1130 (1909).

[222] Walker *v.* Howell, 20 Misc. 236, 45 N. Y. S. 790 (1897).

interest," [223] a "direct right." [224] A New Jersey court has held that this right has a pecuniary value in the eyes of the law, and that anyone who enjoys it can have recourse to the civil courts to obtain its protection.[225] As a consequence, those courts which have followed this line of reasoning have come to consider the fact of belonging to a church as a "real civil right" of which nobody can be deprived, except for an adequate cause, manifested by the laws of the society and after a thorough examination of the case.[226] In this perspective an excommunication remains no longer a question related simply to faith or discipline. It becomes a question of civil rights, over which the tribunals will have jurisdiction to redress injustices.[227]

Section II. Recognition of Ecclesiastical Decisions Concerning Church Property

There is a second question which now must be answered. Under what circumstances will the civil courts question the validity of the decision of a church tribunal? In answer to this question the tribunals will once again reflect a division, depending on which of the two mentioned views they hold. There are, then, those states, including New York, which accept these decisions of the church tribunals as final, and automatically deduce the civil effects which flow from them, without examining if they are just or unjust, as long as they emanate from the legitimate authority and not from a faction. This definitely was the principle enunciated by the U. S. Supreme Court in the extremely important case of *Watson v. Jones*.[228] In the course of this opinion the matters that come before

---

[223] Shannon *v.* Frost, 3 B. Mon. (42 Ky.) 253 (1842).

[224] Mack *v.* Kime, 129 Ga. 1, 58, S. E. 184 (1907); Brunnenmeyer *v.* Burhe, 32 Ill. 183 (1863).

[225] Everett *v.* First Presbyterian Church, 53 N. J. Eq. 500, 142 A. 428 (1895).

[226] Jones *v.* State, 28 Neb. 495, 44 N. W. 658 (1890).

[227] Masbruch *v.* von Oehsen, 163 Wis. 208, 157 N. W. 775 (1916); Watson *v.* Garvin, 54 Mo. 353 (1873); Powanda *v.* Pido, 304 Pa. 42, 155 A. 490 (1931); Gray *v.* Christian Society, 137 Mass. 139 (1884).

[228] 80 U. S. (13 Wall.) 679. (1872).

the courts concerning the rights of church property are classified as follows: (1) property in controversy which by the very terms of the instrument under which it is held, serves for the teaching, the support, or the spread of some specific form of religious doctrine or belief; (2) property which is held by a strictly independent congregation; and (3) property which is held by a congregation that itself is subordinate to some general church organization.[229]

With the first of these categories the topic under discussion has nothing to do. In regard to the third category, the court states that, whenever the questions of discipline, or of faith, or of ecclesiastical rule, custom, or law have been decided by the highest church judicatory to which the particular congregation is subject, and to which the matter has been carried, the legal tribunals must accept such decision as final and as binding on them in their application to the case before them. In regard to the second category, if in such an organization the government is vested in particular officers, their action is conclusive, while otherwise the decision will simply be by majority vote of the members and will have the same effect.[230] Therefore, when a right of property depends on the decision of the Church, the tribunals will let the property go in the direction to which the decision of the Church inclines. The Supreme Court clearly points out that the decisions of competent ecclesiastical tribunals must be accepted by the civil courts, unless they violate the civil law or clearly misapply the ecclesiastical canons, even if they touch directly rights of property which fall under the jurisdiction of the civil courts.[231]

Although emanating from the United States Supreme Court, the ruling of *Watson v. Jones* was not universally received. Those tribunals which believed that the faithful possess rights of pecuniary value over parochial goods were forced logically to adopt another position. In their opinion, when the hierarchy cuts off a member from the Church and the latter feels himself affected adversely in his rights of property by this expulsion, he may have recourse to the civil tribunals, which will not feel themselves constrained by

---

229 Watson *v.* Jones, *loc. cit.* at 722.
230 Watson *v.* Jones, *loc. cit.*
231 Watson *v.* Jones, *loc. cit.*

the judgment of expulsion. They will examine if it has been done regularly, after the necessary warnings, and, if so, they will maintain it; if not, they will pay no attention to it and will give to the complainant the convenient assistance.[232]

While recognizing that the power of imposing an excommunication belongs to the Church alone, these judges affirm, nevertheless, that the faithful "have the right," by the same title as the members of other voluntary associations formed for charitable and benevolent purposes, to invoke the help of the civil tribunal to prevent the use of the property for other than the usages and fiduciary purpose to which it was consecrated, and to guarantee to the associates the enjoyment of their rights as members regarding the use of the property.[233]

This view of other states has been briefly given with the purpose of showing by contrast what is the view of the New York courts. Those courts, including New York, which follow the rule of *Watson v. Jones* affirm that the excommunicated persons have no course but to submit to the decisions of the hierarchy, since upon entering the society they had obliged themselves by implicit contract to obey it. To this the followers of the other view would answer that this contract is not a unilateral pact, which would bind only the faithful and not the Church, but that it was a mutual agreement by which the religious society grants its followers, as a reward for their adherence, certain precise rights which it cannot take away from them except for determinate causes and by a regular procedure forseen by the canons. The State, protector of contracts, would be seriously lacking in its duties, if by a strange partiality it obliged only one of the parties to respect its promises and gave its support to only one of the contractants. It must defend the faithful against the abuses of power on the side of the Church, as well as the Church against the attacks of the faithful. Zollman, one of the best authorities on American Church Law, fell prey to this type of reasoning. He upheld the views that membership in a church includes a prop-

---

[232] Boyles *v.* Roberts, 222 Mo. 613, 121 S. W. 805 (1905); West Koshkonong Congregation *v.* Ottesen, 80 Wis. 62, 49 N. W. 24 (1891); Kerr's Appeal, 89 Pa. 97 (1879).

[233] Fullbright *v.* Higginbothom, 133 Mo. 668, 34 S. W. 875 (1896).

erty right. He then proposed an interesting theory. The temporal property of a church is usually an accumulation in one form or another of the contributions of its members. The property must of necessity belong to someone, and those who contributed the property and who are entitled to its use and enjoyment would seem logically to be the proper owners. If church membership is considered a property right, it should be treated in the same manner as any other property right. The courts should consider that it is based on the initial agreement, by which the petitioner becomes a member.[234]

The reasoning of this second view, as espoused by Zollman and others, would be sustainable if it did not stem from a completely erroneous principle, namely, that the Church is a private association submitted to the control of the State, and not a perfect society entirely independent in its proper sphere. Its authors, if they were logical, should go the end of their argument and give to the State not only the right to break the decisions of the Church, but also that of remaking them, as a real superior tribunal would be empowered to do. That, however, is precisely what they do not do, understanding very well that, if they pushed their principles to their ultimate consequences, they would destroy religious liberty and would eliminate that separation of Church and State which is at the foundation of the American Constitution. So, they claim for the civil forum only the right to examine the *form* of ecclesiastical procedures and not their *basis*, i.e., to see if the sentence was pronounced by competent authority, if the procedure was regular, if the accused could defend himself and enjoy all the appeals which the church law gives him.[235]

As has been seen, the New York courts have adhered to the *Watson v. Jones* decision. Yet, in a recent case involving a Russian Orthodox church a number of decisions have been issued by the courts of this state which somewhat alter the position that New York has taken in the past regarding the *Watson* rule. In the past it had been definitely held in New York that, when disputing fac-

---

[234] Zollman, *American Civil Church Law*, Columbia University Studies, Vol. 77 (New York, 1917), p. 234.

[235] Ghesquières, "La Corporation Paroissiale aux Etats-Unis," *Ephermerides Iuris Canonici*, VIII (1952), 51-52.

tions of a centralized church are involved in civil litigation, the determination of the supreme hierarchical authority is conclusive.[236]

In 1950 there was an attempt on the part of a New York court to avoid application of the *Watson* rule when the central church authority was found to be subject to the secular control of a foreign state.[237] In this case the plaintiff corporation, holder of the cathedral in trust for the use of the faithful of the Russian Orthodox Church, brought an action of ejectment against the Archbishop appointed for the North American Diocese by the Patriarch of Moscow, acknowledged head of the church's hierarchy. The plaintiff contended that another archbishop elected by a convocation of the North American Diocese was the cathedral's proper occupant, relying on a New York statute, which confirmed the administrative autonomy of the North American Diocese, and transferred to it the control of church property within the state.[238] The New York Court of Appeals awarded the plaintiff judgment on the basis of the statute. If this Act is interpreted as simply ordering a transfer of Russian Orthodox property from one disputant group to another, its unconstitutionality seems unmistakable.[239] The majority of the court tried to salvage it by construing it as a declaration that the legislature found it to be a fact that the Moscow Church had been perverted to secular purposes, and that the American faction adhered to the faith to which the property had been dedicated.[240] One writer has commented on this construction of the case as follows: ". . . a gratuitous legislative adjudication of a minor church dispute by 'findings of fact' seems merely an indirect means of achieving an unconstitutional interference with religious freedom tacitly justified by a distaste for Communism. . . ."[241]

[236] Trustees of Presbytery *v.* Westminster Presbyterian Church, 222 N. Y. 305, 118 N. E. 800 (1918).

[237] Saint Nicholas Cathedral *v.* Kedroff, 302 N. Y. 1, 96 N. E. 2d 56 (N. Y., 1950).

[238] *N. Y. Religious Corporations Law*, §§ 105 and 107.

[239] "Constitutional Limitations on State Court Review of Hierarchical Church Judicatory Decisions," *Harvard Law Review*, LXIV (1951), 1361.

[240] Saint Nicholas Cathedral *v.* Kedroff, 302 N. Y. 1, 96 N. E. 2d 56 (1950).

[241] *Harvard Law Review*, LXIV (1951), 1361.

In 1952 the United States Supreme Court reversed and remanded the case, holding that the New York Statute [242] interfered with the free exercise of religion and was therefore repugnant to the due process clause of the Fourteenth Amendment.[243]   On remand in the New York Court of Appeals, the defendant (Moscow-appointed Archbishop) moved for amendment of the *remittitur* to order entry of final judgment in his favor. The decision granted his petition to the extent of ordering a new trial to determine whether the central church authority was freely functioning or was merely a propaganda organ of the Soviet State.[244]

The United States Supreme Court had never before considered the effect of the Fourteenth Amendment upon the power of civil courts to adjudicate ecclesiastical questions, but in *Watson v. Jones* [245] it formulated a common law rule to deal with litigation over church property generated by disputes upon questions of faith, doctrine, or ecclesiastical administration.[246]   In this 1952 case the U. S. Supreme Court found that the purpose of the New York statute was to protect the state's pulpits from the propaganda organ of a foreign power.   In holding the statute unconstitutional the court relied on the rule of *Watson v. Jones,* elevating it to the status of a constitutional requirement.[247]   By overruling the action of the Patriarch of Moscow, the supreme church judicatory, the New York statute conflicted with the *Watson* rule, and the court deemed this an interference with religious liberty.   This interference was not justified by the state's interest in safeguarding its pulpits, and this interest, the court suggested, could more properly be protected by a direct prohibition of subversive utterances from the pulpit than by

[242] Cf. *supra,* p. 85.

[243] Kedroff *v.* St. Nicholas Cathedral, 344 U. S. 94, 99 (1952). The Supreme Court clearly points out here that the principles of the First Amendment on religious liberty are made applicable to the States by the Fourteenth Amendment.

[244] Saint Nicholas Cathedral of the Russian Orthodox Church *v.* Kedroff, 306 N. Y. 38, 114 N. E. 2d 197 (1953).

[245] 80 U. S. (13 Wall.) 679 (1872).

[246] Cf. *supra,* pp. 81-82.

[247] Kedroff *v.* St. Nicholas Cathedral, 344 U. S. 94, 116 (1952).

a transfer of the control of property in violation of the church judicatory's judgment.[248]

On remand the New York Court of Appeals considered the Supreme Court's decision conclusive with reference only to the question of the state's legislative power to transfer control of the property. The court felt that, if the central church authority were found to be dominated by the Soviet state, the New York Courts could use their equitable power to exclude that authority's appointee on the ground that he would not administer the trust property for the benefit of the faithful.[249] The court treated as dictum the Supreme Court's discussion of the *Watson* rule. It denied that the rule had been raised to constitutional stature.[250] The court did not consider its decision inconsistent with early New York cases which accord with the *Watson* rule,[251] for it would qualify the rule to require that the church judicatory be freely functioning before its decision is given binding effect.[252]

This decision of the New York Court of Appeals has been attacked, and it seems rightfully so.[253] Since the Supreme Court considered only whether the New York statute [254] violated the Fourteenth Amendment, it seems clear that its decision makes the *Watson* rule a principle of constitutional law.[255] Thus the action of New York's highest tribunal seems erroneous. By allowing impeachment of the Patriarch's decision upon a finding that it was motivated by a subservience to secular ends, the court has made an unwarranted exception to the *Watson* rule. No basis was estab-

[248] Kedroff *v.* St. Nicholas Cathedral, *loc. cit.* at 109.

[249] Saint Nicholas Cathedral of the Russian Orthodox Church *v.* Kedroff, 306 N. Y. 38, 47, 114 N. E. 2d 197, 202 (1953).

[250] Saint Nicholas Cathedral of the Russian Orthodox Church *v.* Kedroff, 306 N. Y. 38, 50, 114 N. E. 2d 197, 204 (1953).

[251] Connit *v.* Reformed Protestant Dutch Church, 54 N. Y. 551 (1874); Dutch Church in Albany *v.* Bradford, 8 Cow. 457 (N. Y., 1826).

[252] Saint Nicholas Cathedral of the Russian Orthodox Church *v.* Kedroff, 306 N. Y. 38, 51, 114 N. E. 2d 197, 204 (1953).

[253] "Constitutional Limitations of State Court Review of Hierarchical Church Judicatory Decisions," *Columbia Law Review,* LIV (1954), 435-438.

[254] Cf. *supra*, p. 85.

[255] Kedroff *v.* St. Nicholas Cathedral, 344 U. S. 94, 97 (1952).

lished in the Church's fundamental law to require such an examina‑
tion of what had happened to the supreme judicatory.

One may well sum up the discussion of this case with the perti‑
nent observations of the writer in the *Columbia Law Review*: [256]

> The religious guarantees of the constitution extend alike to
> authoritarian and popularly governed churches. Those who do
> not wish to be bound by the decision of church judicatories are
> free to form congregational churches and be governed by a
> majority will. Since the essence of hierarchical church organiza‑
> tion is the supremacy of the judicatory in questions of faith,
> doctrine, and ecclesiastical administration, the civil courts would
> undermine the integrity of hierarchical churches by refusing to
> accord finality to their decision on other matters.
>
> By denying the Watson rule constitutional status, and by
> adding to it a questionable qualification, the instant court seems
> to be attempting to accomplish the same political objectives
> forbidden to the legislature by the Supreme Court's decision.

Section III. Tax Exemption

Although tax exemption of religious and charitable corporations
is universal in this country, it is far from uniform, and for determin‑
ing the extent of the property exempted in particular jurisdictions
one must examine the constitutions or statutory language and judi‑
cial decisions of the various jurisdictions. Before examining the
present situation in New York, one may usefully give a brief his‑
torical survey of the law in this state.

In colonial America such exemptions were justified on the
theory that established churches were governmental agencies; to
tax them would be self-taxation.[257] When dissenting Churches began
to grow up alongside the Established Church, they too received the
benefits of tax exemption.[258] This custom of exempting church
property continued even after the disestablishment of the Church.
In the course of time a more solid foundation was sought for this

---

[256] "Art. cit.," *Columbia Law Review*, LIV (1954), 438.

[257] Torpey, *Judicial Doctrines of Religious Rights in America* (Chapel
Hill: University of North Carolina Press, 1948), p. 171.

[258] Cf. Zollman, "Tax Exemption of American Church Property," *Michigan
Law Review*, XIV (1916), 648. Their private nature was not considered.

custom of tax exemption. With regard to charitable and educational associations, the public nature of the work shouldered voluntarily by these private institutions was looked upon by the courts as a full and sufficient justification for the exemption extended to them.[259]

As to the exemption of property owned by religious bodies (in contradistinction to charitable and educational property), this was justified by the fact that the state is benefited through the influence exerted by the various churches on their members. The religious and moral culture afforded by these societies was deemed to be beneficial to the public, and necessary to the advancement of civilization and the promotion of the welfare of society.[260] The notion soon gained ground in the courts, however, that only such property was tax-exempt as was specifically exempted by provision of law. All states have provided for such exemption either in their constitutions or by statute. It may be stated as a general principle of American Law that the property of churches and religious organizations does not, as a matter of right, enjoy exemption from state, county or municipal taxes, since it is fundamental that all property is liable to such taxation, unless it is specially exempted by constitutional provision, or by statute or charter.[261]

With regard to the exemption of church property from taxation, the constitutions of the various states may be divided into three classes, namely: (1) those which are silent on the matter; (2) those which contain self-executing provisions, and (3) those which contain express powers given to the legislature to pass exemption statutes.[262] Up until 1938 New York was classified among those states whose constitutions contained express powers given to the legislature to pass exemption statutes (the third class just enumerated). The sole limitation placed upon the legislative discretion in

---

[259] *Ibid.*, p. 646.

[260] *Loc. cit.*; People *ex rel.* The Seminary of Our Lady of Angels *v.* Barber, 42 Hun. 27, 30 (N. Y., 1886), *aff'd*, 106 N. Y. 669, 13 N. E. 936 (1887).

[261] Cooley, *The Law of Taxation* (4 vols., Vol. II, 4. ed., Chicago, 1924), II, § 742, p. 1549.

[262] Zollman, "Tax Exemption of American Church Property," *Michigan Law Review*, XIV (1916), 651.

New York was the requirement that exemptions were to be granted only by general law.[263]

In 1938, however, the exemption of New York Tax Law, § 4, subd. 6 was taken into the New York Constitution.[264] The exact content of this exemption will be seen shortly. It suffices now to say that the New York constitution has a mandatory provision concerning tax exemption, and will now be classified among the constitutions of those states which contain self-executing provisions.[265]

It is important to grasp the difference between these two general classifications of constitutional provisions under which the law of New York could be found at different times in its history. Of these two general classes of constitutional provisions the self-executing provision is as complete in itself as any statute can be. It can, therefore, stand alone and will *per se*, without any action by anyone, exempt from taxation such property as it covers.[266] In the absence of a provision giving the legislature power to supersede it, it is beyond the ability of that body to add or detract from it. It is, in other words, the law definitely laid down by the highest law-making power known to our system of government.[267]

Entirely different principles apply to those constitutional provisions which are not self-executing. Such provisions are powers of attorney to the legislature rather than laws. They merely authorize the legislature to act within certain limits, but, with the exception of those which require that the legislature "shall" pass such laws, leave it to the discretion of that body whether it is to act in whole, or in part, or at all.[268] Before the important change of 1938 complete discretion was given to the legislature in New York, except that exemptions were to be granted by general law.[269]

---

[263] *Ibid.*, p. 650.

[264] *N. Y. Constitution*, Art. XVI, § 1.

[265] Cf. *supra*, p. 89.

[266] Cf. *infra*, pp. 91-94.

[267] Zollman, "Tax Exemption of American Church Property," *Michigan Law Review*, XIV (1916), 650.

[268] *Ibid.*, pp. 650-651.

[269] Cf. *supra*, pp. 89-90.

The provisions, whether constitutional or statutory, which grant tax exemption to the property of churches and religious organizations fall naturally into two classes. Some states exempt from taxation property owned by religious societies, regardless of the use to which it is put; [270] others consider only the purpose for which the property is used, regardless of the ownership.[271]

New York, in granting tax exemption, is to be found among those states which consider the purpose for which the property is used. This important point will be considered shortly.[272] The law grants exemption to "the real property of a corporation or association organized exclusively for . . . religious, bible, tract, charitable, benevolent, missionary, hospital, infirmary . . . or cemetery purposes." [273] It is to be noted that the property of religious schools and colleges is not accorded specific statutory recognition in New York. Nevertheless, it is customarily considered included within the scope of exemption clauses applicable to charitable and educational institutions.[274] A New York court has explicitly stated that parochial schools should be exempt on the ground that the state's duty to provide educational facilities is being assumed by others.[275]

In New York the residences of priests and ministers are specifically exempt. A restriction, however, is placed on the value of the property exempted.[276]

Now, assuming that the religious property is of a type for which

[270] Cooley, *The Law of Taxation*, II, § 744, p. 1553.

[271] *Ibid.*, § 745, p. 1554.

[272] Cf. *infra*, pp. 92-93.

[273] *McKinney's Consolidated Laws of New York, Tax Law* (Book 59, Part 1 with 1956 Cumulative Annual Pocket Part, Brooklyn: Thompson, 1949), § 4, subd. 6.

[274] "Constitutionality of Tax Benefits Accorded Religion," *Columbia Law Review*, XLIX (1949), 970-71.

[275] St. Barbara's Roman Catholic Church *v.* New York, 243 App. Div. 371-73, 277 N. Y. S. 538, 541 (2nd Dep't, 1935).

[276] *New York Tax Law*, § 4, subd. 8. "All dwellings—houses and lots of religious corporations while actually used by the officiating clergymen thereof, but the total amount of such exemption to any one religious corporation shall not exceed three thousand dollars. Such exemption shall be in addition to that provided by subdivision six of this section."

exemption is permitted, New York requires that the property be used for the enumerated purposes, and ownership of the property by a religious organization is not sufficient for the establishment of exempt status.[277] Thus it is explicitly provided that the leasing of property for profit, though the property be owned by religious organizations, renders it taxable.[278] This is true, notwithstanding the fact that the income so received is used for religious, educational, or charitable purposes.[279] There is a conflict of authority in various states on whether the general rule applies when the lessee is also a religious institution.[280] The New York law provides that the property does not lose its exemption, if it is leased to other exempt organizations, provided that no more rent be charged than what is necessary to pay carrying, maintenance and depreciation charges.[281]

In New York, then, to determine the extent of tax exemption, the basic question that must be answered is what is to be considered a religious use of property. It is clear that a church building, primarily used for public worship, will be exempt from taxation,[282] together with land actually covered by the building and such adjacent land as is reasonably necessary for convenient access, light and air, and appropriate ornamentation.[283] Also it may reasonably be expected that other buildings, such as parish houses, mission houses, and chapels which supplement the functions of the main church building, and are primarily used for what may be called the

[277] Cf. Hebrew Free School Assn. *v.* Mayor etc. of New York, 99 N. Y. 488, 2 N. E. 399 (1875).

[278] *New York Tax Law,* § 4, subd. 6.

[279] Board of Foreign Missionaries *v.* Board of Assessors, 244 N. Y. 42, 154 N. E. 816 (1926).

[280] "Constitutionality of Tax Benefits Accorded Religion," *Columbia Law Review,* XLIX (1949), note 21, pp. 973-4.

[281] *New York Tax Laws,* § 4, subd. 6.

[282] People *ex rel.* Church of St. Mary *v.* Feitner, 168 N. Y. 494, 61 N. E. 762 (1901).

[283] "Exemption of Property Owned or Used by Religious Organizations," *Minnesota Law Review,* XI (1927), 544.

contributory purposes of religion, will be exempt, unless the actual wording of the statute makes the exemption impossible.[284]

Greater difficulty is encountered when property is used partly for religious and partly for secular purposes. If it is possible to divide the property with reference to the space that is used, the New York rule seems to be that the portion used primarily for religious purposes is exempt from taxation, while the remainder is not. This rule is certainly true when that part of the property which is used for exempt purposes is in a different building or on a different lot, fully separate from the rest.[285] This rule will have to be qualified if the division is within one building, e.g., among the floors or the rooms. Because of a particular statute which speaks of an *exclusive* use of such property,[286] the New York courts have refused to consider any such division of the building, and have declared the entire property subject to taxation.[287]

Most states hold that vacant land held by the Church as an investment is not in use for any religious purpose and therefore is not tax exempt.[288] New York is an exception to this rule. It provides that the lots "shall be so exempt, though not in actual use . . . if the construction of such buildings or improvements is in progress, or is in good faith contemplated." [289]

In accordance with this statute a New York court has ruled that lots purchased by a religious society, which in good faith contemplated the erection of buildings for purposes which would be exempt, but delayed its execution because of the high cost of construction, were not subject to taxation.[290]

[284] *Ibid.,* pp. 544-45.

[285] Board of Foreign Missions *v.* Board of Assessors, 244 N. Y. 42, 154 N. E. 816 (1926).

[286] *New York Tax Law,* § 4, subd. 6. The statute specifies that there should be no exemption, "unless the same shall be exclusively used for such purposes and exclusively the property of a religious society."

[287] *In re* Congregation Kal Israel Anschi Poland *v.* New York, 52 Hun. 507, 5 N. Y. S. 608 (N. Y. 1889).

[288] "Exemption of Property Owned by Religious Organizations," *Minnesota Law Review,* XI (1927), 548.

[289] *New York Tax Law,* § 4, subd. 6.

[290] Board of Foreign Missions *v.* Board of Assessors, 244 N. Y. 42, 154 N. E. 816 (1926).

It must also be kept in mind that constitutional provisions exempting religious institutions from property taxes have uniformly been held inapplicable to taxes imposed on the transfer of property to such institutions.[291] Dispositions to religious institutions are, however, almost always exempted from statutes imposing inheritance, estate, and gift taxes. New York exempts such transfers unconditionally.[292] The New York courts have given a liberal interpretation of such exemptions.[293]

This ruling of the New York courts brings up an interesting question. What can be said in general as to the construction of tax exemption statutes? The general rule of strict interpretation has been iterated and reiterated by the courts in probably a majority of cases.[294] Yet one New York court has taken the view that the importance to the public of religious, charitable, and educational activities warrants a relaxation of the ordinary rule that exemption provisions be strictly construed.[295] It also has been pointed out that the object of exemption statutes is to foster religious societies, and that accordingly they should be reasonably construed in furtherance of this object and should not be frustrated by finely drawn technicalities.[296]

The propriety and expediency of the governmental policies underlying such tax exemptions has been questioned by some. Most of the adverse criticisms of the policy have been founded on the conclusions reached by Mr. Philip Adler.[297] This attack on tax exemp-

---

[291] "Constitutionality of Tax Benefits Accorded Religion," *Columbia Law Review*, XLIX (1949), p. 974.

[292] *New York Tax Law* (Book 59, part 2), § 249-s.

[293] Cf. *In re* Mergentime's Estate, 129 App. Div. 367, 373-74, 113 N. Y. S. 948, 953 (1st Dep't 1908), *aff'd without opinion* 195 N. Y. 572, 88 N. E. 1125 (1909).

[294] Zollman, "Tax Exemption of American Church Property," *Michigan Law Review*, XIV (1916), 653.

[295] St. Barbara's Roman Catholic Church *v.* New York, 243 App. Div. 371, 373, 277 N. Y. S. 538, 541 (2d Dep't, 1935).

[296] Shari Berocho *v.* New York, 60 N. Y. Super. Ct. (28 Jones and S.) 479, 18 N. Y. S. 792 (1892).

[297] The work was originally entitled "Origin of the Exemption from Taxation of Charitable Institutions," and was published in 1922, by the West-

tion was answered most competently by Mr. John Godfrey Saxe.[298] The whole problem of religious and charitable exemptions in New York is well presented in a study made under the auspices of religious and charitable agencies and presented to the Legislature of New York in 1934.[299]

Section IV. Cemeteries

Certificates of cemetery corporations must contain special information, and must be filed with the Clerk of each county in which any part of the cemetery lies, as well as in the offices specified in the General Corporation Law.[300] A religious corporation may take and hold, for cemetery purposes, any personalty or realty given it by purchase, grant, gift, bequest, or devise, either absolutely or in trust.[301] The management of such cemetery property is regulated by Religious Corporations Law §§ 7, 8, 9, 5a, and 12, subd. 7, and is subject also to other general laws.[302]

To go into the particular requirements of these laws is beyond the scope of this work. It seems apropos, however, to note one interesting fact. It has been pointed out that a religious corporation in New York cannot sell any of its real property without leave of the Supreme Court.[303] A special exception is made with regard to cemeteries owned by religious corporations. New York law permits sale of plots or burial permits in such a cemetery without permission of the court, and it permits conveyance of the cemetery

chester Chamber of Commerce, under the title, "Tax Exemption on Real Estate, an Increasing Menace."

[298] Saxe, *Charitable Exemption from Taxation in New York State on Real and Personal Property* (New York, 1933).

[299] Tobin, Hannan, Tolman, *The Exemption from Taxation of Privately Owned Real Property Used for Religious, Charitable and Educational Purposes in New York State* (Albany, 1934-1938).

[300] *N. Y. Membership Corporation Law*, § 11, subd. 3.

[301] *N. Y. Religious Corporations Law*, § 7.

[302] *N. Y. Membership Corporations Law*, § 60 ff.; *N. Y. Real Property Law*, §§ 291, 292, 451; *N. Y. Public Health Law*, §§ 24 and 375; *N. Y. Code of Civil Procedure*, § 1395.

[303] Cf. *supra*, p. 75.

from the religious corporation to a cemetery corporation without the court's leave. It forbids, however, mortgages of any cemetery lands held by a religious corporation.[304]

Some decisions of the New York courts shed further light on this matter. It has been expressly held that religious organizations may not only establish cemeteries exclusively denominational, but may also guard and protect them by such rules and regulations as make effective the object and purpose of their organization.[305] They, therefore, can determine who is to be buried there. These rules and regulations will enter into and become a part of every contract for a lot in such cemetery, unless the proof is clear and convincing that a contract of a different kind was properly made with the lot owner by a duly authorized agent of the organization.[306]

> When a party applies for a burial plot at the office of a distinctly Roman Catholic cemetery, it is with the tacit understanding that he is either a Roman Catholic, and as such eligible to burial, or at least that he applies on behalf of those who are in communion with the Church. The entire business is transacted on that basis.[307]

It follows that the mere payment of fees and charges confers the privilege of sepulchre only "in a mode used and permitted by the corporation."[308] A person who, according to the decision of the Church, has ceased to be a member of it is not entitled as a matter of right to be buried in such a cemetery, though he had contributed to it while still a member.[309] Further, a member of

---

[304] *N. Y. Religious Corporations Law*, § 12, subd. 7.

[305] People, *ex rel.* Coppers *v.* Trustees of St. Patrick's Cathedral, 21 Hun. 194, 198 (N. Y. 1880).

[306] Windt *v.* German Reformed Church, 4 Sandf. Ch. 471, 474 (N. Y. 1847).

[307] People *ex rel.* Coppers *v.* Trustees of St. Patrick's Cathedral, 21 Hun. 184, 194 (N. Y. 1880).

[308] Windt *v.* German Reformed Church, 4 Sand. Ch. 471, 474 (N. Y. 1847).

[309] McGuire *v.* Trustees of St. Patrick's Cathedral, 3 N. Y. S. 781, *aff'd* 54 Hun. 207, 7 N. Y. S. 345 (N. Y. 1889).

the religious organization may not be buried with ceremonies which are objectionable to it.[310]

As to the nature of the title which the owner of a lot in a cemetery has, it is the New York ruling that the "certificate" or "receipt" given to the purchaser of a lot creates only a license,[311] or easement,[312] or usufructuary right,[313] and entitles the holder of such privilege only to have the bodies that are interred in such ground "remain undisturbed so long as the cemetery shall continue to be used as such, . . . and also the right in case the cemetery shall be sold for secular purposes, to have such remains removed and properly deposited in a new place of sepulchre."[314]

It has been held that "every person purchasing . . . a grave in a church yard, appendant to a church, does so with the full knowledge and implied understanding that a change in circumstances may, in time, require a change of location; and that the law . . . looking to such exigency, authorizes the corporation when it arrives . . . to sell the soil in absolute fee, discharged of all easements, and to make some other more appropriate investment or disposition of the proceeds."[315]

A very fundamental principle underlying this whole matter is that the State, for the protection of the public health, may under police power regulate and prohibit the use of land for burial purposes.[316] It has been pointed out that a religious corporation, although under its charter it was entitled to be protected against impairment of contract, was, nevertheless, subject to the police

[310] People *ex rel.* Coppers *v.* Trustees of St. Patrick's Cathedral, 21 Hun. 184, 233 (N. Y. 1880).

[311] McGuire *v.* St. Patrick's Cathedral, 3 N. Y. S. 781, *aff'd* 54 Hun. 207, 7 N. Y. S. 345 (N. Y. 1889).

[312] Richards *v.* North West Protestant Dutch Church, 32 Barb. 42, 20 How. Pr. 317, 11 Abb. Pr. 30 (N. Y. 1859).

[313] Windt *v.* German Reformed Church, 4 Sand. Ch. 471 (N. Y. 1847).

[314] Windt *v.* German Reformed Church, *ibid.*, at 474.

[315] Richards *v.* North West Protestant Dutch Church, 32 Barb. 42, 46, 20 How. Pr. 317, 322, 11 Abb. Pr. 30, 38 (N. Y. 1854).

[316] Moritz *v.* United Brethrens' Church on Staten Island, 269 N. Y. 125, 199 N. E. 29 (1935).

power of the state, regardless of the provisions of the charter.[317] It has also been held that the general power conferred by the Religious Corporations Law upon religious corporations to take and hold real property for cemetery purposes does not vest in such corporations the power to locate and maintain at will cemeteries in towns, but confers such power subject to the exercise of the police power of the state, as corporations generally exercise their enumerated powers subject to such police power, including the legitimate exercise of the powers of boards of health in towns.[318]

Section V. Liability of Charitable Corporations

The liability of a charitable corporation for the torts of its servants has long been a topic for discussion in the courts of New York. An examination of New York cases clearly shows that the courts in this state are restricting more and more the cases wherein charitable corporations can claim immunity from such tort actions. One writer has summed up the reason for this trend in the following way:

> The rule of exemption from liability arose when charitable organizations, having their origin in donations of benevolent persons or in grants from the state, were supported by a few individuals and their resources were limited. It was, therefore, in the best interests of the public that such institutions were nurtured. Today charity is dispensed by large well-endowed corporations, whose modern multiplication has apparently reduced this danger and rendered more equitable the payment of compensation to those so injured. Thus the demands of the public welfare, for protection from liabilities for wrongs committed in their conduct, have become less imperative as compared with the needs of the injured individual. Their economic aspects are non-profit rather than charitable.[319]

The New York cases are concerned with the personal injuries sustained by the beneficiaries and employees of the charity and by

[317] Moritz *v.* United Brethrens' Church on Staten Island, *loc. cit.*

[318] Morton *v.* St. Patrick's Roman Catholic Church Soc., 56 Misc. 71, 105 N. Y. S. 1100 (1907).

[319] Larber, "Liability of Hospitals for the Negligence of Their Employees," *St. John's Law Review*, XV (1941), 276-77,

strangers. New York enforces ordinary tort liability against charitable organizations when employees[320] or strangers[321] are injured. With regard to beneficiaries, the matter is not so clear cut. There is need for a more thorough examination of the cases to reflect the present law with regard to these.

Various theories have been advanced with a view to freeing charitable corporations from liability for the torts of their servants. One is the "Trust Fund" theory. It holds that the fund created by the benefactors of a charity was intended as a trust, and that there would be an illegal diversion of the trust *res* from the purposes for which it was set apart, if it was employed for the paying of damages caused by the negligence of the charity's employees.[322] The "Trust Fund" theory has never been accepted in New York[323]

The courts of New York have held that a recipient of charity implicitly exempts his benefactors by contract from liability for injuries inflicted upon himself by the servants of the charitable corporation.[324] While this theory did serve as the basis for the decisions just referred to, it soon began to be attacked by the New York courts. It was pointed out that it was logically weak, since it rested on the patent fiction that a patient had voluntarily relinquished a known right by coming to the hospital or any other charitable institution for aid.[325] A somewhat earlier case[326] had stated quite explicitly that the use of such a theory had come to an end.

---

[320] Hordern *v.* Salvation Army, 199 N. Y. 233, 92 N. E. 626 (1914).

[321] Kellogg *v.* Church Charity Foundation of Long Island, 203 N. Y. 191, 96 N. E. 406 (1911).

[322] Zollman, *American Law of Charities,* p. 542.

[323] Cf. Hordern *v.* Salvation Army, and Kellogg *v.* Church Charity etc., *supra,* notes 320 & 321.

[324] Joel *v.* Woman's Hospital, 89 Hun. 73, 35 N. Y. S. 37 (N. Y. 1895); Collins *v.* New York Post-Graduate Medical School, 59 App. Div. 63, 69 N. Y. S. 106 (1907); Schloendorff *v.* Society of N. Y. Hospital, 211 N. Y. 125, 105 N. E. 92 (1914); Van Tassel *v.* Manhattan Eye and Ear Hospital, 39 N. Y. St. R. 781, 15 N. Y. S. 620 (1918).

[325] Phillips *v.* Buffalo General Hospital, 239 N. Y. 189, 146 N. E. 199 (1924).

[326] Hamburger *v.* Cornell University, 226 N. Y. 625, 123 N. E. 868 (1919).

In New York a special application of, or exception to, the doctrine of *respondeat superior* has been adhered to. The courts point out that doctors and nurses are not mere servants and agents of a charitable corporation, but are rather independent contractors for whom the hospital has provided a place to aid the suffering.[327] The hospital undertakes not to heal or attempt to heal through the agency of others, but merely to supply others who will heal on their own responsibility.[328] It follows, then, that the doctrine of *respondeat superior* could not be invoked, since there was no relationship of master and servant upon which to predicate it. The hospital, therefore, could not be held for the wrongs of these parties.

The hospital's immunity from liability for the errors of its physicians and nurses was applied in the case of a university, also held to be a charitable institution. Here a like immunity from liability for wrongs of professors, instructors, or other members of its staff of teachers was declared to exist.[329] The only burden placed upon the shoulders of the hospital or school was the duty to select the doctors and nurses, or the faculty, with due care. The question, however, of whether or not there would be liability for the ordinary acts of administrative agents acting in an administrative capacity was an undecided one until the case of *Sheehan* v. *North Country Community Hospital*[330] came before the New York Court of Appeals.

The exact question brought before the court was whether a charitable institution should be exempt from liability to a beneficiary for personal harm caused by the negligence of one acting as its mere servant or employee. The issue was raised in an action brought by a patient of the defendant hospital, a charitable institution, to recover for personal injuries sustained through a collision between the ambulance in which she was riding and another vehicle, alleged to have been occasioned through the negligence

[327] Wilson *v.* Brooklyn Homeopathic Hospital, 97 App. Div. 37, 89 N. Y. S. 619 (1904); Cunningham *v.* Sheltering Arms, 135 App. Div. 178, 119 N. Y. S. 1033 (1909); Bernstein *v.* Beth Israel Hospital, 236 N. Y. 268, 140 N. E. 694 (1923).

[328] Schloendorff *v.* Society of N. Y. Hospital, *supra,* note 324.

[329] Hamburger *v.* Cornell University, 226 N. Y. 625, 123 N. E. 868 (1919).

[330] 273 N. Y. 163, 7 N. E. 2d 28 (1937).

of both. The defense appealed to the doctrine that a charitable corporation is immune from liability to a beneficiary for an injury caused by the negligence of its servants or agents. The court ruled "that to impose liability is to beget careful management; and that no conception of justice demands that an exception to the rule of *respondeat superior* be made in favor of the resources of a charity against the person of a beneficiary injured by the tort of a mere servant or employee functioning in that character."

Note that *Sheehan* v. *North Country Community Hospital* said nothing concerning the charitable institution's liability for negligences of its doctors and nurses. There was no change in the law here. Therefore in New York a charitable corporation was held liable for the torts of its mere servants and agents, but not for those whom the court considered to be independent contractors, i.e., doctors and nurses.

This law was criticized. It was claimed that there was a "juggling" of the doctrine of *respondeat superior*. How could there exist the doctrine that a charitable corporation was liable for the tort actions of its employees when a servant was performing a menial function, and then mysteriously disappear when the act was termed "professional?" The criticism conclusively pointed out that, if the relationship of master and servant existed for one purpose, it was a retreat from realism to say that it was lacking for another purpose.[331]

A very recent decision of the highest tribunal in New York is noteworthy.[332] The court of Appeals in this State abandoned what had come to be called the "Schloendorff Rule,"[333] under which the liability of hospitals for injuries suffered by a patient, through the negligence of its employees, depended upon whether the injury-producing act was administrative or medical.

In this very recent case the negligent injury-producing act was that of a nurse employed by a private hospital. The trial jury,

---

[331] Larber, "Liability of Hospitals for the Negligence of Their Employees," *St. John's Law Review*, XV (1941), 277.

[332] Bing *v.* Thunig, 2 N. Y. 2d 656, 143 N. E. 2d 3 (1957).

[333] Cf. Schloendorff *v.* Society of N. Y. Hospital, 211 N. Y. 125, 105 N. E. 92 (1914).

under a proper *Schloendorff* rule instruction, brought in a verdict for the plaintiff. The Appellate Division reversed, finding as a matter of law that the act was a medical act. The Court of Appeals, recognizing that the act of the nurse "might, perhaps, be denominated an administrative default," nevertheless did not consider it either wise or necessary again to become embroiled in the disputation as to whether it should be labelled administrative or medical. Instead it proceeded to re-examine the present basis of the rule itself. It reached the following conclusion:

> Hospitals should, in short, shoulder the responsibilities borne by everyone else. There is no reason to continue their exemption from the universal rule of *respondeat superior*. The test should be for these institutions, whether charitable or profit-making, as it is for every other employer, was the person who committed the negligent injury-producing act one of its employees and, if he was, was he acting within the scope of his employment.
>
> The rule of non-liability is out of tune with the life about us, at variance with modern-day needs and with concepts of justice and fair dealing. It should be discarded.[334]

[334] Bing *v.* Thunig, 2 N. Y. 2d 656, 143 N. E. 2d 3 (1957).

CHAPTER III

CHARITABLE AND RELIGIOUS GIFTS IN THE CODE

ARTICLE 1. CANONICAL NOTION OF A PIOUS CAUSE

THE dedication of property to a good purpose, a dedication which enjoys the favor of the law, is designated by the Code of Canon Law with the phrase *ad pias causas*.[1] The expression *causa pia* seems to have been chosen by the Code in the light of a tradition in force for many centuries. In this traditional sense, *causa pia* includes all pious, religious and charitable works favored by the Church.[2]

Causa pia also has a more restricted sense. It is used to signify something stable and abiding, as an institute or foundation by means of which pious works are carried on.[3] Here it connotes more than a pious finality; it stands for a body of goods actually dedicated to a pious end. There are many canons that speak of *causa pia* in this substantive sense.[4] In this work the term *pious cause* will be used in its more extensive connotation. The term, therefore, includes all works which, either by reason of their direct purpose or by reason of the intention of the donor, are destined for a supernatural end.[5]

Gifts made for the celebration of Mass, for the performance of other acts of religion, for works of spiritual charity—all these are pious because they are destined to ends that are pious by their nature, and thus the works themselves are intrinsically pious.[6] A

---

[1] Cans. 1513, § 1; 1516, § 1; 2348.

[2] Visser, "De Solemnitatibus Piarum Voluntatum in Iure Canonico," *Apollinaris*, XX (1947), 61.

[3] *Ibid.*, p. 60.

[4] Cf. cans. 1421; 1653, § 4; 1757, § 3, n. 1; 2347, n. 2.

[5] Bouscaren-Ellis, *Canon Law* (Milwaukee: Bruce, 1946), p. 755.

[6] Cf. Visser, "art cit.," *Appollinaris*, XX (1947), 65: " . . . determinatio utrum voluntas aliqua sit pia necne, provenit (a) Primarie ex elemento externo: si dispositio dirigitur ad aliquod institutum vel actum obiective pium, semper est voluntas pia."

103

gift to any moral personality in the Church is a *pious* gift. This can be seen from the fact that all property in the ownership of moral personalities in the Church is ecclesiastical property in the technical sense,[7] and all such property is destined by law to purposes of "piety."[8] This last statement demands further clarification.

Ecclesiastical goods are dedicated to piety by the canons governing the nature and constitution of moral personalities in the Church. Every moral personality in the Church which is constituted by the very operation of the law[9] performs, or makes possible the performance of, one or more of the divinely established functions of the Church itself.[10] Among these purposes are: the worship of God,[11] the preaching of the Gospel,[12] the religious government of the members of the Church,[13] the pursuit of Christian perfection,[14] the administration of the sacraments,[15] and the exercise of spiritual and temporal charity toward men.[16] These are the purposes for which by the divine law the Catholic Church and the Apostolic See were established. These are the purposes for which the Church establishes provinces, dioceses, parishes, benefices, seminaries and universities, tribunals, and religious communities, etc.

---

[7] Can. 1497.

[8] It may be said that the terms "piety" and "pious," as used in the Code, point to every good work undertaken for the love of God or of neighbor. At times the canons use these terms to describe acts directly referred to God (cf., e.g., cans. 1268, §4; 1385, §1, n. 2; 1535; 1587, §2; 931). In two canons (cans. 707, § 1; 1544, §1) "piety" is used along with the term "charity" when reference is made to acts of worship and to acts in aid of human necessity. Here it might seem that "piety" had the restricted meaning of works directed toward God and "charity" the exclusive connotation of works directed toward the neighbor. This is not so, however, since both kinds of works are indicated with the single term "pious" in other canons (cf., e.g., cans. 250, § 2; 497, §2; 622, §3; 1492).

[9] Cf. *supra,* pp. 21-22.

[10] Cf. *supra,* p. 20.

[11] Can. 1255.

[12] Cans. 1322, §2; 1327.

[13] Cans. 218; 329; 1553, §1.

[14] Cans. 487; 488; 673.

[15] Can. 371.

[16] Cans. 497, §2; 1473; 1489.

Finally, all of the institutes and associations which are granted moral personality by way of special concession [17] may and can be constituted exclusively for purposes of religion or charity."[18]

There are, however, other works, which in their internal character are "indifferent" as regards piety. Such works, and also the gifts in aid of them, cannot be established as pious through any application of the standard of intrinsic piety. Here a work of beneficence which is intrinsically indifferent as regards piety will be determined as pious or not by the intention of the doer of the work, or of the person who makes a gift in aid thereof.[19] The work is pious if motivated by the love of God. It is not pious, if it has a merely "humanitarian" or "philanthropic" motivation.[20] In this latter case, the work and any gift in aid thereof will belong to the civil, and not to the canonical jurisdiction.[21] In the former case, though the quality of "piety" is lacking in the intrinsic nature of the work, that quality is supplied by the will of the worker or of the giver.[22] This "will" is a fact not externally obvious, and is to be determined in each case from the terms of the act of the gift, or from other legal proofs and presumptions of the donor's will. The policy of Christian piety is imposed by the law of the Church upon works undertaken by those institutions and associations which are constituted juridical entities by Canon Law.[23] With regard to institutions and associations approved indeed by Church authority, but not established as juridical entities in the Church,[24] that same policy is warranted in consequence of the official act of ecclesiastical

[17] Cf. *supra*, pp. 28-28.

[18] Can. 100, §1.

[19] Cf. Visser, "art cit.," *Apollinaris*, XX (1947), 65-66: " . . . determinatio utrum voluntas aliqua sit pia necne, provenit . . . (b) Secundarie ex elemento interno: si dispositio dirigitur ad aliquod institutum vel actum obiective indifferentem, ita ut possit esse pium vel non, voluntas est pia vel non pia secundum intentionem iuridicam disponentis i.e. secundum voluntatem eam dirigendi ad finem Ecclesiae vel Status."

[20] Wernz-Vidal. *Ius Canonicum*, Tomus IV, Vol. II, n. 781, p. 259; Coronata, *Institutiones*, II, n. 1024.

[21] Wernz-Vidal, *loc. cit.;* cf. Visser, ibid., pp. 67-68.

[22] Cf. *supra*, note 19.

[23] Cf. *supra*, pp.104-105.

[24] Cf. *supra*, p. 19.

approval.[25] If all public works of beneficence and education were carried on by the Church, or by agencies constituted or approved by the Church, any gift for these purposes would presumably be directed to an administration under ecclesiastical jurisdiction. In a society, however, wherein such works are carried on also by civil or secular agencies, such presumptions are unwarranted.[26]

ARTICLE 2. DESTINATION OF GOODS TO A PIOUS CAUSE

Section I. *Pia Voluntas*

Private property is destined to pious causes by means of an act of the owner's will, called *pia voluntas*.[27] The obligation imposed by a *pia voluntas* upon the recipient of such goods to use them for pious purposes is analogous to the obligation of a trustee for charity in New York law.[28] There is, however, a difference also. The canonical concept of the recipient's duty differs from the trust theory in that the former does not rely so distinctly upon the notion of responsibility to a beneficiary.[29] The canons which *ex professo* set forth the recipient's duty and provide for its enforcement by authority refer explicitly and directly to the fulfillment of the *pia voluntas* of the *donor*;[30] only indirectly and implicitly do these canons refer to the beneficiary of the *causa pia*.[31]

[25] Cf. cans. 684; 696; 1591, §1.

[26] Cf. Visser, *ibid.*, pp. 67-68.

[27] Cf. cans. 1514-1517; Visser, *ibid.*, p. 60: "Vox *voluntas pia* in Iure Canonico semper considerata est plene identica cum ea: *dispositio ad causas pias*, vel *dispositio in favorem causae piae*." In footnote 3 on the same page the author refers to a case on inheritance handled by the Sacred Congregation of the Council in 1927.

[28] Cf. *infra*, pp. 145-152.

[29] Cf. *infra*, p. 145, note 48.

[30] Cf. can. 1514: "Voluntates fidelium facultates suas in piis causis donantium vel relinquentium . . . diligentissime impleantur . . ."; can. 1515, §1: "Ordinarii omnium piarum voluntatum . . . executores sunt . . ."; can. 1515, § 2: "ut piae voluntates impleantur . . ."; can. 1516, §2: "pro executione piae voluntatis . . ."; can. 1517, §2: ". . . servatata . . . fundatoris voluntate. . . ."

[31] Cf. can. 1516, §3, where the character of the beneficiary determines the competence of ordinaries; can. 1517, §2, where it is directed that beneficiaries be consulted before any condonation of a pious will.

Section II. General Canonical Sanction to Fulfill Will of Donor

A general canonical sanction is given in canon 1514 to all obligations arising under an act of the will by which a man dedicates his goods to pious causes.[32] The canon commands that the directions of the person who made the dedication be carried out most diligently. It does not limit in any way the extension of the obligation imposed. It therefore binds all those who have anything to do with the administration or distribution of the goods thus dedicated to pious purposes. This obligation extends not only to the fulfillment of the purpose to be served by the property in question, but also to the carrying out of the donor's directions as to the specific manner in which the pious work or gift is to be managed and directed to the purpose thus designated.

This sanction has one exception. Any direction, when found in an *ultima voluntas*,[33] which attempts to deny the power of ordinaries as executors [34] over *pious wills* is to be disregarded in the assessing of obligations on the part of persons charged with receiving, administering, or distributing such goods. It might be well to examine the effect of this exception. The exception is expressed in canon 1514 in its reference to canon 1515, § 3, a canon which treats of the power of ordinaries as executors over *pious wills*.[35]

The clause which prescribes that such directions be disregarded reads as follows: *"tanquam non appositae habeantur."* There are two other canons in the Code with similar wording. Both these canons have the clause, *"non adiecta habeatur."* The first of these canons points out that if a person has in any way ordered that his body be cremated, it is illicit to obey such instructions. It goes on

[32] Can. 1514.—Voluntates fidelium facultates suas in pias causas donantium vel relinquentium, sive per actum inter vivos, sive per actum mortis causa, diligentissime impleantur etiam circa modum administrationis et erogationis bonorum, salvo praescripto can. 1515, §3.

[33] This term as used in Canon Law designates the last act by which a man determines what shall be done after his death, particularly with respect to the disposition of his property. Cf. Wernz-Vidal, *Ius Canonicum*, Tomus IV, Vol. II, n. 800, p. 280.

[34] Cf. *infra*, p. 109.

[35] Can. 1515, §3: "Clausulae huic Ordinariorum iuri contrariae, ultimis voluntatibus adiectae, tanquam non appositae habeantur."

to point out that if such a provision occur in a contract, last testament, or in any document whatsoever, it is to be disregarded.[36] The second of these canons is concerned with future conditions annexed to marital consent when these conditions are either inexorable or unachievable or evil, but are not contrary to the very substance and essence of marriage.[37]   The clauses just noted in these two canons do seem to express the same idea as that expressed in canon 1515, § 3. The force of the clause in canon 1092, n. 1, has been explained by many commentators, and there seems to be no reason why the same force should not be applied to the clause contained in canon 1515, § 3.

Commentators point out that the phrase in canon 1092, n. 1, creates a presumption of law [38] that the conditions in question are not expressed seriously.[39] If the expressed condition hinges on something impossible or evil, the extant presumption will nevertheless yield to the proof that the condition was seriously made. With that proof established, the judgment must be that the condition was effective in suspending the marital consent. This suspension will last until the evil condition has become verified, or it will last indefinitely if the expressed condition is truly impossible of achievement. This same doctrine seems to be applicable to the clause *"tamquam non appositae habeantur"* of canon 1515, § 3. Consequently, when a condition contrary to the ordinary's rights is expressed seriously and is antecedent to the will to dedicate the goods to a pious cause, the dedication is invalid, if the condition is not fulfilled. Such a condition, certainly, cannot be observed legally, so any *voluntas* which has been made subject to a firm and antecedent condition of this kind becomes invalid as a *pious will*.

[36] Can. 1203, §2: "Si quis quovis modo mandaverit ut corpus suum cremetur, illicitum est hanc exsequi voluntatem; quae si adiecta fuerit contractui, testamento aut alii ciulibet actui, tanquam non adiecta habeatur."

[37] Can. 1092: "Conditio semel apposita et non revocata: 1°. Si sit de futuro necessaria vel impossibilis vel turpis, sed non contra matrimonii substantiam, pro non adiecta habeatur; . . .

[38] Cf. can. 1826.

[39] Bouscaren-Ellis, *Canon Law,* p. 511; Abbo-Hannan, The Sacred Canons (St. Louis: Herder, 1952), II, 330. Capello, *De Sacramentis* (3 vols., Vol. III, Romae: Marietti, 1923), III, n. 629, p. 663.

Certain important points must always be kept in mind. The law can establish presumptions for the interpretation of private acts; the law can also command acts; but the law cannot supply the donor's will to give, any more than it can supply any man's will to marry. If no proof avails for dislodging the law's presumption that the objectionable condition is not serious, or at least that it arose only subsequently to the will to make a pious gift, then the act is juridically a *pious will*. The recipient of the property in question is, therefore, free of any duty to observe the specified condition in his acceptance, administration, or distribution of the goods.[40]

Section III. Canonical Duties of Executors of Pious Wills

Ordinaries are the executors of all pious donations made in contemplation of death (*mortis causa*) or during the lifetime of the donors (*inter vivos*).[41] An executor is one who is charged with administering and distributing, according to the deceased owner's will and in accord also with the law, the property left by the decedent. A distinction must be made between the *executor delegatus*[42] and the *executor natus*, who is the ordinary.[43] The *executor delegatus* may be the executor named by the decedent, or he may be the one named by a civil authority, or, in default of either, by the ordinary himself.[44] His duty is to receive and to manage, to pay over or to use, according to the owner's directions, property dedicated under a *pious will*.[45] The ordinary, as *executor natus*, does not supersede the *executor delegatus*;[46] but the latter is subject to the vigilance and to the visitation of the ordinary in connection with his duties, and he is obliged to render an account to the ordinary on the completion of his duties.[47]

---

[40] Wernz-Vidal, *Ius Canonicum*, Tomus IV, Vol. II, n. 795, p. 276.
[41] Can. 1515, § 1.
[42] Can. 1515, § 2.
[43] Cf. Beste, *Introductio in Codicem*, p. 753.
[44] Bouscaren-Ellis, *Canon Law*, p. 760.
[45] Cf. 1514.
[46] Beste, *op. cit.*, p. 753.
[47] Can. 1515, §2.

In New York Law a trustee of goods destined to a pious purpose is not called an executor,[48] yet his position is within the scope of the canonical concept of *executor delegatus*,[49] and he is, therefore, subject to the same vigilance and visitation, and is chargeable for an accounting when his task is accomplished.

Section IV. Canonical Duties of Certain Trustees

Very similar in effect to the "charitable trust" in New York Law [50] is the canonical *fiducia* (*fideicommissum*).[51] The latter exists when property is given, by donation or by testamentary act, to a person (*fiduciarius*—"trustee") on whom is imposed the obligation of using that property for pious purposes or of delivering it to a moral personality in the Church.[52] Many canonists hold that there

[48] Cf. *N. Y. Real Property Law*, §§ 100 and 113, subd. 1.

[49] Cf. Bouscaren-Ellis, *op. cit.*, p. 760.

[50] Cf. *infra*, pp. 145-152.

[51] It must be kept in mind, however, that the canon law notion of *fiducia* is not the same as the common law concept of the *trust*. They do not represent the same concept, even though they are quite similar in effect. As one author puts it, "The chief difference appears to lie in the fact that the Roman or canonical notion of a trust is concerned with an obligation to transfer to another the title to the property involved or to spend it for some pious cause, while the Anglo-American concept of trust involves the trustee's continued holding of the title to the trust property while conferring the benefit of that property upon another or for the accomplishment of some charitable purpose. Thus the Anglo-American concept of a trust is a specific mode of holding property which does not have a canonical counterpart."—Byrne, *Investment of Church Funds*, The Catholic University of America Canon Law Studies, n. 309 (Washington, D. C.: The Catholic University of America Press, 1951), p. 92.

[52] Wernz-Vidal, *op. cit.*, Tomus IV, Vol. II, n. 796. Beste recounts four elements as inherent in every canonical trust: (1) A trustee must be designated. This trustee can be either a moral personality or a physical person. This trustee is given ownership (*titulus vel dominium*) of the property that constitutes the trust, but he has the added obligation of administering and managing that same property for some other person or pious cause. (2) A beneficiary must be designated. This may be either a physical person, or a moral personality, or a pious cause, but always distinct from the trustee. The property is to be applied for the benefit of the former according to the mind

is no canonical trust, though there is still a pious gift, when the property given is a determined sum of money which is to be used immediately for a stated pious purpose. In such a transaction the recipient does not "manage" or "administer" the property.[53]

When, however, the recipient is to convert or invest the property, or to hold it for a considerable time, or when he is to use the property, or pay out its income, for a specified purpose over any period of time, in all these cases there is a pious trust. On the contrary, a gift of money which is to be used or paid over immediately, or a gift of property to a moral personality in the Church, apart from any specific direction as to how that property shall be held or used, is not a trust at Canon Law.[54]

Canonists commonly teach that any lay fiduciary for pious causes is subject to the duties of an *executor delegatus* as described in canon 1515, § 2.[55] Canon 1516 imposes special duties on clerics

of the donor of such property. (3) There must be property which is to be transferred and applied in trust. (4) Such property must be actually handed over to the trustee. Cf. Beste, *op. cit.*, p. 750.

[53] Wernz-Vidal, *op. cit.*, Tomus IV, Vol. II, n. 797, p. 277, note 9; Coronata, *Institutiones*, II, n. 1056, p. 480. These authors assert that a gift of a definite sum of money to be used for a determined end, when no administration is required, does not come under the provisions of canon 1516. Beste, citing a particular case, seems to agree with their view. Cf. Beste, *op. cit.*, p. 754. This can also be seen in his elaboration of the elements that constitute a canonical trust. Cf. *supra*, p. 110, note 52. Cf. also Cocchi, *Commentarium in Codicem Iuris Canonici* (8 vols., Vol. VI, 5. ed., 1937, Taurinorum Augustae: Marietti), VI, n. 195; Prümmer, *Manuale Iuris Canonici* (5. ed., Friburgi Brisgoviae: Herder, 1927), p. 525, note 5.

[54] Cf. Beste, *op. cit.*, p. 750: "Hinc non habetur fideicommissio vel fiduciaria acceptatio, sed simplex donatio, si bona directe legentur vel tradantur alicui personae morali cum obligatione iisdem in sui ipsius favorem utendi. . . ."

[55] This canon states: "Hoc ex iure Ordinarii vigilare possunt, ac debent, etiam per visitationem, ut piae voluntates impleantur, et alii exsecutores delegati debent, perfuncti munere, illis reddere rationem." Cf. Vermeersch-Creusen, *Epitome*, II, n. 836, p. 584; Wernz-Vidal, *op. cit.*, Tomus IV, Vol. II, n. 797; Beste, *op. cit.*, p. 753. These authors hold that lay fiduciaries do not come under the regulations of canon 1516, which treats of clerical and religious fiduciaries. Coronata seems to deny this when he states: ". . . attamen, quia difficilius contra laicos in hoc neglegentes poenis procedi poterit, ideo Codex *specialem* (in canon 1516) clericis et religiosis circa hoc obligationem

and religious who accept in trust goods destined for pious causes. A cleric is a man who has received tonsure, and thereupon has not lapsed from the ecclesiastical state; [56] a religious is a man or a woman who upon profession remains under the obligation of public vows.[57]

The duties imposed by canon 1516 are additional to the obligations sanctioned in canon 1514.[58] The cleric or religious must advise his ordinary of the pious trust he has received, giving an inventory of all the property, personal or real, which is subject to the trust, and stating the duties imposed by the trust. If the donor expressly and absolutely forbade such a report to the ordinary, the cleric or religious must not accept the trust.[59] In addition to the trustee's duties of submitting his management to the vigilance of the ordinary, and of accounting to the ordinary on the completion of his task, the religious or cleric as trustee has a further duty to obey the ordinary's directions regarding the depositing and investing of the funds held in trust.[60]

Section V. Canonical Duties of Moral Personalities in the Church as Trustees for Pious Causes

When property is given to ecclesiastical moral personalities apart from any implied duty to use that property for a specified pious

imponit, quo tamen, ni fallimur, laicos ab eadem absolvi non putamus."— *Institutiones*, II, n. 1056, p. 479.

[56] Cf. cans. 108, § 1; 211-213.

[57] Cf. cans. 488, n. 7; 637-672.

[58] Cf. *supra*, p. 107.

[59] Can. 1516, § 1. Beste makes a distinction between property received in trust for a pious cause by donation (*inter vivos*) and property received by reason of a last will and testament. With regard to the former, if the donor refuses to retract the specification that militates against this canon, the trust is to be refused. With regard to the latter, he holds that such a restriction should not be observed in accordance with the requirements of canon 1516, § 3, and the trust, therefore, could be accepted. Cf. Beste, *op. cit.*, p. 754.

[60] Can. 1516, § 2. A secular cleric is not obliged to hand over the trust goods to his ordinary, but a religious may be required to do so because of religious discipline and the vow of poverty, not, however, in virtue of this canon. Cf. Cappello, *Summa Iuris Canonici* (3 vols., Vol. I, 4. ed., Romae: Apud Aedes Universitatis Gregorianae, 1945), I, n. 599, 2.

purpose or to administer or distribute it in a particular way, the general sanctions of canons 1514 and 1515 are to be observed.[61] When, however, the donor directs specifically the manner of administration and distribution of the property, or directs its use for particular pious purposes over a period of time, there is a pious trust.[62] If the property is given for the founding of a moral personality in the Church, or for the establishing of a pious foundation, there are special provisions of law, which will be considered shortly.[63] When the purpose of the fund is neither of these, the law prescribes the giving of special consideration to the settlor's will in two eventualities: when there is to be a division of the goods or the territory of the moral personality holding the trust,[64] and when the goods of that moral personality are distributed upon its extinction.[65]

Section VI. Special Obligations of Trustees Under a Gift Made for the Founding of a Moral Personality in the Church

When a gift is made for the founding of a pious institute,[66] the founder's wishes regarding the purpose of the institute, its constitution, its government and administration, the use of its income, and the disposition of its funds, if it becomes extinct, should be incorporated in the charter of foundation.[67] The founder of a benefice may, at the time of the foundation, and with the consent of the ordinary, establish any proper conditions, even conditions contrary to the common law, provided that they are not repugnant to the nature of the benefice.[68]

The law directs that these wishes are to be respected in the dividing of the goods of the territory of the moral personality,[69] and in the determining of succession to the goods of the moral person-

---

[61] Cf. *supra*, pp. 107-110.
[62] Cf. *supra*, pp. 110-111.
[63] Cf. *infra*, pp. 113-115.
[64] Can. 1500.
[65] Can. 1501.
[66] Cf. *infra*, p. 121.
[67] Can. 1490, § 1; cf. also cans. 1492, § 2; 1494.
[68] Can. 1417, § 1.
[69] Can. 1500.

ality upon its extinction.[70] The founders wish may determine whether the consent, or only the advice, of the diocesan council of administration will be required for the ordinary acts in regulating and supervising the administration of the goods of the moral personality.[71] The founder also may determine the manner of expenditure of the income deriving from invested funds,[72] and his wishes may affect the policy to be followed in future alienations of valuable property,[73] and in giving mortgages or in contracting other debts.[74]

Section VII. Special Obligations of Trustees Under a Gift Made for Creating a Pious Foundation

When any kind of property is given to a moral personality in the Church in any manner whatsoever with the attached obligation of using the annual income either for the celebration of Masses, or for carrying out certain defined ecclesiastical functions, or for the performance of some works of piety and charity, there is constituted what is known technically as a *pious foundation.*[75] Certainly any gift for the establishment of such a foundation is a pious gift,[76] and constitutes a species of canonical trust.[77] Pious foundations have certain characteristics which distinguish them from other types of canonical trusts. These distinguishing marks can be seen in three points: (1) pious foundations must be given in ownership to a moral personality in the Church; (2) they permit the use of the income only, and (3) they must be established in perpetuity or for a long time.[78]

---

[70] Cans. 494, § 2; 1501.

[71] Can. 1520, § 3.

[72] Can. 1523, n. 3.

[73] Can. 1532, §§ 2 and 3.

[74] Can. 1538, § 1.

[75] Can. 1544.

[76] Cf. *supra,* pp. 103-104.

[77] Cf. *supra,* p. 110.

[78] Authors disagree on the period of time that may be considered sufficiently protracted to make a pious foundation of the endowment to which a prolonged burden is attached. Most authors hold to a period of forty or fifty years, though some place it as low as ten years. Cf. Abbo-Hannon, *The*

Moral personalities in the Church are bound to observe the rules established by their ordinaries[79] regarding the minimum requisite value of the property offered for pious foundations, and regarding the due proportion between income and obligations.[80] Before the foundation is accepted, the ordinary's consent must be obtained in each case, and that consent must be expressed in writing.[81]

The moral personality accepting the foundation has custody and management of the foundation property, but is obliged to follow the ordinary's directions in the matters indicated in the law. These directions must be followed in the choice of a place for the deposit of the liquid funds given and of the moneys accruing from the sale of realty received for the endowment of the foundation. They also must be followed in the selecting of safe and profitable investments for the trust funds.[82] Founders and administrators of pious funds may offer suggestions regarding the deposit and investment of such funds, but the final decision rests with the ordinary.[83] The investment is to be made for the benefit of the moral personality and an explicit mention of the obligations involved is to be made in the document of investment. The amount of income to be made available for the fulfillment of each obligation is to be determined specifically, as well as the time during which the obligations are binding upon the moral personality.[84]

Sacred Canons, II, 748; Bouscaren-Ellis, *Canon Law,* p. 788; Coronata, *Institutiones,* II, n. 1079, p. 509.

[79] Cf. cans. 1545-1550. Canon 1550 clearly points out that when there is question of pious foundations in the churches of exempt religious, even though they be parochial churches, the rights and duties of the local ordinary mentioned in canons 1545-1549 pertain exclusively to the major religious superior. Cf. can. 488, n. 8, and *AAS,* XVIII (1926), 393.

[80] Can. 1545.

[81] Can. 1546, § 1. Authors are in disagreement concerning whether this consent is required for the validity or merely for the permissiveness of the acceptance. Cf. Byrne, *Investment of Church Funds,* pp. 135-137.

[82] Can. 1547.

[83] Bouscaren-Ellis, *op. cit.,* p. 790.

[84] Bouscaren-Ellis, *loc. cit.* On this matter there is 'some dispute among canonical authors. Some affirm and others deny that in the case of movable property (e.g., bonds) the endowments can be aggregated so that each insures the others, i.e., so that an increase in the value of one set of bonds might

Article 3. Power and Duties of Ecclesiastical Authority regarding Pious Wills

Section I. Power to Enforce Such Wills

A. *General Considerations*

Ordinaries[85] are by law executors (*executores nati*) of all pious wills.[86] The respective jurisdiction of local and religious ordinaries is determined according as the pious work has been given its specific direction by the will in question. When the work depends on a local jurisdiction, the local ordinary is the *executor natus* of the will; when the work is subject to the religious ordinary, he is to be the executor of the will.[87] The exact function of these ordinaries will now be seen.

The ordinary has the generic duty and right of supervising the fulfillment of all the obligations mentioned in Canon 1514.[88] In the exercise of this supervision, he is empowered to avail himself of a canonical visitation of all the persons and things affected by the obligations deriving from the pious will.[89] He is also empowered to exact from delegated executors of pious wills[90] and from all fiduciaries for pious causes[91] an accounting of their accomplished

---

compensate for a decrease in the value of another set, both sets containing a portion of the pooled endowment funds which represented various original endowments. Cf. Abbo-Hannan, *The Sacred Canons*, II, 749; Byrne, *op. cit.*, pp. 141-146.

[85] Canon 198 clearly points out who come under the term "ordinary." A distinction is here made between ordinaries for their respective territories (local ordinaries) and ordinaries for their own subjects. Included under the former designation will be the residential bishop (not however an auxiliary bishop) and the vicar-general (can. 366); under the latter, the major superiors (can. 488, n. 8) in clerical religious institutes (can. 488, n. 4) which are exempt (can. 615).

[88] Cf. *supra*, p. 107.

[87] The word "will" here is used to designate *pia voluntas*, i.e., the destination of private property to pious causes by the act of the owner's will.

[88] Cf. *supra*, p. 109.

[89] Cf. cans. 345, 346, 513 for the norms of procedure in the act of visitation.

[90] Cf. *supra*, p. 109.

[91] Cf. *supra*, pp. 111-112.

commissions.[92] It is he who must warn neglectful heirs.[93] Those persons who, in consequence of the civil defeat of a pious will, obtain possession of the decedent's property which in the terms of his will should go to pious causes are the *heredes* mentioned in canon 1513, § 2. The fact that the word *moneantur,* as used in this canon, obliges the ordinary to warn the heirs was never called into dispute.[94] There was for some time a difference of opinion among canonists on whether this canon did or did not confirm the existence of an obligation in conscience. That dispute was settled by the reply of the Pontifical Commission for the Authentic Interpretation of the Code of Canon Law.[95] The canon is preceptive and the obligation is, therefore, confirmed. The warning *per se* is not penal in the sense of canons 2307, 2233, § 2, and 2242, § 2, or procedural in the sense of canons 2143, 2168, 2176, etc. It is a paternal warning, as contemplated in canons 588, § 1, 467, § 2, and 1348. Since, however, the ordinary can punish recalcitrant heirs by means of censures according to canon 2348, he may in so doing impose penal warnings, as contemplated in canons 2233, § 2, and 2242, § 2.[96]

B. *Power to Enforce Certain Pious Trusts*

In respect to pious trusts when accepted by individual clerics or religious the ordinaries have additional powers. The ordinary is to receive from any such fiduciary notice of his acceptance of the trust, together with an inventory of the trust property and a full statement of the fiduciary obligations.[97] In the case of such trusts the ordinaries not only exercise vigilance and receive a final accounting from the fiduciary, but they also direct him in depositing and investing the trust property.[98]

[92] Can. 1515, § 2.

[93] Can. 1513, § 2.—In ultimis voluntatibus in bonum Ecclesiae serventur, si fieri possit, sollemnitates iuris civilis; hae si omissae fuerint, heredes moneantur ut testatoris voluntatem adimpleant.

[94] Visser, "De Solemnitatibus Piariem Voluntatum in Iure Canonico," *Apollinaris,* XX (1947), 118.

[95] *AAS,* XXII (1930), 196.

[96] Visser, *ibid.,* p. 117.

[97] Can. 1516, § 1.

[98] Can. 1516, § 2.

C. *Special Regulations Regarding Religious*

The investment of property by religious must always be undertaken in accord with the constitutions of their community.[99] In some cases religious will need the local ordinary's consent for the investment and reinvestment of funds held by the community or by its members. In the same cases the religious must account for the administration of those funds to the diocesan ordinary. The local ordinary's supervision of the administration of ecclesiastical property, however, does not usually extend to properties held by persons and institutions exempt from his jurisdiction.[100] These exempt properties are under the supervision of other authorities, especially the superiors of religious congregations and orders.[101]

The law requires the consent of the local ordinary for the investment and reinvestment of funds, and it requires an accounting of the administration of the funds held by religious in the following cases: (1) All funds held for any purpose by communities of nuns,[102] or women religious of diocesan approval, [103] or individual members of such communities; [104] (2) Funds held by communities of women religious of pontifical approval, as the dowry for their professed members; [105] (3) Funds donated to the houses of religious congregations for purposes of divine worship or benevolence to be executed in that very place; [106] (4) Funds held by any religious, even regulars, when the funds were given to a parish or a mission, or were given to the religious for the benefit of a parish or a mission.[107]

---

[99] Can. 532, § 1.

[100] Cans. 1519, § 1; 500, § 1.

[101] Can. 502.

[102] Can. 488, n. 7.

[103] Can. 488, n. 3.

[104] Cans. 533, § 1, n. 1; 535, § 1, n. 1, and § 3, n. 1.

[105] Cans. 533, § 1, n. 2; 535, § 2. Cf. also can. 549.

[106] Cans. 533, § 1, n. 3; 535, § 3, n. 2. Authors dispute the exact extent of this provision. Some would not include under it funds donated for these purposes to the province or the institute itself; others exclude houses of regulars (can. 488, n. 7 and 2) and even those of exempt congregations (cans. 488, n. 2; 500, § 1). Cf. Abbo-Hannan, *The Sacred Canons*, I, 547-548.

[107] Cans. 533, § 1, n. 4; 535, § 3, n. 2.

Written consent of the local ordinary is required for alienation of the property of nuns or women religious of diocesan approval, and the same consent is needed if those communities are to contract debts or incur other obligations, when the sum or value involved is less than five thousand dollars.[108] If the value is above that sum, the permission of the Holy See is required.[109]

D. *Power Over Ecclesiastical Administrators*

The administration of all ecclesiastical property located in his diocese and not exempted from his jurisdiction is subject to the supervision of the local ordinary.[110] This is a most important principle, but it must be correctly understood. The local ordinary is the *immediate* administrator of all property which constitutes the episcopal benefice (*mensa episcopalis*),[111] as well as of any funds held in common (*massa communis*) for the benefit of the diocese as such. He is also the immediate administrator of all funds belonging to the diocesan seminary.[112] He is likewise the immediate administrator of the property of the cathedral church.[113] The thing to note is that canon 1519, § 1,[114] does not refer to these properties, but to others which have their own immediate administrators.[115] The local ordinary is to exercise careful and diligent vigilance over such administrators; but he may not take upon himself the immediate administration of any church property which

108 Can. 534, § 1. Cf. *AAS,* XLIII (1951), 602; Bouscaren, *Canon Law Digest,* Supplement under cc. 534 and 1532.

109 *Loc. cit.*

110 Can. 1519, § 1. If ecclesiastical property is exempted from local jurisdiction, e.g., the property of an exempt clerical religious institute, it will be subject to the vigilance of a religious superior, who will supervise its management according to the religious constitutions. Cf. can. 532.

111 Can. 1483.

112 Cf. cans. 1357 and 1359.

113 Can. 1182, § 1.

114 The canon states: "Loci Ordinarii est sedulo advigilare administrationi omnium bonorum ecclesiasticorum quae in suo territorio sint nec ex eius iurisdictione fuerint subducta, salvis legitimis praescriptionibus, quae eidem potiora iura tribuant."

115 Bouscaren-Ellis, *Canon Law,* p. 765.

by law has its own administrator.[116] With regard to such property, i.e., property having its own administrator, the local ordinary, by law, has the right of visitation, of demanding reports, and of prescribing the method of administration. A more particular examination of these powers is now in order.

The local ordinary is empowered to make rules that will govern the management of such property. In so doing he must keep within the limits of the common law and take into consideration the rights of various persons and legitimate customs and circumstances.[117] He is to appoint administrators of the properties of any church, institution, or other ecclesiastical entity which does not have an administrator appointed by the law or by its charter;[118] direct the investment of any funds which are surplus above the operating expenses of the churches or other institutions of his diocese;[119] authorize the reinvestment of funds;[120] demand an annual accounting of all such administration;[121] permit or refuse permission for administrators to enter or to contest suits regarding the property in their charge;[122] grant or refuse authorization for any act which exceeds the limits of ordinary administration.[123] The license of the diocesan ordinary or of the Holy See is required for the alienation of church property subject to his jurisdiction,[124] and also for the assumption of obligations;[125] for giving mortgages or contracting

---

[116] *Loc. cit.*

[117] Can. 1519, § 2.

[118] Can. 1521, § 1.

[119] Can. 1523, n. 4.

[120] Can. 1539, § 2.

[121] Can. 1525.

[122] Can. 1526.

[123] Can. 1527. For a clear and rather thorough discussion of what constitutes "ordinary administration" cf. Huot, "Bonorum Temporalium apud Religiones Administratio Ordinaria et Extraordinaria," *Commentarium pro Religiosis et Missionariis,* XXXIV (1955), 60-61.

[124] Cans. 1530-32. Cf. *AAS,* XLIII (1951), 602; Bouscaren, *Canon Law Digest,* Supplement under can. 1532.

[125] Can. 1533. It must be always kept in mind that the phrase "acts of alienation," as employed by the Code, includes not only sale, but any other contract by which a third party acquires any right to the real or personal property belonging to an ecclesiastical moral personality. Inasmuch as the

debts—here the ordinary establishes the rate of amortization; [126] for refusing gifts; [127] and for giving leases.[128] It obviously follows from what has been said that any funds given to a moral personality in the Church will be safeguarded by the ordinary in his exercise of the powers just enumerated.

E. *Power Over Ecclesiastical Institutes*

When funds are given or bequeathed for the purpose of founding ecclesiastical institutes, e.g., hospitals, orphanages, schools, and other agencies which carry on works of religion or of spiritual or temporal charity, it is in the power of the local ordinary to give authoritative approval to such foundations,[129] or to establish those institutes as moral personalities in the Church.[130] He is forbidden by law to approve such institutes unless their purpose be truly useful and the sum offered be sufficient in the given circumstances for the purpose contemplated.[131] The founder is permitted to have his directions regarding certain matters of administration incorporated in the foundation charter.[132] If, however, the institute is

ownership or usufruct or some right is transferred to another by the act of alienation, there results a certain weakening of the assets of the moral personality, thereby making them less secure and placing a burden upon the Church. Cf. Woywod, *A Practical Commentary on the Code of Canon Law* (revised by Callistus Smith, revised and enlarged edition, 2 vols., New York: Jos. F. Wagner, Inc., 1948), II, n. 1524, p. 208.

[126] Can. 1538.

[127] Can. 1536, § 2.

[128] Cans. 1541-1542.

[129] Cf. Abbo-Hannan, *The Sacred Canons*, II, 699-700. Without ecclesiastical approval such institutes remain lay institutes, even though they prosecute the very aims of the Church and act from the same supernatural motives, e.g., the St. Vincent de Paul Society. Such lay institutes, however, do remain subject to the supervision of the local ordinary. This is not true of purely philanthropic institutes, i.e., such as are based on pure humanitarianism, even though many of their patrons or officials be Catholics. Cf. also Vermeersch-Creusen, *Epitome*, II, n. 812, p. 562. The quinquenial report which bishops are required to send to the Sacred Consistorial Congregation provides in chapter 11 for information concerning lay (not philanthropic) institutes. Cf. *AAS*, X (1918), 487.

[130] Can. 1489, § 1. Cf. *supra*, p. 19.

[131] Can. 1489, § 2.

[132] Can. 1490, § 1.

constituted as a moral personality, the management of its property is subject to the laws regarding ecclesiastical administration, and its administrators are responsible to the local ordinary in accordance with the norms of the general law of the Church.[133] If the institute is not constituted as a moral personality, but is entrusted to a religious house of diocesan approval, the administration is fully subject to the local ordinary.[134] If it is entrusted to a religious house of pontifical approval, the institute is subject to the local ordinary's vigilance only in matters of religious and moral teaching and practice.[135] By law, all ecclesiastical institutes are subject to the local ordinary's visitation,[136] and he is especially charged to see that the wishes of the founders, as expressed in the charters of these institutes, are carried out.[137] Even though a pious institute may have been rendered exempt from the jurisdiction and the visitation of the local ordinary at the time of its foundation, or by the running of prescription, or through an Apostolic privilege, the diocesan ordinary is authorized by law to demand an accounting of its administration.[138] If the founder should wish that the administrators be not bound to render an accounting to the local ordinary, the foundation is not to be accepted.[139] Without the permission of the Holy See, these institutes cannot be suppressed, united, or diverted to uses foreign to the intentions of the founders, unless the agreement or charter drawn up at the time of their foundation provides otherwise.[140]

F. *Power Over Pious Foundations*

When funds are given or bequeathed for the establishing of a pious foundation,[141] the ordinary's consent must be obtained before

---

[133] Can. 1480, § 3. Cf. *supra*, pp. 119-121.
[134] Can. 1491, § 2.
[135] *Loc. cit.*
[136] Can. 1491, § 1.
[137] Can. 1493.
[138] Can. 1492, § 1. Cf. also can. 1509, nn. 3 and 7.
[139] Can. 1492, § 2.
[140] Can. 1494.
[141] Cf. *supra*, p. 114.

acceptance of the foundation by any moral personality in the Church.[142] If the foundation is offered to an ecclesiastical moral personality, even a parish church, which is the property of exempt religious or which is united completely (*pleno iure*) [143] to a religious house, then this right which centers in the giving of the requisite consent, along with all the other rights described as belonging to the ordinary in connection with pious foundations, belongs to the major religious superior, and not to the local ordinary.[144]

With this exception, the local ordinary has power over all pious foundations. Before consenting to the acceptance of a pious foundation, the ordinary must ascertain that the moral personality can satisfy the obligations arising from the new foundation as well as the ones already undertaken. He must especially see that the income from the foundation corresponds fully to the imposed obligations, according to the custom of the respective diocese.[145] The ordinary is also to prescribe the regulations regarding the limits below which a pious foundation cannot be accepted, and regarding the proper distribution of the income from the endowment.[146]

It belongs to the local ordinary to direct the deposit and the investing of the personal property accepted for a pious foundation, or realized from the sale of immovable property so accepted.[147] The investment is to be made according to the good judgment of the

---

142 Can. 1546, § 1.

143 Cf. cans. 452, § 1; 1425, § 2. A parish is completely (*pleno iure*) united to a religious institute when the union is such that the moral personality itself (the religious society) holds the title of pastor of the parish and governs the parish through its vicar. Cf. Bouscaren-Ellis, *Canon Law*, p. 192.

144 Can. 1550: "Si agatur de piis fundationibus in ecclesiis, etiam paroecialibus, religiosorum exemptorum, iura et officia Ordinarii loci, de quibus in can. 1545-1549, exclusive competunt Superiori maiori." Note that in accordance with the norm of canon 1498 the word *ecclesia* is here used in reference to any moral personality in the Church, and not only to a "church" in the restricted meaning of canon 1161. The power given to the religious superior in canon 1550 does not extend to secular parishes merely entrusted to a religious society. Cf. Cappello, *Summa Iuris Canonici*, II, n. 630, p. 589; Bouscaren-Ellis, *op. cit.*, p. 197.

145 Can. 1546, § 1.

146 Can. 1545.

147 Can. 1547.

ordinary, after he has consulted both the interested parties and the diocesan board of administration.[148] and is to be made in favor of the foundation, with the ordinary enumerating explicitly and individually the obligations attached to the foundation.[149] The final judgment, however, in this matter always rests with the ordinary. His vigilance will extend to demanding periodic accounts of the record books which the administrator of the foundation is bound to keep.[150]

Up to this point the powers of the ordinaries to enforce the obligations of a *pious will* have been discussed. There remains for consideration their power to change, diminish, or remit these obligations.

Section II. Power to Remit, Diminish, or Change Obligations Arising from Pious Wills

When the property given or left for a pious purpose has perished altogether, without fault of the person managing it for such a purpose, his obligation to perform pious works ceases entirely.[151] When the property is totally unproductive, obligations to use its income for pious works naturally cease, unless and until the property is again productive.[152] Neither principal nor income is subject to prescription, because possession adverse to the rights of one who cannot defend or assert his rights (the decedent founder) would be in violation of natural equity.[153]

There are three distinct types of changes that possibly might be made with regard to the obligations arising from a last will and testament.[154] Relaxation (*reductio*) reduces the number of the pious works intended. Specification (*moderatio*) reduces the propor-

---

[148] Can. 1520.

[149] Can. 1547. Cf. *supra*, p. 115.

[150] Can. 1549, § 2.

[151] Wernz-Vidal, *Ius Canonicum*, Tomus IV, Vol. II, n. 790, p. 270.

[152] Cappello, *Summa Iuris Canonici*, II, n. 600, 3.

[153] Wernz-Vidal, *op. cit.*, Tomus IV, Vol. II, n. 790, pp. 270-271. Cf. can. 1509, 1°.

[154] Cf. can. 1517, § 1. This canon refers to these three types of changes as *reductio, moderatio* and *commutatio*.

tions of the plan. This is just another way of saying that there is a moderation of the secondary or accessory conditions specified for the performance of the works in question. Finally, modification (*commutatio*) substitutes acts, plans, or beneficiaries. In this latter case there is a substitution of a work different in nature or object from the work intended.[155]

The power given by law to the ordinaries[156] encompasses a possible change of the obligations under a pious will when the fulfillment of these obligations has become impossible, whether from diminished income of the dedicated property or from any other cause, provided that the impossibility does not result from the fault of the property's administrator.[157] This power extends to the obligations arising from pious foundations.[158] Moral impossibility seems to suffice;[159] and so does any legal impossibility arising from prohibitions of canon law or secular law.[160] If simply some condition as attached to the gift is unlawful, or if it is impossible of fulfillment, it is to be considered as not attached.[161]

In exercising this power the ordinary may relax the obligations or specify their conditions.[162] He may not substitute works of a different kind or works in aid of different beneficiaries, unless the performance of the type of work intended has become truly impossible, or unless works of the specified kind can no longer aid the beneficiaries indicated.[163] In effecting any such change the ordinary

---

[155] Abbo-Hannan, *The Sacred Canons*, II, 722; Vromant, *De Bonis Ecclesiae Temporalibus*, n. 174, p. 155; Wernz-Vidal, *op. cit.*, Tomus IV, Vol. II, n. 790, pp. 271-272.

[156] Regarding the respective competency of religious and local ordinaries, cf. *supra*, pp. 116-124.

[157] Can. 1517, § 2.

[158] Can. 1551, § 1.

[159] Abbo-Hannan, *op. cit.*, II, 723; Cappello, *Summa Iuris Canonici*, II, n. 600, 2.

[160] Abbo-Hannan, *loc. cit.*

[161] *Loc. cit.*

[162] Reference is here made to what is called *reductio* and *moderatio* in canon 1517, § 1. Cf. *supra*, pp. 124-125.

[163] Cappello, *Summa Iuris Canonici*, II, n. 600, 2. The ordinary cannot so act, if it is merely a question of adopting a plan that seems more practicable. Cf. Abbo-Hannan, *op. cit.*, II, 723.

is bound to seek the advice of interested persons.[164] He is not, however, bound to follow their advice.[165] These interested persons will include the administrators of the funds, the living heirs of the founder, the person carrying on or directing the works prescribed by the founder, the representatives of the designated beneficiaries.[166] The ordinary is obliged to conform as closely as possible to the donor's will in exercising his power to change the attached obligations.[167]

The law permits the ordinary[168] and any other person[169] to use powers given them by the founder or donor to change these obligations. In the exercise of such powers the ordinary or other authorized person is bound to adhere to the owner's will regarding the manner and the extent of the changes to be made.

The Holy See has extensive power to make changes in pious wills.[170] The law requires here a just and inevitable cause.[171] A decidedly greater utility of the work to be substituted would be a sufficient cause for the requesting of such a change.[172] Accordingly a petitioner may properly suggest what changes would be most expedient, giving reasons for the preference.

For a clear understanding of this matter one must keep in mind an important distinction. *Interpretation* of a pious last will is not the same as *commutation*. Since the ordinary is the executor of all pious wills,[173] he has the right to interpret them if necessary.[174] This he is to do by determining the exact wishes of the donor as

---

[164] Can. 1517, § 2.

[165] Cf. can. 105. n. 1.

[166] Cappello, *Summa Iuris Canonici*, II, n. 660, 2.

[167] Can. 1517, § 2.

[168] Can. 1517, § 1.

[169] Cappello, *Summa Iuris Canonici*, II, n. 600, 1, p. 569.

[170] Can. 1517, § 1.

[171] *Loc. cit.*

[172] Coronata, *Institutiones*, II, n. 1057, p. 481; Bouscaren-Ellis, *Canon Law*, p. 762.

[173] Can. 1515, § 1. Cf. *supra*, p. 109.

[174] Coronata, *op. cit.*, II, n. 1057, p. 481; Bouscaren-Ellis, *op. cit.*, p. 762.

expressed in the document establishing the foundation, or as expressed in his last will and testament, even though it be invalid at civil law, or as determined by the testimony of trustworthy witnesses, etc.[175]

The Holy See alone can change obligations arising from a pious will when these have become incorporated into the charter of an ecclesiastical institute[176] or of a pious foundation,[177] except when a person exercises powers, duly given him in the charter, for changing the purpose of the institute or for suppressing it, or for uniting it with another ecclesiastical person, or for effecting any change in the provisions of the charter.[178]

When the Holy See has granted an indult permitting the reduction of founded Masses,[179] that faculty does not in and of itself include any authority for the reduction of Mass obligations assumed by contract;[180] nor does such an indult grant the power for reducing founded obligations which are distinct from the obligations attaching to Mass foundations.[181] An indult which contains the grant of a general power to reduce obligations under pious foundations, must be understood, unless the contrary is evident, as binding the holder of the indult to exercise his powers primarily for the reduction of obligations other than those of Masses. Accordingly the reduction of Mass obligations is not to be undertaken until the very purposes of the indult could otherwise not be achieved.[182]

---

[175] Bouscaren-Ellis, *loc. cit.*

[176] Cf. *supra,* pp. 121-122.

[177] Cf. *supra,* p. 114.

[178] Cf. cans. 1494; 1551, § 1.

[179] Can. 826, § 3: ". . . stipendia quae ex fundationum reditibus percipiuntur, appellantur *fundata* seu *Missae fundatae.*"

[180] Masses assumed by contract are those for which *stipendia,* either *manualia* or *ad instar manualium* (cf. can. 826, §§ 1 and 2) have been given and accepted. Cf. can. 828: "Tot celebrandae et applicandae sunt Missae, quot stipendia etiam exigua data et accepta fuerint."

[181] Can. 1551, § 2.

[182] Can. 1551, § 3. Bishops in their quinquennial faculties, under certain

ARTICLE 4. ACTS BY WHICH GOODS ARE DEDICATED TO PIOUS CAUSES

Section I. Classification of Terms

Up to this point there have been considered in this chapter the obligations arising from pious wills in which the property of the donors has been dedicated to charity. In this final section will be considered the various acts by which a man may bring it about that, after his death, his property shall be dedicated to pious purposes.

The term *ultima voluntas* as used in Canon Law[183] refers to the last act by which a man determines what shall be done after his death, especially with regard to the disposition of his property.[184] Acts of this kind are denominated in some canons with the phrase *actus mortis causa*,[185] and in other canons with the term *testamentum*.[186] In opposition to the terms just noted the Code also uses the expression *actus inter vivos*.[187] All acts categorized under this last expression are acts the performance of which are accomplished and perfected in the lifetime of their author.[188]

Some further clarification is necessary. An *actus inter vivos* may here be defined as any donation or other contract by which ownership of property is transferred irrevocably to another for a pious cause. It is called an *actus inter vivos* because ownership is transferred at once, in total abstraction from the death of the donor as

circumstances, can reduce, for five years, on account of diminished revenue, perpetual Mass obligations to the number that can be celebrated on the basis of the relation of the income to the diocesan stipend. Cf. Bouscaren, *Canon Law Digest,* I, 66. These same faculties authorize them, under certain limitations, to tranfer, for five years, the celebration of Masses to other days, churches, or altars. Cf. Bouscaren, *loc. cit.* These specific faculties have remained unchanged up to the present. Cf. *Index Facultatum,* IV, 1-3, in Beste, *Introductio in Codicem* (4. ed., Neapoli: D'Auria, 1956), pp. 1073-1074.

[183] Cf. cans. 1513, § 2; 1515, § 3; 1517, § 1.

[184] Wernz-Vidal, *Ius Canonicum,* Tomus IV, Vol. II, n. 800, II.

[185] Cf. cans. 1513, § 1; 1514; 1515, § 1.

[186] Can. 1516, § 1.

[187] Cf. cans. 1513, § 1; 1514; 1515, § 1; 1516, § 1.

[188] Vermeersch-Creusen, *Epitome,* II, n. 834, I, p. 581.

a condition essential for the act.[189] With regard to *ultima voluntas* there is some difficulty in terminology, since authors vary in the use of this term. The term is often used synonymously with the term *actus mortis causa*.[190] No matter what term or expression is used, such an act can take two forms: (a) A donation in consideration of death (*donatio mortis causa*), by which a gift of certain property is made during the lifetime of the donor, but is subject to revocation on his part at any time before his death. While the beneficiary must accept it to give it effect, the ownership of the property is not transferred to him in consequence of his acceptance of it, but only at the death of the donor, provided that the latter has not revoked it during his lifetime.[191] (b) A last will and testament (*testamentum*), which is the final declaration of a person's intentions regarding the disposition of his property which he wills to be made after his death. Hence such a will is an act, not a contract, and it is essentially revocable. It requires no acceptance on the part of the beneficiary, and it takes effect only on the death of the person who made it.[192]

Sometimes the law itself, without any action of the owner, determines who shall have his goods when he has died. If this is accomplished through a legal designation of the "necessary heirs," who take the decedent's property in spite of any attempt of his to dispose of it otherwise by donation or testation,[193] he can make no effective transfer of the property by means of an *ultima voluntas*.

---

[189] Bouscaren-Ellis, *Canon Law*, p. 756.

[190] Cf. Wernz-Vidal, *op. cit.,* Tomus IV, Vol. II, n. 800, II as compared with Vermeersch-Creusen, *op. cit.,* II, n. 834, I, p. 581 and Bouscaren-Ellis, *op. cit.,* p. 756. The latter two works use the expression *actus mortis causa* to designate what the first work calls *ultima voluntas,* i.e., the act by which provision is made for the transfer of property to take place on the death of the donor.

[191] Bouscaren-Ellis, *loc. cit.*; cf. Vermeersch-Creusen, *loc. cit.*; Cappello, *Summa Iuris Canonici,* II, n. 594, p. 564.

[192] Bouscaren-Ellis, *loc. cit.* Further confusion in terminology is seen in the fact that this work uses the term *ultima voluntas* here while other authors use the term *testamentum.* Cf. Vermeersch-Creusen, *loc. cit.*; Cappello, *loc. cit.*

[193] Cf. *infra,* pp. 134-136.

Section II. Can Any Civil System Be Regarded as
Suppletory Law in Pious Wills?

In the Decretals [194] the Roman Law was regarded as suppletory to the Canon Law.[195] Pre-Code authors disputed concerning the extent of the obligation of this rule.[196] In general it may be said that, when no contrary disposition was expressed by Canon Law, the civil law (Roman Law) was to be observed.[197]

With this principle applied to the matter of pious wills, an interesting development can be seen in the Canon Law in the pre-Code era. In the pre-Code legislative texts there is no general rejection of Roman Law as a suppletory norm in regard to this particular question.[198] Nevertheless, pre-Code authors all seemed to agree that pious wills, apart from the canon law itself, were to be ruled by the natural law, and not by any civil law.[199] One of the fundamental reasons adduced by these authors for the exclusion of the civil law

[194] The reference here is made to the letters and decrees of the popes of the Middle Ages, which helped to form that pre-Code compilation of Church law known as the *Corpus Iuris Canonici*. Cf. Beste, *Introductio in Codicem*, pp. 26-29, nn. 27-32.

[195] The celebrated text on this matter is the letter of Pope Lucius III (1181-1185) to a bishop who had asked what he should do when there was no canonical law on some point. The Pope replied: "Quia vero, sicut leges non dedignantur sacros canones imitari, ita et sacrorum statuta canonum principum constitutionibus adiuvantur . . . negotium ipsum, secundum legum et canonum statuta non differas terminare." C. 1, X, *de novi operis nunciatione*, V, 32; Jaffé, n. 15189; cf. c. 7, X, *de sententia et re indicata*, II, 27; Jaffé, n. 1210; c. 28, X, *de privilegiis et excessibus privilegiatorum*, V, 33; Potthast, n. 7848.

[196] Cf. Visser, "De Solemnitatibus Peariem Voluntatum in Iure Canonico," *Apollinaris*, XX (1947), 72-73.

[197] "Quidquid sit de intentione Decretalium, de facto expressiones auctorum tam largae sunt et tam fere concordes in hoc puncto, *ut saltem ex generali consuetudine et praxi larga interpretatio ut legitima et obligatoria* consideranda sit."—Visser, *ibid.*, p. 73.

[198] Visser, *loc. cit.*

[199] ". . . haec generalis exceptio (causae piae) a Iure Civili exorta est non ex canonibus expressis hoc Ius reicientibus sed ipsa natura spiritualis actus per constantem traditionem iuridicam hanc reiectionem imposuit et sine haesitatione applicavit."—Visser, *ibid.*, p. 80.

in these matters was the spiritual nature of all pious wills.[200] The suppletory norms of Roman Law were accepted only for profane matters,[201] and not for those that had a spiritual character.[202]

If one now look to the present law of the Code, one will see that, with regard to pious wills, the same conclusion can be reached, but in a much more direct way than was possible in the older law. In the present law of the Church no civil law system is regarded as furnishing a suppletory norm.[203] It follows, therefore, that the force of any civil law in respect to pious wills is not be presumed, but needs to be proved as an exception.[204]

The civil law on contracts is explicitly canonized, but with this reservation, "unless it be contrary to the divine law or unless some contrary provision be made in the canon law."[205] Contrary provisions have been made regarding pious wills, which, as such, are not contracts, anyway, but simply acts.

Section III. Solemnities in Pious Wills

At this point it seems necessary to determine what is meant by the term "solemnities" as used in the Code.[206] "Solemnities" are the external modes in which acts are to be performed, and circumstances are to be observed in the performance of these acts. All

---

[200] Cf. *supra,* pp. 103-106.

[201] ". . . ex contextibus clare apparet, canonistae non intendunt res profanas secundum nostram terminologiam hodiernam (i.e. de rebus subiectis regimini Status Civilis) sed de *rebus temporalibus de quibus Ecclesiae ius est.*" —Visser, *ibid.,* p. 74. A contract entered into by the Church was to be considered "profane." Cf. Visser, *ibid.,* p. 76.

[202] Visser, *ibid.,* pp. 76-80.

[203] Can. 20; cf. Visser, *ibid.,* p. 108; Van Hove, *Commentarium Lovaniense in Codicem Iuris Canonici* (1 vol. in 5 toms., Tom. I, *Prolegomena,* 2. ed., 1945, Mechliniae-Romae: H. Dessain), I, nn. 110-112.

[204] ". . . requiritur positivus actus legislatoris Ecclesiae, quo aut lege generali ius civile tamquam fons subsidiarius iuris canonici declaratur, aut lege speciali ordinatio quaedam particularis iuris civilis in foro ecclesiastico recipitur et approbatur."—Wernz, *Ius Decretalium* (6 vols., Vol. I, 2. ed., Romae, 1905), I, n. 195, II. Cf. Visser, *ibid.,* p. 109.

[205] Can. 1529.

[206] Can. 1513, § 2.

this is called for in addition to the declaration or manifestation of a person's will, and pertains to the completion of the declaration or manifestation of that will in such a manner that the will is not lawful, or perhaps even not valid, without them.[207] Such are the common law requirements of delivery in the act of gift,[208] and the statutory requirements relating to the form of acts transferring realty [209] and of testamentary acts.[210] The canon law nowhere prescribes "solemnities" for the act of pious wills,[211] although it does in some cases urge compliance with the civil law in this respect.[212]

Canon 1513, § 2, directs that *"in ultimis voluntatibus in bonum Ecclesiae"* the solemnities of the civil law are to be observed, if that can be done. Since the word *ecclesia* in this section of the Code denotes any moral personality in the Church,[213] civil solemnities

[207] Visser, *ibid.*, p. 59.

[208] Cf. Ridden *v.* Thrall, 125 N. Y. 572, 26 N. E. 627 (1891). Judge Earl here wrote: "To consummate a gift, whether *inter vivos* or *causa mortis*, the property must be actually delivered and the donor must surrender the possession and dominion to the donee."

[209] In New York it is clearly pointed out that gifts of real estate cannot be created by a parol gift *inter vivos*; nor by the devise of "gift *causa mortis*," because that devise is accomplished by parol and it confers a necessarily revocable and defeasible title. Gifts of realty can be made only by delivery of a deed or grant in writing, and these instruments take effect immediately when delivered, conferring title on the donee according to the terms of the instrument. Cf. *N. Y. Real Property Law*, §§ 242-246.

[210] Cf., e.g., *N. Y. Decedent Estate Law*, §§ 10, 15, 21. A typical example to show the importance of these statutory regulations in their civil effects can be seen in the fact that a will is not valid in New York if not signed at the end. Cf. *In re* Bongiovanni, 140 Misc. 436, 251 N. Y. S. 723 (1931).

[211] Visser, *ibid.*, p. 112; Wernz-Vidal, *Ius Canonicum*, Tomus IV, Vol. II, n. 794; "Ius ecclesiasticum ad validas donationes et testamenta aliosque actus ultimae voluntatis pro causis piis nullam specialem requirit solemnitatem, sed sola contentum est disponentis voluntate clare expressa et certo modo probata."

[212] Cf. Visser, *ibid.*, p. 109: "In materiis magis technici, praesertim in regimine de bonis temporalibus Ius Canonicum facilius recipit Ius Civile, quia istud saepe bonum est et practice paulum tantum corrigi eique adiici posset, quod fieri poterit canonibus particularibus derogatoriis vel suppletoriis; inutile esset creare systema proprium parallelum, cum insuper saepe damnosum esset propter probabiles difficultates cum potestate civili."   .

[213] Can. 1498.

are to be observed in all last wills which benefit any ecclesiastical moral personality. Does this obligation extend to other last wills for pious causes in which the beneficiary is not a moral personality in the Church? This point is disputed by canonists.[214] At any rate, the directive does not affect the validity of the last will made without such solemnities. There are some authors who seem to go so far as to say that pious wills in which the beneficiary is not a moral personality in the Church would be invalid if the solemnities were not observed.[215] Even granted that such pious wills do not come under canon 1513, § 2, this contention does not seem to be true. First of all, in canon law an act is said to be invalid only when the effect of invalidity is stated in the law, either expressly or equivalently.[216] Laws, moreover, do not oblige *in dubio iuris*.[217]

It certainly does not appear from the law under consideration, and it seems nowhere else to appear in the Code, that pious wills when made without civil solemnities would be invalid.[218] The most cogent argument against the invalidity of informal last wills for pious causes is that the persons who might take the property on defeat of such an act have a conscientious and canonical[219] obliga-

---

[214] The following authors hold that all pious wills are here included: Vromant, *De Bonis Ecclesiae Temporalibus*, n. 161, p. 145; Vermeersch-Creusen, *Epitome*, II, n. 835, p. 583, note 2; Hannan, *The Canon Law of Wills*, The Catholic University of America Canon Law Studies, n. 86 (Washington, D. C.: The Catholic University of America 1934), p. 473. The following authors hold that the directive of canon 1513, § 2, contemplates only last wills made in favor of ecclesiastical moral personalities: Visser, *ibid.*, p. 114; Gillet, "De Piis Fidelium Voluntatibus," *Collectanea Mechlinensia*, XVI (1927), 87; Larraona, "De Paupertate Simplici," *Commentarium pro Religiosis*, II (1921), 10.

[215] Gillet, "art. cit.," p. 84; Cance, *Le Code de Droit Canonique* (3 vols., Vol. III, 7. ed., Paris: Gabalda, 1946), III, n. 146.

[216] Can. 11.

[217] Can. 15.

[218] Cf. Visser, *ibid.*, pp. 115-117; 119-120.

[219] Those who attach a restrictive meaning to canon 1513, § 2, and at the same time hold for the validity of *all* informal pious wills, would deny the presence of any canonical obligation to carry out the pious will. They do admit, however, the presence of an obligation binding in conscience to carry out such a will. Cf. Visser, *ibid.*, p. 114: "Secundum comma huius paragraphi

tion to carry out the pious will. Since their obligation to carry out the pious will is certain, the pious will must be in effect.

Canon 1513, § 2, directs that when the civil solemnities have not been observed by the maker of an *"ultima voluntas in bonum Ecclesiae,"* the "heirs" are to be warned to fulfill the maker's will. The ordinary as *executor natus* of all pious wills[220] is bound to give this warning, and the heirs are under an obligation in conscience to carry out the pious purpose manifested by the decedent.[221]

Section IV. Rights of "Necessary Heirs" Against Pious Causes

In assessing the obligation of heirs who take property dedicated to pious causes by a last will which is invalid at civil law for want of solemnities, canonists commonly hold that in such a case the "necessary heirs" are obliged to surrender only that portion of the property which was "civilly disposable."[222]

One may well seek here to establish who are some of these "necessary heirs" in New York Law.[223] Under the law of this State some widows have dower rights which are good even against the hus-

---

hae si ommissae . . . [he is here referring to the canonical obligation of fulfilling the obligation of a last will as mentioned in canon 1513, § 2] non est primus finis obiectivus canonis sed tantum disposito hypothetica. In recto § 2 imponit ut serventur solemnitates civiles in ultimis voluntatibus in favorem personae moralis ecclesiasticae; ut tamen vitetur possibilis conclusio quod hae solemnitates necessariae essent ad inducendam obligationem heredi, adiungitur quod omissio earum non tollit hanc obligationem. Consequenter unicus effectus exclusionis aliarum piarum voluntatum ab hac paragrapho est, quod Ecclesia pro illis non explicite imponit observantiam solemnitatum civilium; et ideo nec necessarium est iis applicare secundam partem paragraphi."

[220] Cf. *supra,* p. 109.

[221] Cf. *supra,* p. 117.

[222] Wernz-Vidal, *Ius Canonicum,* Tomus IV, Vol. II, n. 793, note 4; Vermeersch-Creusen, *Epitome,* II, n. 835, p. 583; Cappello, *Summa Iuris Canonici,* II, n. 595, note 2; Bouscaren-Ellis, *Canon Law,* p. 759.

[223] The expression "necessary heirs," which describes persons whose rights of inheritance cannot be denied or abridged by testamentary dispositions made in favor of other persons, is not used in the New York Law. There are, however, rights of inheritance which are guarded by this law against the effect of certain testamentary dispositions which might be adverse to such rights.

band's will.[224] Many surviving spouses now have the right of electing to take a certain share of the estate of the decedent spouse, rather than to accept the dispositions of the will in their regard.[225] Surviving spouses, children, descendants and parents have the right to recover from any legatee for charity their intestate shares in that part of the charitable legacy which exceeds one-half of the net estate of their decedent spouse, parent, grandparent or child.[226] Certain wills, if made before the testator's marriage or before the birth of his child, are revoked to give the spouse or after-born child a share of the estate such as he would have under the rules governing intestacy.[227] In line with the common teaching of the canonists[228] it seems clear that all these persons may take their share of the estate, even against a disposition of the will in favor of charity.

A favored survivor may take action under *N. Y. Decedent*

---

[224] Cf. *N. Y. Real Property Law*, §§ 190-207. Where a marriage took place before September 1, 1930, the wife who survives her husband has consummate dower rights in his real property. Those rights extend to any lands in which the husband had an inheritable estate at any time subsequent to the marriage and prior to September 1, 1930 (*N. Y. Real Property Law*, § 190), and to certain other property by way of exception (*N. Y. Real Property Law*, §§ 191-207).

[225] *N. Y. Decedent Estate Law*, § 18. This right is conferred upon the surviving spouse when the other died after August 31, 1930, and left a will made after that date. The surviving spouse is permitted to elect either to take the share due under the rules of intestacy (cf. *N. Y. Decedent Estate Law*, § 83), or to take a legacy under the will.

[226] *N. Y. Decedent Estate Law*, § 17; cf. *infra*, p. 163.

[227] *N. Y. Decedent Estate Law*, § 35. If, after making any will, the testator marries and the husband or wife survives the testator, that will shall be deemed revoked as to the surviving spouse, unless provision has been made for the survivor in an ante-nuptial agreement in writing. This affects only such wills as had been made before Sept. 1, 1930. *N. Y. Decedent Estate Law*, § 26, provides for an after-born child. It provides that any child of the testator, when its birth followed upon the making of the will, and no provision was made for it by settlement, or in the will, or in any way mentioned in the will, shall succeed to the same share of his parent's estate as if that parent were intestate (cf. *N. Y. Decedent Estate Law*, § 83). He shall have the right to recover that share from the persons who take under the will, in proportion to the parts of the estate so given them.

[228] Cf. *supra*, p. 134.

Estate Law, § 17, for avoidance of the statutory excess of a charitable legacy, not only for the purpose of obtaining a distribution of that excess gift among persons of the favored class, but even to permit that excess to be distributed by an alternative or residuary clause of the will to persons not of that favored class.[229] It seems, however, that a favored survivor who would take action for the second purpose would go contrary to his conscientious and canonical obligations, unless it were certain that the testator intended to give nothing to charity beyond the statutory half. Anyone thus violating his obligations, and also the person who would take the excess as an alternative or residuary legatee, should be warned regarding his obligations.[230]

[229] Cf. *infra*, pp. 167-168.
[230] Can. 1513, § 2 ; cf. *supra*, p. 117.

CHAPTER IV

CHARITABLE GIFTS IN NEW YORK LAW

ARTICLE 1. HISTORY OF CHARITABLE TRUSTS IN NEW YORK

THE first matter to be considered is the validity of charitable trusts in the State of New York. For a proper understanding of this important matter, a brief survey of the history of charitable trusts in this state is absolutely called for.

In 1601 the English Parliament enacted the Statute of Charitable Uses.[1] This statute authorized the Anglican bishops of every diocese, and also certain others, to investigate the cases wherein property had been given for charitable purposes, and to make such orders, judgments and decrees as should be necessary to carry out the purposes for which the donors had given the property. These orders, judgments, and decrees were to be valid until altered by the chancellor. In short, the statute provided machinery for the enforcement of charitable trusts. The statute, nevertheless, soon fell into disuse. Its preamble, however, containing an enumeration of charitable purposes, was to exert an influence on judicial decisions for centuries. The statute recognized the existence of certain charitable uses [2] and provided for their enforcement.

The State of New York in 1788 repealed the English Statute of Charitable Uses (Statute of Elizabeth).[3] In the Revised Statutes of 1829 there was a codification of the law of trusts in New York. This statute abolished all trusts except as expressly authorized and modified by the legislature of that State.[4] It provided for only four

---

[1] 43 Eliz. c. 4 (1601).

[2] Cf. Bogert, *Handbook of the Law of Trusts* (2. ed., St. Paul: West Publishing Co., 1942, § 195, no. 26, for an enumeration of the purposes mentioned in the Statute.

[3] Laws of New York, c. 46, § 37.

[4] *The Revised Statutes of the State of New York* (2 vols., Vol. I, Albany, 1829), I, 727.

classes of express trusts in land [5] and said nothing of charitable trusts.

Did the Revised Statutes abrogate the charitable trusts because they failed to mention them? At first it was believed that they did not. The question arose in 1844, and the court was startled by the contention, "so contrary to the public interests and so repugnant to the spirit of the age," that all charitable trusts springing from benevolent and not from interested motives should be abolished by a statute which did not even mention them. The court, accordingly, denied the contention on the ground that such trusts were not within the purview of the lawmakers; that the evils for which a remedy was sought were not incident to them; that the provisions enacted to preserve what was useful and beneficial in private trusts were inapplicable to the administration of charities, and that therefore the statute referred solely to private trusts, and simply cut down those intricacies and refinements in the dealings of individuals with real estate which had perplexed conveyances and filled the courts with litigation.[6]

The State Supreme Court in 1850 severely criticized this construction of the court as judicial legislation. It pointed out that the language of the statute was plain, distinct, emphatic, and signified that there should be a thorough and radical reform of this branch of the law and a total abrogation of express trusts for any and every purpose except as authorized therein.[7]

In 1853 the leading case of *Williams* v. *Williams* [8] came before the Court of Appeals. It is classic in the determination of the position of charities in New York Law. The conclusion arrived at was that "the law of charities was, at an indefinite but early period in English judicial history, engrafted from the common law; that its general maxims were derived from the civil law as modified in the later periods of the Empire by the ecclesiastical element introduced by Christianity; and that the Statute of Charitable Uses was not

[5] These four can now be found in *N. Y. Real Property Law,* § 96.

[6] Shotwell *v.* Mott, 2 Sand. Ch. 46, 51 (N. Y. 1844).

[7] Yates *v.* Yates, 9 Barb. 324, 341 (N. Y. 1850); cf. Voorhees *v.* Presbyterian Church of Amsterdam, 17 Barb. Ch. 103, 105 (N. Y. 1853).

[8] 8 N. Y. 548, 4 Seld. 525 (1853).

introductory of any new principles, but was only a new and less dilatory and expensive method of establishing charitable donations which were understood to be valid by the laws antecedently in force." [9] The conclusion was, therefore, that the original jurisdiction of the courts of chancery ought to enable the courts to support charitable trusts, irrespective of the Statute of Charitable Uses. It follows, then, that even the repeal of that statute would not necessarily affect the question in the least.

The charitable gift considered in the *Williams* case was directed to a trustee competent at law. This decision, therefore, did not determine the question whether a charitable donation made without naming a trustee, or made to an incompetent trustee, might be maintained by the equity jurisdiction. Three years later that question was decided by the court in *Owens* v. *Missionary Society of the M. E. Church*.[10] Here the association to which the gift had been directed was incapable of taking for its own benefit, and the court held there was no trust regarding the application of the fund. The court argued the absence of a trust from the fact that the association named to receive the gift was legally incompetent to act as trustee. The holding admitted the principle established in the *Williams* case, namely, that failure to nominate definite beneficiaries of a charitable gift does not invalidate that gift; but the court here distinguished the present case from the *Williams* matter, where a competent trustee had been named.[11]

In short, the joint authority of the *Williams* decision and the *Owens* decision established the following principles in the matter of charitable gifts: "(1) That a gift for charity is maintained in this state if made to a competent trustee, and if so defined that it can be executed, as made by the donor, by a judicial decree, although it may be void, according to the general rules of law, for want of an ascertained beneficiary; (2) that in other respects the rules of law applicable to charitable uses are within those which apply to trusts in general; (3) that the *cy pres* power which . . . is exercised in

9 Williams *v.* Williams, 4 Seld. 525, 542 (N. Y. 1853).

10 14 N. Y. 380 (1856).

11 This analysis of the *Owens* case is to be found in Holland *v.* Alcock, 108 N. Y. 312, 16 N. E. 305 (1888).

determining gifts to charity where the donor has failed to define them, and in framing schemes of approximation near to or from the donor's true design, is unsuited to our institutions, and has no existence in the jurisprudence of our state." [12]

Other decisions followed the trend of the *Owens* case, not indeed overruling the *Williams* decisions, but narrowly limiting the application of its doctrine to the precise circumstances therein contemplated. The repeal of the Statute of Elizabeth at a time when the law of charities was thought to rest on it, and the subsequent abolition of the law of uses and trusts, except as re-enacted in the repealing statute, were circumstances which were going to militate against the views expressed in the *Williams* case.[13]

In 1865 the court assailed the *Williams* case. The court vigorously maintained that the English system of charities was palpably incongruous with the state's political system and the principles that lie at the basis of its government and institutions, not adapted to its social conditions and impracticable of execution, and that by the repeal of the Statute of Elizabeth it was not intended that "indefinite trusts of every kind and description, however irrational or absurd, superstitious, fanatical or idolatrous, should become valid in equity and that the property of donors, without limit or restraint, might at their own will and for the promotion of such objects, be withdrawn and put in mortmain away from the general uses of society." [14]

The New York courts for the next twenty-five years followed this same line of reasoning.[15] As one writer put it, it was pointed out by the courts during this time "that the Revised Statutes as far as the abolition of trusts were concerned must be construed strictly; that it had unqualifiedly abolished all trusts except those

[12] Holland *v.* Alcock, 108 N. Y. 312, 16 N. E. 305, 313 (1888).

[13] Zollman, "The Development of the Law of Charities in the United States," *Columbia Law Review,* XIX (1919), 101.

[14] Levy *v.* Levy, 33 N. Y. 97, 114, 116 (1865).

[15] Boscom *v.* Albertson, 34 N. Y. 584 (1886); Burrel *v.* Boardman, 43 N. Y. 254 (1871); Holmes *v.* Mead, 52 N. Y. 332 (1873); Holland *v.* Alcock, 108 N. Y. 312, 16 N. E. 305 (1888); Tilden *v.* Green, 130 N. Y. 29, 28 N. E. 880 (1891).

specifically authorized; that charitable trusts, especially where the trustee named was an individual, were not authorized and that general charitable gifts could still be made to corporations expressly organized under the statutes to dispense charity." [16]

The result of this wrecking process may be summarized in a few words. All organized charities as distinguished from corporate charities were now abolished in New York. The only method by which a testator could devise his property to charity was to give it to a charitable corporation either as an absolute gift (when the corporation was in existence) or as an executory devise (when it had not yet been formed).[17] All attempts to induce the court to return to the doctrine of the *Williams* case were useless.[18] There was need of legislative action to alter the situation.

In 1893 the legislature did take action when it passed a most important law, which came to be known as the "Tilden Act." [19] This act provided that gifts for "religious, educational, charitable, or benevolent uses," which are otherwise valid according to the laws of the State, shall not be deemed invalid "by reason of the indefiniteness or uncertainty of the persons designated as the beneficiaries thereunder in the instrument creating the same." It declared that all gifts made without the designation of a trustee should vest in the supreme court, and directed the attorney general to enforce them by proper court proceedings. The act was amended in 1901 through the added provision that permitted a gift to be applied *cy pres* with the consent of the donor or grantor, if living, or, if dead, after the expiration of twenty-five years from the date of the execution of the instrument when a literal compliance with the terms of the gift had become impracticable or impossible.[20]

This twenty-five year limit was stricken out, so that the court is now at liberty to make such application at any time upon a proper showing, provided that no such order is made without the

---

[16] O'Toole, *Law of Trusts* (Brooklyn, 1933), p. 50.

[17] Zollman, "art. cit.," *Columbia Law Review*, XIX (1919), 102.

[18] Cottman *v.* Grace, 112 N. Y. 299, 19 N. E. 839 (1889); Fosdick *v.* Town of Hempstead, 125 N. Y. 581, 26 N. E. 801 (1891).

[19] Laws of 1893, c. 701.

[20] Laws of 1901, c. 292, §§ 1 and 2.

consent of the donor or grantor of the property, if he be living.[21]
Further amendment in 1931 conferred upon the Surrogates the
power of *cy pres* construction, which up to that time had been
reserved to the Supreme Court.[22]

The Tilden Act, with its various amendments, is now contained
in § 113 of the New York Real Property Law and in § 12 of the
Personal Property Law. Its effect was to restore the law as it was
declared in *Williams* v. *Williams,*[23] and it reversed the previous
policy of the state.[24] The indefiniteness of the beneficiary could no
longer be a sound objection to the validity of a charitable bequest.[25]
The *cy pres* doctrine which had been inapplicable before this
statute [26] now became effective.[27]

ARTICLE 2. CHARITABLE PURPOSE

Although it has been said that the "Tilden Act" [28] applies only
to "gifts for purposes specified in the law," [29] the courts have not
been relieved of the task of determining whether a concrete gift be
within the purposes contemplated by the law. In making such a
determination, the court needed to settle upon some general criterion
of charity.

"A charity in the legal sense may be more fully defined as a
gift to be applied consistently with existing laws for the benefit of
an indefinite number of persons, either in bringing their minds and

---

[21] Laws of 1909, c. 144, §§ 2 and 22.

[22] Laws of 1931, c. 562, §§ 8 and 9.

[23] Bowman *v.* Domestic and Foreign Missionary Society, 182 N. Y. 494,
75 N. E. 535 (1905), *modifying* 100 App. Div. 29, 90 N. Y. S. 898 (1904),
reversing 42 Misc. 574, 87 N. Y. S. 621.

[24] Washington Ave. Baptist Church *v.* Clark, 158 App. Div. 230, 142
N. Y. S. 1089 (1913), *reversing* 80 Misc. 306, 141 N. Y. S. 1.

[25] Star *v.* Selleck, 205 N. Y. 545, 98 N. E. 1116 (1911); *in re* Groot, 226
N. Y. 576, 123 N. E. 867 (1919); Matter of Morris, 227 N. Y. 141, 124 N. E.
724 (1919).

[26] Lock *v.* Mayer, 50 Misc. 442, 100 N. Y. S. 837, 840 (1906).

[27] *In re* MacDowell's Will, 217 N. Y. 454, 465, 112 N. E. 177 (1916).

[28] Cf. *supra,* p. 141.

[29] Fralick *v.* Lyford, 107 App. Div. 546, 95 N. Y. S. 433 (3d Dept. 1905),
aff'd without opinion, 187 N. Y. 524, 79 N. E. 1105.

hearts under the influence of education or religion, by assisting them to establish themselves in life, or by creating and maintaining public buildings or works or otherwise lessening the burdens of government." [30] Three general norms could serve to indicate how a charitable purpose according to New York State law is to be determined:

(1) It must be founded upon a humanitarian view looking to the improvement and well-being of mankind.[31]

(2) The beneficiaries must of necessity be indefinite and uncertain as an element of the definition of any charitable trust.[32]

(3) It must be for some public purpose as distinguished from a purely selfish or private purpose in the guise of charity.[33]

With regard to this third norm, one should keep in mind that the distinction between "public use" and "private purpose" is not always obvious. New York courts have maintained, as charitable, gifts in which the beneficiary institution charged fees for its services, or required persons whom it had aided to repay sums of money advanced to them. The institution in question was judged by its general character, and if that was charitable, it was not altered by the practice of charging fees or requiring repayment of loans.[34] Also maintained as charitable were gifts in which the trustees were directed to give preference to certain of the testator's relatives and

---

[30] Jackson *v.* Phillips, 14 Allen (Mass.) 539, 556 as quoted in People *v.* Fitch, 154 N. Y. 14, 32, 47 N. E. 983 (1897). These are the words of Lord Eldon in Morice *v.* Bp. of Durham, 9 Ves. 299, 10 Ves. 522 (a leading English case).

[31] Tilden *v.* Green, 130 N. Y. 29, 28 N. E. 880 (1892). In this case the phrase "well-doing and well-being of mankind" served for denoting the purpose of the charitable trust.

[32] Bowman *v.* Domestic etc. Society, 182 N. Y. 494, 75 N. E. 535 (1905). *In re* MacDowell's Will, 217 N. Y. 454, 112 N. E. 197 (1916); Stewart *v.* Frouchetti, 167 App. Div. 541, 153 N. Y. S. 453 (1st Dept. 1915).

[33] *In re* Shattuck's Will, 193 N. Y. 446, 86 N. E. 455 (1908); *In re* Robinson 203 N. Y. 380, 96 N. E. 925 (1911); In the matter of Frosch, 245 N. Y. 174, 156 N. E. 656 (1927).

[34] *In re* MacDowell's Will, 217 N. Y. 454, 112 N. E. 177 (1916); *In re* Davidge, 200 App. Div. 440, 193 N. Y. S. 245 (2d Dept. 1922).

friends, these persons being within the general class to be aided by the gift.[35]

In conveying property for charitable purposes the motive of the one conveying the property is of no significance.[36] The civil law is interested in the effects of his action, not in the motives that lie behind it. A New York ruling has clearly pointed out that the donor's motive, or his purpose of conferring a general benefit does not, of itself, bring a trust within the terms of the "Tilden Act." [37] The courts will judge whether the purpose which will be served, when the gift is executed according to the donor's directions, is actually a charitable purpose or not.

There is now in order an examination of the New York cases which reflect how the court could arrive at this judgment.

The intent of a testator that his property be devoted to charitable purposes will be judged, ordinarily, from the language of his will.[38] The use in a will of such terms as "charity," "charitable," "need," "aiding," "assisting," are indicative of charitable purpose.[39] Yet, a provision in a will which directed the distribution of certain funds of a trust "to any charitable institution or to any person, persons, individual or individuals" was not upheld as a gift to charity, since authority was given the trustees to distribute those funds for private purposes if they chose to do so.[40] The word "church" will be taken by the courts to refer to a religious use.[41] When the language of the will is susceptible of more than one meaning, the court, pursuant to the general rule of benign interpre-

[35] *In re* MacDowell's Will, 217 N. Y. 454, 112 N. E. 177 (1916); *In re* Gugenheim's Estate, 168 Misc. 1, 5 N. Y. S. 2d 137 (1938).

[36] Scott, *The Law of Trusts* (4 vols., Boston: Little, Brown and Co., 1939), III, § 368.

[37] *In re* Carpenter's Estate, 163 Misc. 474, 297 N. Y. S. 649 (1937).

[38] Wait *v.* Society for Political Study, 68 Misc. 250, 123 N. Y. S. 637 (Supreme Ct. 1910).

[39] Utica Trust and Deposit Co. *v.* Thompson, 87 Misc. 47, 149 N. Y. S. 392 (Supreme Ct. 1914); Matter of Robinson, 203 N. Y. 380, 96 N. E. 925 (1911); Sawyer *v.* Dearstyne, 139 N. Y. S. 955 (Supreme Ct. 1912).

[40] *In re* Sheifer's Estate, 178 Misc. 340, 34 N. Y. S. 2d 302 (1942).

[41] *In re* Werner's Will, 181 N. Y. S 534 (Supr. Ct. 1919).

tation, will adopt that interpretation which requires the property to be devoted to charitable purposes.[42]

The "Tilden Act" itself clearly points out that under the term "charitable" are included educational, religious, and benevolent purposes.[43] The terms "charitable" and "benevolent" are practically synonymous.[44] "A gift for the promotion of education or learning is a gift for charitable uses. . . . Charity ministers to the mind as well as to the body."[45] The education intended to be conferred may be "special or specific," and includes any department or extent of education, primarily and fairly calculated to make the recipient self-supporting.[46] New York courts even before the "Tilden Act" always affirmed that the concept of charity included religious purposes.[47]

ARTICLE 3. CHARITABLE TRUST IN PRESENT NEW YORK LAW

Section I. General Notions

When one who has ownership of goods is under obligation to use his rights over those goods for a charitable purpose, the law will protect and enforce that obligation. In New York law such an obligation is created and enforced on the pattern of the trust,[48] except that a corporation formed for charitable purposes may be bound to use gifts for determined ends within its corporate purposes, without application of the legal form of a "trust."

It is important to note the precise question under discussion in this present section. The nature and properties of charitable

---

[42] *In re* Robinson, 203 N. Y. 380, 96 N. E. 925 (1911); *In re* Tiffany's Estate, 157 Misc. 873, 285 N. Y. S. 791 (1935).

[43] *N. Y. Real Property Law*, § 113.

[44] *In re* Rockefeller, 177 App. Div. 791, 165 N. Y. S. 154 (1st Dept. 1917).

[45] Butterworth *v.* Keeler, 219 N. Y. 449, 114 N. E. 803 (1916).

[46] *In re* Robinson, 203 N. Y. 380, 96 N. E. 925 (1911).

[47] Cf. Williams *v.* Williams, 8 N. Y. 548, 4 Seld. 525 (1853); Levy *v.* Levy, 33 N. Y. 87 (1865); Holland *v.* Alcock, 108 N. Y. 312, 16 N. E. 305 (1888).

[48] "A trust is a right of property held by one party for the benefit of another."—Gifford *v.* Rising, 51 Hun. 1, 3 N. Y. S. 392 (N. Y. 1889).

corporations have already been seen.[49] This present section is concerned with the nature and the consequences of the fiduciary gift for charity.

So dominant is the idea of a trust in connection with the law of charities, that it has been said that a charity necessarily involves a trust.[50] Where an absolute gift is made to a charitable corporation, the law of the corporation's charter supplies the elements of a trust,[51] even though there be no trust in a technical sense.[52]

It will be seen that the law of New York protects charitable trusts from the peril of certain general rules on trusts.[53] The law of this state, however, does something more fundamental than that. It casts any charitable gift, when it is not destined to a competent corporate charity or to a competent charitable trust, into the form of a charitable trust of which the Supreme Court is trustee.[54] It may be said that upon any charitable gift, when it is not subject to a valid express charitable trust or is not protected by the law of corporate charity, the "Tilden Act"[55] raises a trust. "If in the instrument creating such a gift, grant or devise (to religious, educational, charitable, or benevolent uses) there is a trustee named to execute the same, the legal title to the lands or property given . . . for such purposes shall vest in such trustee. If no person be named as trustee, then the title to such lands or property shall vest in the Supreme Court."[56]

Section II. Elements of Trust Applied to Charitable Trust

There is a decision of a New York court referring directly to express trusts which, nevertheless, seems to afford a clear and authoritative description of the elements essential to the creation

---

[49] Cf. *supra,* chap. II, *passim.*

[50] Owens *v.* Missionary Society of M. E. Church, 14 N. Y. 384 (1856).

[51] *In re* First Presbyterian Society of Buffalo, 106 N. Y. 251 (1887).

[52] Fowler, *The Law of Charitable Uses, Trusts, and Donations in New York* (New York: Diossy Law Book Co., 1896), p. 91.

[53] Cf. *infra,* pp. 152-154.

[54] *N. Y. Real Property Law,* § 113.

[55] Cf. *supra,* p. 141.

[56] *N. Y. Real Property Law,* § 113, subd. 1.

of any legal trust. It mentions four elements: (1) A designated beneficiary; (2) a designated trustee, who must not be the beneficiary; (3) a fund or other property, sufficiently designated or identified to enable title to pass to the trustee, and (4) the actual delivery of the fund or other property, or a legal assignment thereof, to the trustee, with the intention of passing legal title thereto to him as trustee.[57]

Any charitable gift comprises these elements, at least in an imperfect sense, and without all of the refinements necessary to the legal device of a trust. In charity the legal owner is deprived of the full enjoyment of his property, and that benefit of which he is deprived is reserved to the furtherance of a charitable purpose. When a man, for a charity, makes over his property to an individual or to a profit-making corporation, the donor's will, with the sanction of law, limits the donee's enjoyment of the property. When the charitable gift is made to a charitable corporation, the members and directors thereof are bound by the law of their charter to use the gift for charity, and this general duty may be more definitely specified by the donor's will. An examination of these four elements of the trust as applied to charitable trusts is now in order.

There is not much difficulty with the third and fourth element. Certainly, designation of the trust property is as necessary in a gift to charity as in a gift to any other purpose. Delivery of the trust property to the trustee is subject to some particular rules when the gift is made to charity. The Supreme Court will take title, not only when no trustee or no competent trust is named,[58] but also when a corporation named as trustee has ceased to exist before the trust comes into operation.[59]

There is need, however, of a somewhat more extended treatment with regard to the first two elements. With regard to the first element, the beneficiary of a charitable trust need not be definitely and certainly designated in the act which creates that gift. "No gift, grant, or devise to religious, educational, charitable or benevolent uses, which shall in other respects be valid under the laws of

---

[57] Hodgman *v.* Cobb, 202 App. Div. 259, 195 N. Y. S. 428 (1922).

[58] *N. Y. Real Property Law,* § 113, subd. 1.

[59] *In re* Deming, 112 N. Y. S. 170 (1908).

this state, shall be deemed invalid by reason of the indefiniteness or uncertainty of the persons designated as the beneficiaries thereunder in the instrument creating the same." [60] A trust with indefinite beneficiaries is held not invalid, since enactment of the Tilden Act restored the law of charitable uses as it existed at the time of the American Revolution, removing restrictions against indefiniteness of beneficiaries.[61]

A religious corporation can be made the beneficiary of a trust though such power is not granted by its certificate of incorporation.[62] In an earlier decision, however a devise was held void where it was made to a bishop to be held in trust by him for the use of his church, because that church was not authorized by charter or statute to take devises of property.[63] A devise in trust for a charitable organization, unincorporated at the time of the execution of the will, is valid if the organization is incorporated before the money becomes payable.[64] Non-residents of this State may be beneficiaries of a charitable trust established in New York.[65]

One element remains to be discussed, viz., a designated trustee. Property may generally be devoted to charitable purposes not only by means of its transfer to a trustee in order that it be used for charitable purposes, but also by means of its transfer to corporations specifically organized for the accomplishment of charitable purposes.[66]

A very important question is next to be considered. The courts in this country have been divided on the question whether the property given to charitable corporations is to be considered as being held absolutely, or whether it is to be considered as held in trust for the purposes or some of the purposes for which the corporation was organized. Some decisions have unequivocally denominated

[60] *N. Y. Real Property Law,* § 113, subd. 1.

[61] *In re* Tiffany's Estate, 157 Misc. 873, 285 N. Y. S. 971 (1935); cf. *supra,* p. 141.

[62] *In re* Johnson, 148 Misc. 218, 265, N. Y. S. 395 (1933).

[63] McCaughal *v.* Ryan, 27 Barb. Ch. 376 (N. Y. 1857).

[64] Philson *v.* Moore, 23 Hun. 152 (N. Y. 1880).

[65] *In re* Robinson, 203 N. Y. 380, 96 N. E. 925 (1911).

[66] *Restatement of the Laws of Trust* (2 vols., Vol. II, St. Paul: American Law Institute, 1935), II, 1093.

gifts to charitable corporations as conveyances of mere legal title to the corporation as trustee.[67] Others have regarded such gifts as held by the charitable corporation without the character of a technical trust.[68]

A more detailed look at the law in New York is now in order. In this state it has been held in the past that, with regard to a gift to a charitable corporation, a donor's words of restriction or direction regarding its use were precatory only, and did not impose an obligation enforceable against the corporation.[69] There are specific New York cases wherein the courts construed gifts to charitable corporations as outright gifts, even when the terms of the gift contained express trust language or other words importing a charitable use.[70] It was held that such gifts were not "true trusts" because of the identity of trustee and beneficiary. Where the estate of the trustee and that of the beneficiary merge in one entity, the trust is extinguished and the trustee-beneficiary takes the estate.[71]

In *Lutheran Hospital of Manhattan* v. *Goldstein*,[72] the restriction placed upon a charitable corporation, namely, that the property be used for endowment, was presupposed as enforceable in this case as a technical trust provision, and therefore the court refused to exercise its *cy pres* power to permit the endowment principal to be spent for current expenditures.[73]

This reference to the *cy pres* power brings up an interesting difficulty. If gifts to a charitable corporation that were expressed to be in trust or for specified purposes actually did not partake of the nature of a trust or use, then the doctrine of *cy pres* would be inapplicable, and many gifts to charity would necessarily fail of

[67] Cf. Byrne, *Investment of Church Funds*, p. 166.

[68] Cf. Byrne, *loc. cit.*

[69] Wetmore *v.* Parker, 52 N. Y. 450 (1873); Corporation of the Chamber of Commerce of N. Y. *v.* Bennett, 143 Misc. 513, 257 N. Y. S. 2 (1932).

[70] St. John *v.* Andrews Institute, 191 N. Y. 254, 83 N. E. 981 (1908); Tabernacle Baptist Church *v.* Fifth Ave. Baptist Church, 60 App. Div. 327, *aff'd*, 172 N. Y. 598, 64 N. E. 1126 (1902).

[71] Sherman *v.* Richmond Hose Co., 230 N. Y. 462, 130 N. E. 613 (1921).

[72] 182 Misc. 913, 46 N. Y. S. 2d 705 (1944).

[73] Cf. also Application of Brooklyn Children's Aid Society, 269 App. Div. 789, 55 N. Y. S. 2d 323 (1945).

accomplishing the benevolent purposes which the donors contemplated. It has been held that the courts will not use their *cy pres* power with respect to outright gifts, but only where the gift, grant, devise or bequest is for a religious, educational, charitable or benevolent trust or "use." [74]

Having held that restricted gifts to charitable corporations, even when expressed as trusts, were not trusts but outright gifts, and having refused to apply the *cy pres* principle to outright gifts, the courts were confronted with an embarrassing problem in the handling of cases which called for the application of the *cy pres* doctrine, in order that the donor's charitable intention might be continued after the original donee had ceased to exist, or where for some other reason it became impossible for the original donee to execute the donor's charitable intent.

In 1921 the New York Court of Appeals squarely met this issue in *Sherman* v. *Richmond Hose Co.*[75] It held that, while the trust was not an ordinary trust created by the donor, it was nevertheless a trust created by the charter of the charitable corporation, and *cy pres* could be applied as to a charitable trust. The case in question contained no trust language, but the will of the testatrix specified that the fund should be held by the corporation and the income used for its corporate charitable purposes. This was the first clear indication in New York that the courts will find a "use" within the meaning of the Tilden Act even where, as in the case of a charitable corporation, the legal and equitable titles have merged.[76] The *Sherman* case, therefore, held the gift in question to be a trust established by the corporate charter, and not by the donor. A later New York case arrived at substantially the same result, holding that there was an implied trust, but no formal trust.[77]

Subsequently a very important decision of the New York Court

[74] Fralick *v.* Lyford, 107 App. Div. 543, *aff'd,* 187 N. Y. 524, 79 N. E. 1105 (1907).

[75] 230 N. Y. 462, 130 N. E. 613 (1921).

[76] Taylor, "A New Chapter in the New York Law of Charitable Corporations," *Cornell Law Quarterly,* XXV (1940), 386.

[77] *In re* Walter, 150 Misc. 512, 269 N. Y. S. 402 (1934).

of Appeals [78] seemed to abandon the theory that there is a trust, actual or implied. As one writer put it, this decision arrived at a "position midway between a charitable corporation holding a gift absolutely and holding it in trust." [79]

The case concerned a bequest of money to the hospital which, by the terms of the will, was "to be held as an endowment fund and the income used for the ordinary expenses of maintenance." The hospital asked the court to declare that such a bequest was not a trust fund but an absolute gift to the hospital, which it might use to discharge a first mortgage on the hospital property. It was held that the fund could not be diverted from the purpose specified by the testator, and that it could not be used in a manner different from the manner prescribed. As has been said, the court considered the gift as something midway between property held by absolute title and property held in trust. It did point out that the court could apply the *cy pres* principle.

The bequest was considered as absolute, the words of the testator as indicating the gift to the charitable corporation as his primary purpose, and the specific use to be made of it as a secondary purpose. The testator's general intent was to help the charitable corporation. By the designation of the specific manner of the use, the gift neither was made less absolute nor was created as a trust. The court did not classify the obligation arising from this gift.

Various answers have been given. One answer suggests that, while possibly it has some elements of a contractual obligation, more likely it seems that restrictive gifts to charitable corporations in New York are henceforth to be recognized as creating a fiduciary relationship which is *sui generis*.[80] Another answer implies that, in effect, the testator's language here resulted in an absolute gift, which had attached to it certain equitable restrictions respecting its use.[81]

[78] St. Joseph's Hospital *v.* Bennett, 281 N. Y. 115, 22 N. E. 2d 305, 130 A. L. R. 1092 (1939).

[79] Byrne, *Investment of Church Funds*, p. 173.

[80] Taylor, *ibid.*, p. 388.

[81] Cloppers, "Charities—Absolute Gift to Public Charitable Corporation," *Boston University Law Review*, XIX (1940), 657.

There is a further clarification of this matter in a case that arose four years later.[82] Here a testator left an endowment to a hospital. The income from the endowment was to be used for the hospital's general purposes. It was held that the court would permit the use of the principal, if it appeared that otherwise the hospital would be forced to close. It was stated that the court was here using the power of *cy pres,* which enables it to permit this deviation from the terms of the bequest establishing the property as an endowment. The fact that such exercise of *cy pres* was deemed necessary indicates that the restriction established by the testator was enforceable. The thing to note is that this restriction was enforceable whether it was a trust provision or not, and *cy pres* could be applied in either case.[83]

Section III. Statutes Saving Charitable Trusts from Prohibitions Affecting Trusts in General

A. *Perpetuities*

Suspension of the absolute power of alienation of property for long periods of time, if it become general, would work serious disadvantages to society. The absolute power of alienation is suspended when no living persons can give a perfect title to property.[84] Under the common law, it was permitted to suspend the power of alienation during the continuance of a life or any number of lives in being at the creation of the estate, and for twenty-one years thereafter; and nine months in addition, for the birth of a posthumous child.[85]

Suspension beyond that period made the grant void as a "perpetuity." Now the "vice of perpetuity" attaches to a trust in New York if that trust is created for a period not measured by a life or two lives in being at the time of its creation; a minority is deemed part of a life, and not an absolute term of years; lives in being in-

---

[82] Knickerbocker Hospital *v.* Goldstein, 181 Misc. 540, 41 N. Y. S. 2d 32 (1943).

[83] Knickerbocker Hospital *v.* Goldstein, *loc. cit.*

[84] Williams *v.* Montgomery, 148 N. Y. 519, 43 N. E. 57 (1896).

[85] Stewart *v.* McMartin, 5 Barb. Ch. 438 (N. Y. 1849).

clude a child begotten but not born when the trust is created. A trust, if not limited as stated, is void.[86]

A trust, however, for charitable purposes, if not limited or measured as aforesaid, is held not to be invalid, since passage of the Tilden Act restored the law of charitable uses as it existed at the time of the American Revolution, thus removing restrictions against perpetuities.[87] The law explicitly declares that trusts for cemetery purposes, which the law deems "for charitable and benevolent uses," shall not "be deemed invalid as violating any existing laws against perpetuities or suspension of the power of alienation of title to property." [88]

B. *Accumulations*

Similar in intent to the prohibition of "perpetuities" are the statutes against "accumulations." For the purpose of increasing the value of their gifts, donors have sometimes provided that no use shall be made of a gift or of its income during a period of time in which the income on the gift shall accumulate and be added to the original sum of the gift. The duration of the period of accumulation has been measured by a stated term of years, or by lives or minorities, or by specification that the accumulation shall continue until a certain value is reached.

The New York Statutes limit such accumulations generally to the minority of a beneficiary,[89] but make notable exceptions when the gift is made to a charity. Accumulations are permitted when the purpose of the fund is a charitable one.[90] Even these, however, may not continue at the will of the donors or at the pleasure of the persons or corporations holding such properties. When a gift is made in trust to a religious, educational, charitable or benevolent corporation, for one or more of its corporate purposes, a limited accumulation is permitted. In such a case no more than one-fourth part of the gift, and in no event more than fifty thousand dollars in

---

[86] *N. Y. Real Property Law,* § 42.

[87] *In re* Tiffany's Estate, 157 Misc. 873, 285 N. Y. S. 971 (1936).

[88] *N. Y. Real Property Law,* § 114a.

[89] *N. Y. Real Property Law,* § 61, subd. 1.

[90] *N. Y. Real Property Law,* § 61, subd. 3.

value may be committed to accumulation. The accumulation shall end, and the whole sum shall be available to the uses of the corporation, in a manner subject to the directions of the donor, when the accumulation shall have reached the value of one hundred thousand dollars.[91]

Article 4. Power and Duties of Public Authorities Concerning Charitable Gifts

Section I. Power of Courts

The powers and duties of the public authorities regarding charitable gifts may be summarized under four points: (1) To raise a charitable trust when no trustee is named by the donor of a charitable gift; (2) to provide for the succession of trustees; (3) to regulate the management of the trust property; and (4) to apply the *cy pres* doctrine when conditions warrant it.

With regard to the first point, this power is vested in the New York Supreme Court. Reference has already been made to this important power.[92] There is no need of further discussion here.

As to the second power, when a trustee dies, the property held by him in trust does not, under New York law, descend to his heirs, but vests in the Supreme Court, and that Court appoints a new trustee to administer the trust.[93] The Court also takes title and appoints a new trustee when it accepts a trustee's resignation, or when it removes him as being unsuited for administering the trust, or when he is impeded from his trust duties by engagement in war services.[94]

In the management of trust property, any trustee will need an order of the Supreme Court in order to accomplish certain conveyances, leases and encumbrances of the real property held in trust.[95] The Court has special powers regarding realty held for charitable

---

[91] *Loc. cit.*

[92] Cf. *supra*, p. 146; *N. Y. Real Property Law*, § 113, subd. 1.

[93] *N. Y. Real Property Law*, § 111.

[94] *Ibid.*, § 112.

[95] *N. Y. Real Property Law*, §§ 105-107.

uses. The Supreme Court may authorize sale or mortgage of any real property granted or devised to charitable uses, or any real property held or owned by any corporation charged with such uses, or held so that income therefrom is bound to any charitable use. Such authority is given to the trustee, or to the person or corporation holding title to the property.

The Supreme Court will authorize such sale or mortgage whenever the court is satisfied that the property or any portion thereof appears to be in jeopardy for one of these reasons: that it has become or is likely to become unproductive, or that it has depreciated or is likely to depreciate in value, or that it is advisable to raise money to improve or erect buildings on the property, or that the sale or mortgage is advisable for any other reason. This power of the Court does not restrict such powers as the trustee or corporation may have by law or by grant of the donor of the property.[96]

With regard to the power of *cy pres,* one must always keep certain fundamental notions in mind. The doctrine of *cy pres* has two branches, viz., *judicial cy pres* and *prerogative cy pres.* The former is the authority of Equity to apply property that was designated for a charity to as nearly a similar purpose as is possible, when the carrying out of the original trust becomes impossible or inexpedient, in view of changed conditions, or when the settlor has imperfectly outlined the scheme for his charity.[97] This power is possessed by the New York courts by virtue of statute.[98]

The *prerogative cy pres* power is the authority of the crown in England, in consequence of its position as *parens patriae,* to dispose of property to such charitable uses as it sees fit in two cases: (a) where bequests are made to particular uses, charitable in their nature but illegal, and (b) where the original charity is too vague to be enforced, and there are no trustees to make it certain.[99] This *prerogative cy pres* power is not possessed by any courts in the

---

[96] *Ibid.,* § 113, subd. 4.

[97] Bogert, *Trusts,* p. 225.

[98] *N. Y. Real Property Law,* § 113, subd. 2.

[99] 14 C. J. S. Charities, § 51.

United States, but is vested in the several legislatures.[100] As the United States Supreme Court points out: "Here the legislature is the *parens patriae* and, unless restrained by constitutional limitations, possesses all the powers in this regard which the sovereign possesses in England."[101] The courts of this country cannot take it upon themselves to exercise this *prerogative cy pres* power unless the legislature has expressly given them authority to do so. The New York statute, from which the courts derive their *judicial cy pres* power, states that they may exercise it, "whenever it shall appear that circumstances have so changed since the execution of an instrument containing a gift, grant or bequest to religious, educational, charitable or benevolent uses, as to render impracticable or impossible compliance with the terms of such instrument."[102] The conclusion is inescapable that, if the trust is invalid in its inception, then the court may not exercise this power.

One may thus sum up these general notions on the *cy pres* power. The *prerogative cy pres* does not exist in New York. It was found necessary by special enactment (the Tilden Act) to establish the *judicial cy pres* power. As yet the New York legislature has not seen fit to delegate its power as *parens patriae* to the courts to exercise the *prerogative cy pres* power.

Looking more particularly to the application of the *judicial cy pres* power in New York, one may well point out that this power is possessed by the New York Supreme Court.[103] Concurrent with the jurisdiction of the Supreme Court is the *cy pres* power of the Surrogate's Court of the county where a will containing a charitable gift is probated.[104] A decree of the Surrogate, however, in applying the *cy pres* doctrine and declaring the existence of a charitable trust, is not a *res iudicata* as against a proceeding in the Supreme Court to open and modify such a decree. It was so held in a case

[100] Church of Jesus Christ *v.* United States, 136 U. S. 1, 10 Sup. Ct. 792 (1890).

[101] Church of Jesus Christ *v.* United States, 136 U. S. 1, 56.

[102] *N. Y. Real Property Law*, § 113, subd. 2.

[103] *N. Y. Real Property Law*, § 113, subd. 2.

[104] *Loc. cit.*

wherein a Surrogate, finding the testator's plan for charity impracticable, ordered *cy pres* administration, in spite of the clause in the will which directed that, in the event of failure of the specified charitable purpose, the gift should pass to the lineal descendants of the testator's sister.[105]

An examination of a few New York decisions will clarify the extent of the *cy pres* power and the manner of its operation. A trust created by will and bequeathed to a church which had ceased to exist was turned over to a general convention of the same denomination, which served purposes similar to those served by the extinct church.[106] A bequest to a missionary society no longer existing was properly claimed by its "parent body."[107] Where certain wills indicated that only certain charitable purposes might be chosen, it was held that the wills were within the statute, and the trusts could be enforced by judicial decrees, and that the trustees could be compelled to carry out the purposes indicated.[108]

A corporation cannot be selected as a beneficiary of a charitable gift, unless the corporation accepts the gift as a charitable one, and is in need and worthy of it.[109] A devise of real estate to a ladies' aid society, which was unable to take because it was an unincorporated society, was held not void, but a valid gift in favor of the incorporated church of which the society was a branch.[110] If a specific charitable purpose is indicated so definitely as not to admit an alternative, the gift is not within the *cy pres* power of the statute. If that specific purpose should fail, no other purpose may be substituted by the court.[111]

---

[105] In *re* Merritt's Will, 171 Misc. 812, 14 N. Y. S. 2d 103, *aff'd* 258 App. Div. 188, 16 N. Y. S. 2d 1 (1939).

[106] Graff *v.* Harrington, 137 Misc. 712, 244 N. Y. S. 307 (1930).

[107] *In re* Dering, 140 Misc. 357, 152 N. Y. S. 193 (1931).

[108] *In re* Cunningham, 206 N. Y. 601, 100 N. E. 437 (1912); Matter of Robinson, 203 N. Y. 380, 96 N. E. 925 (1911).

[109] *In re* Groot, 173 App. Div. 436, 159 N. Y. S. 1003 (1916).

[110] First Methodist Church of Penn Yan *v.* Putnam, 189 Misc. 519, 72 N. Y. S. 2d 70 (1947).

[111] *In re* Merritt's Will, 280 N. Y. 391, 21 N. E. 2d 365 (1939).

Section II. Power of the Attorney General

One may well conclude this discussion of the powers and duties of public authorities regarding charitable gifts by pointing out very briefly the function of the Attorney General of the State. The New York Statutes clearly define his function. He is to represent the beneficiaries in all cases wherein a charitable gift lacks a named beneficiary, or trustee, or wherein the donor's plan of execution has become impossible. It will be his duty then to enforce such trusts by proper proceedings in the courts.[112] His rights and duties in applications to sell or mortgage realty that is held for charitable purposes are clearly pointed out.[113] There he represents the State, the beneficiaries of a charitable trust, and all persons who might benefit from the property held for charity.

When a trust agreement is capable of execution, the trustee is competent, and the beneficiaries are of a definite class, the Attorney General is neither a necessary nor a proper party to a proceeding therein.[114] Since the Statutes require the Attorney General to act in a capacity other than that of a trustee, it is improper to appoint him as trustee of a charitable trust.[115]

ARTICLE 5. LIMITATION ON ABILITY TO TAKE A CHARITABLE GIFT

Section I. Ability of Corporations to Take Testamentary Gifts

There is a very important New York statute which states: ". . . no devise to a corporation shall be valid, unless such corporation be expressly authorized by its charter, or by statute, to take by devise."[116] In spite of the declaration of § 14, subd. 3, of the General Corporation Law, which states that every corporation has power to acquire by devise such property as the purposes of the corporation shall require, the New York courts have held that when a question arises on whether a particular corporation has authority

---

[112] *N. Y. Real Property Law,* § 113, subd. 3.

[113] *Ibid.,* subd. 4 and 5.

[114] *Opinion of Attorney General,* 51 State Department Reports 295 (1934).

[115] Manley *v.* Fiske, 139 App. Div. 665, 124 N. Y. S. 149, *aff'd without opinion,* 201 N. Y. 546, 95 N. E. 1133 (1910).

[116] *N. Y. Decedent Estate Law,* § 12.

or power to take a testamentary gift, it is incumbent on the donee
to show by affirmative proof that power to take has been conferred
by its charter or the act under which it was incorporated, and that
the restrictions imposed by general laws have no application to the
gift in question.[117] As the New York Court of Appeals observed in
Matter of McGraw:[118]

> The will does not take effect until the testator's death, and then,
> if his property is not legally devised or bequeathed, no title
> vests for a single moment in the devisee or legatee, but it rests
> instantly in the heir or next of kin; and the corporation claim-
> ing under the will asks the aid of the law to give the property to
> it, and in so doing it must show the authority it has to take.

It will be helpful here to delineate, at least very briefly, the
background to Section 12 of the New York Decedent Estate Law.
The original Statute of Wills, passed in the reign of Henry VIII,
excepted corporations from those who were able to take real property by devise.[119] The re-enactment of the statute by the Laws of
1787 embodied an exception in respect to bodies politic and corporate,[120] as did the act concerning wills passed in New York in
1813.[121]

The Revised Statutes declared that "no devise to a corporation
shall be valid, unless such corporation be expressly authorized by
its charter, or by statute, to take by devise."[122] This provision
has been continued without change, and now exists as Section 12
of the New York Decedent Estate Law.

This New York law is a statute of mortmain.[123] The purpose of
such statutes is to prevent the accumulation of property in the hand

[117] Hughes *v.* Stoutenburgh, 168 App. Div. 522, 154 N. Y. S. 65 (1st
Dept. 1915).

[118] 111 N. Y. 110, 19 N. E. 233 *aff'y* 45 Hun. 354 (1888).

[119] Downing *v.* Marshall, 23 N. Y. 383, 23 How. Pr. 4 (1861).

[120] *In re* Tone, 186 App. Div. 365, 174 N. Y. S. 391, *aff'y* 103 Misc. 618,
170 N. Y. S. 844 (1st Dept. 1919), and *aff'd on opinion below* 226 N. Y. 696,
123 N. E. 892.

[121] White *v.* Howard, 46 N. Y. 163, *aff'y* 52 Barb. 294 (1871).

[122] Cf. White *v.* Howard, *loc. cit.*

[123] *In re* McGraw, 111 N. Y. 107, 19 N. E. 233, *aff'y* 45 Hun. 354 (1888).

of institutions which take no part in the productive activity of the community.[124] Such statutes act upon the power of corporations to receive and hold, not on the power of the testator to give.[125] New York courts have held that the legislature has full power to impose limitations and restrictions upon the capacity of corporations to take property by devise or bequest,[126] and that it has plenary power to alter, restrict, or revoke the right of the individual to devise or bequeath his estate.[127]

The word "expressly" in the statute under discussion is significant. In determining the validity of a particular devise, one may not base on probability the finding of an intent on the part of the legislature to empower the corporation to take the property. Authority must be vindicated in clear and positive terms. It must be express, not implied.[128]

The language of the statute is sufficiently broad to include every interest or estate which may be subject to devise. Consequently, trusts and uses on realty when made in favor of corporations come under this statute.[129] The same is undoubtedly true concerning liens on real estate.[130] This statute does not, however, affect the power of the corporation to take personalty which is produced by a conversion of real estate,[131] nor does it apply to gifts of personal property by will or otherwise.[132]

---

[124] *In re* McGraw, *loc. cit.*

[125] Amherst College *v.* Ritch, 151 N. Y. 333, 45 N. E. 876, *aff'y* 91 Hun. 509 (1897).

[126] Smith *v.* Havens Relief Fund Society, 118 App. Div. 686, 103 N. Y. S. 770, *aff'y* 44 Misc. 594, 90 N. Y. S. 168, and *aff'y without opinion*, 190 N. Y. 557, 83 N. E. 1132 (1st Dept. 1907).

[127] Ayers *v.* Methodist Episcopal Church, 3 Sandf. 361 (N. Y. Sup. Ct. 1849).

[128] Ayers *v.* Methodist Episcopal Church, *loc. cit.*

[129] Downing *v.* Marshall, 23 N. Y. 386, 80 Am. Dec. 290 (1861).

[130] Theological Seminary of Auburn *v.* Childs, 4 Paige 419 (N. Y. Ch. Ct. 1834).

[131] Theological Seminary of Auburn *v.* Childs, *loc. cit.*; *In re* McGraw, 111 N. Y. 107, 19 N. E. 233, *aff'y* 45 Hun. 354 (1888).

[132] Sherwood *v.* American Bible Society, 40 N. Y. 1, (1864).

Section II. Testamentary Gifts to Unincorporated Groups

Testamentary gifts to voluntary or unincorporated associations, when they exist and are maintained for charitable purposes, were sustained under the rule developed by the common law.[133] That rule is recognized in some States of the Union,[134] and the earliest New York decisions were in accord with it.[135]

From the time, however, of the enactment of the Revised Statutes of 1830 until the passage of the Tilden Act in 1893, it was beyond question that an association which does not exist as a legal entity by virtue of incorporation cannot receive a testamentary gift to charitable uses.[136] A few years after the Tilden Act, it was held that an unincorporated association has power to take and hold a charitable bequest either absolutely or as trustee.[137] But the contrary is held in all subsequent cases touching the point.[138]

Recent decisions have affirmed that an unincorporated association or society is incompetent to take or hold property by bequest or devise.[139] The law states that testamentary dispositions which are neither expressed to be for charitable purposes, nor held in trust, cannot be sustained in favor of a society, association or institution which does not exist as a legal entity by virtue of incorpora-

[133] Cf. Powell, "Land Capacity of Unincorporated Groups," *Columbia Law Review*, XLIX (1949), 301.

[134] *Loc. cit.*

[135] Wright *v.* Trustees of M. E. Church, 1 Hoff. 263 (N. Y. Ch. Ct. 1839); Hornbeck *v.* American Bible Society, 2 Sandf. Ch. 135 (1844); Owens *v.* Missionary Society of the M. E. Chnrch, 14 N. Y. 386 (1856); Mount *v.* Tuttle, 183 N. Y. 367, 76 N. E. 873 (1906).

[136] Murray *v.* Miller, 178 N. Y. 231, 70 N. E. 870 (1904); Matter of Graves, 171 N. Y. 47, 63 N. E. 787 (1902).

[137] *In re* Fitzsimmons, 29 Misc. 204, 61 N. Y. S. 485, and 29 Misc. 731, 62 N. Y. S. 1009 (1899).

[138] *In re* Lyon, 280 N. Y. 391, 21 N. E. 2d 265 (1939); *In re* Collier, 97 Misc. 543, 163 N. Y. S. 402 (1916); *In re* Scott, 31 Misc. 85, 64 N. Y. S. 577 (1900); Fralick *v.* Lyford, 107 App. Div. 543, 95 N. Y. S. 433, *aff'd without opinion,* 187 N. Y. 524 (1907).

[139] Fisher *v.* Lister, 130 Misc. 1, 223, N. Y. S. 321 (1927); *In re* Winburn, 139 Misc. 5, 247 N. Y. S. 583 (1931).

tion.[140] The circumstance that the purpose of the association or
institution is charitable does not import that the gift is in trust for
such purposes, even when the society administers such a charity as a
home or hospital for crippled children.[141]

It seems that the observation made by the Court of Appeals in
1856 states the reasoning of the New York courts in this matter:

> Those purposes may change with the will of the associates.
> They may be pious today and impious tomorrow. There is no
> law to prevent or restrain such changes. It is difficult to see,
> therefore, how a bequest to such an association can be deemed
> to create a charitable use, unless the purpose to which it is to be
> devoted is pointed out by the testator.[142]

A devise to an unincorporated association which carries on
charitable works is not confirmed to the association by incorporation after the testator's death, nor by a subsequent amendment of
its charter authorizing it to take the property, when it had no
authority to do so at the time of the testator's death.[143] A devise,
however, of property to certain corporations which became effective after the death of the testator's wife was valid where the corporations, though not in existence at the testator's death, had been
formed prior to the death of the testator's wife, and were then
capable of taking the property.[144]

A devise in trust for a charitable organization which was unincorporated at the time of the execution of the will is valid if the
organization is incorporated before the money becomes payable.[145]
The court has said that "there is no reason why property cannot be
given to a corporation to be formed after the death of the testator
and within the restricted period, any more than there is why prop-

---

[140] Trustees of Sustentation Fund *v.* Hoosac School, 192 App. Div. 745,
183 N. Y. S. 585 (3rd Dept. 1920); Wait *v.* Society for Political Study, 68
Misc. 250, 123, N. Y. S. 637 (Sup. Ct. 1910).

[141] Mount *v.* Tuttle, 183 N. Y. 367, 76 N. E. 873 (1906).

[142] Owens *v.* Missionary Society of the M. E. Church, 14 N. Y. 385 (1856).

[143] White *v.* Howard, 46 N. Y. 144, *aff'y* Barb. Ch. 294 (1871).

[144] Shipman *v.* Rollins, 98 N. Y. 311, 15 Abb. N. Cas. 288 *reversing* 33
Hun. 89 (1885).

[145] Philson *v.* Moore, 23 Hun. 152 (N. Y. 1880).

erty should not be given to descendants or other persons thereafter to be born." [146] The "restricted period" referred to is the duration of two lives in being at the creation of the trust as has been pointed out above.[147]

ARTICLE 6. LIMITATION ON AMOUNT OF TESTAMENTARY GIFTS FOR CHARITY

The present New York statute on this matter reads as follows:

No person, having a husband, wife or child or descendant or parent, shall, by his or her last will and testament, devise or bequeath to any benevolent, charitable, literary, religious or missionary society, association, corporation or purpose, in trust or otherwise, more than one-half part of his or her estate, after the payment of his or her debts, and such devise or bequest shall be valid to the extent of one-half and no more. The validity of a devise or bequest for more than such one-half may be contested only by a surviving husband, wife, child, descendant or parent.[148]

It must be kept in mind that the present statutory provision has within it two important additions which are not to be found in the original provision. This basic law was amended in 1923 [149] by the addition of the words "or purpose" after "society, association or corporation." This amendment sought to offset the rule of law laid down in *Allen* v. *Stevens* [150] to the effect that the old law did not restrict a testamentary gift to individuals in trust for a charitable purpose. In New York, prior to the amendment, it was held that this statute in limiting the testamentary capacity of a person did not include a testamentary gift to individuals in trust for a charitable purpose, notwithstanding the fact that the will also authorized, but did not compel, the trustees to create a corporation.[151]

[146] St. John *v.* Andrews Institute, 191 N. Y. 254, 83 N. E. 981 (1908).
[147] Cf. *supra,* p. 152.
[148] *N. Y. Decedent Estate Law,* § 17.
[149] Laws of 1923, c. 301.
[150] 161 N. Y. 122, 52 N. E. 568 (1899).
[151] 68 C. J. 553; cf. *In re* Blumenthal, 124 Misc. 850, 854, 208 N. Y. S. 682, 686 (Surr. Ct. 1925).

It has now been definitely established that this section cannot be evaded by agreement of the prospective legatee with the testator to devote the legacy to charitable purposes desired by the testator, or by charging the gift to one entitled to invoke the section, with trust obligations to devote it to charity.[152] An important question at once arises. If the legatee is under no legal obligation to use the property for charity, but actually does so or proposes to do so because he feels so obliged in conscience, would the New York courts find here a violation of the Statute? There is no New York case covering this particular point.

There is a Pennsylvania ruling [153] which could well supply a norm to the New York courts, if this situation should arise in the State of New York. In the Pennsylvania case the testator gave his estate to certain designated charities, but declared in his will that, if he died within a month, all his property should go "absolutely" to Archbishop Ryan of Philadelphia. The Pennsylvania Statute invalidates wills for charity which are made only within thirty days before the testator's death.[154] The testator here was evidently trying to evade the Statute. The Archbishop declared in court that he had never seen, or even heard of, the testator; that he entered into no agreement with the testator regarding the use of his property; but that he found himself obliged in conscience to use the property for the charities indicated in the will.

The Pennsylvania court stated:

> There could be no fuller acknowledgment of a moral obligation, nor a stronger avowal of an intention to discharge it, but our decrees do not go out to compel the performance of a mere moral duty. In *foro conscientiae*, conscience is the sole chancellor, whose decrees we are as powerless to enforce as we are to provide penalties for their violation.[155]

---

[152] *In re* Watson's Estate, 177 Misc. 308, 30 N. Y. S. 2d 577 (1941).

[153] Flood *v.* Ryan, 220 Pa. St. 450 (1908).

[154] *Purdon's Pennsylvania Statutes Annotated, Decedents' and Trust Estates* (Title 20 with 1956 Cumulative Annual Pocket Part, Philadelphia: Bisel, 1950), § 180.7, subd. 1.

[155] Flood *v.* Ryan, 220 Pa. St. 450 (1908).

Consequently, even though the legatee was under no legal obligation to use certain property for charity, but actually proposed to do so, because he felt obliged in conscience, the Pennsylvania court found no violation of any statute.

Before reference is made to the second amendment to the statute under discussion (N. Y. Decedent Estate Law, § 17), certain preliminary notions must be kept in mind. Where surviving members of a protected class of relatives did not contest a devise violating a charitable bequest statute, the question arose whether the bequest could be challenged by individuals who, although not members of the specific class, were nevertheless adversely affected by the devise. Most courts, having a similar type of statute, have refused to permit such persons to contest charitable bequests.[156]

Until 1930 New York formed the sole exception to this rule. In this jurisdiction persons who were not members of the preferred class were permitted to contest such wills, provided that they would benefit by avoiding the charitable bequest.[157] For example, a collateral heir was in a position to contest an excessive devise to charity, even though the testator's spouse was willing to allow it to stand.[158]

In 1930, however, New York amended its charitable bequest statute by explicitly limiting the power to contest voidable charitable devises to specific heirs, thereby bringing its law into line with that of other jurisdictions which have passed on this question.[159] The following sentence was added to the statute: "The validity of a devise or bequest for more than such one-half may be contested only by a surviving husband, wife, child, descendant or parent."

One may with profit examine some of the rulings of the courts on the construction of this statute as it exists today in New York.

---

[156] "Standing to Contest Wills Violating Charitable Bequest Statutes," *Columbia Law Review*, L (1950), 96.

[157] Trustees of Amherst College *v.* Ritch, 151 N. Y. 282, 45 N. E. 876 (1897); Decker *v.* Vreeland, 220 N. Y. 326, 115 N. E. 989 (1917); Matter of Mosley, 138 Misc. 847, 247 N. Y. S. 520 (N. Y. Sur. Ct. 1931).

[158] Decker *v.* Vreeland, *loc. cit.*; Matter of Mosley, *loc. cit.*

[159] Laws of 1929, c. 229, § 3.

The term "child" in the Statute includes adopted children.[160] The word "descendant," as used in this Statute, refers to the issue of a deceased child of the testator, which issue is living at the time of the testator's death, but it does not include the children of a parent who is still living.[161]

This statute regulates and controls testamentary dispositions only.[162] New York has explicitly rejected a California ruling[163] that permits non-conforming charitable devises to be challenged only by those among the surviving specified relatives who would otherwise have taken the property so bequeathed.[164]

This statute is not a mortmain act.[165] One ruling has stated:

The decisions under the mortmain acts of England are equally inapplicable when the difference between those acts and the act of 1860 (c. 360) (i.e. the charitable bequest statute) is borne in mind. That statute is of a different character than any of those mentioned. It does not prevent charitable corporations from taking, but forbids a testator who has a wife, etc., from giving more than one-half of his estate. . . . It does not prohibit charitable gifts altogether, but only under certain circumstances, to a certain extent and by a certain method.[166]

This statute constitutes a limitation on testamentary power; it does not disqualify the devisee or legatee to take the testamentary gift. To put it in another way, this statute does not operate on the capacity of the corporations, institutions, or individuals to take

[160] *In re* Mawhinney, 146 Misc. 30, 261 N. Y. S. 334, *aff'd* 239 App. Div. 874, 264 N. Y. S. 984 (1933).

[161] *In re* Plaster's Will, 266 App. Div. 439, 43 N. Y. S. 2d 1, *aff'd,* 293 N. Y. 822, 59 N. E. 2d 181 (1943).

[162] Robb *v.* Washington etc. College, 185 N. Y. 485, 78 N. E. 359 (1906).

[163] *West's Annotated California Codes, Probate Code* (Vol. 52, St. Paul: West Publ. Co., 1956), § 44.

[164] *In re* Logossa, 163 Misc. 628, 297 N. Y. S. 730 (N. Y. Sur. Ct. 1937).

[165] *In re* Watson's Estate, 177 Misc. 308, 30 N. Y. S. 2d 577 (1941).

[166] Trustees of Amherst College *v.* Ritch, 151 N. Y. 282, 333, 45 N. E. 876 (1897).

charitable testamentary gifts,[167] nor does it prescribe or limit the amount of property a corporation may take.[168]

There are further considerations. The fact that one of the persons named therein, and on whose survival the operation of the statute depends, has an ample estate of his own does not authorize a construction of the statute favorable to a charitable or benevolent organization claiming under the will.[169] It has been held also that this statute, applicable to gifts "for charitable and benevolent" purposes, includes an "educational" purpose.[170] Prior to the amendment of the New York Statute, which added the word "purpose" after "society, association or corporation," it was held that a gift to a bishop for the erection of a parochial school was not within the statutory provision.[171]

Following the amendment of 1930 the courts of New York have affirmed that only those persons who are specified in the statute may question a testamentary gift on the grounds that it is in excess of the amount permitted by statute.[172] Such authority is a personal privilege,[173] and should be narrowly restricted.[174] Other persons who might be enabled to gain a share of the estate may not contest the gift, notwithstanding the survivorship of a person or persons specified.[175] A person so specified may waive his right to invoke the statute.[176] It should be noted, however, despite the amendment of 1930, that if the spouse, for example, should contest the bequest, it might still result that some of the property undisposed of could

[167] Chamberlain *v.* Chamberlain, 43 N. Y. 424, *modifying* 3 Lans. 348 (1871).

[168] Trustees of Amherst College, 151 N. Y. 282, 333, 44 N. E. 876 (1897).

[169] *In re* Rowland's Will, 225 App. Div. 118, 232 N. Y. S. 127.

[170] *In re* Rowland's Will, *loc. cit.*

[171] Vanderveer *v.* McKane, 25 Abb. N. C. 105, 11 N. Y. S. 808 (N. Y. 1890).

[172] *In re* Plaster's Estate, 179 Misc. 80, 37 N. Y. S. 2d 299, *aff'd* 266 App. Div. 439, 43 N. Y. S. 2d 1, *aff'd* 293 N. Y. 822, 59 N. E. 2d 181 (1943).

[173] *In re* Sonderling's Will, 157 Misc. 231, 283 N. Y. S. 568 (1935).

[174] *In re* Plaster's Estate, 179 Misc. 80, 37 N. Y. S. 2d 299, *aff'd* 266 App. Div. 439, 43 N. Y. S. 2d 1, *aff'd* 293 N. Y. 822, 59 N. E. 2d 181 (1943).

[175] *In re* Korzencewska's Estate, 163 Misc. 323, 297 N. Y. S. 997 (1937).

[176] *In re* Watson's Estate, 177 Misc. 308, 30 N. Y. S. 2d 577 (1941).

pass to distributees who under existing law had no right to contest the bequest in the first instance.[177]

It has been pointed out by the courts that it is the purpose of the charitable bequest statute to protect the natural rights of the testator's relatives by shielding them against his making improvident gifts to their neglect.[178] This view has been attacked [179] because of the fact that the testator may still donate all his property to charity during his lifetime, even though the gift be made in contemplation of and within a few hours of his death,[180] and in an effort to evade the statute.[181]

Another author [182] has pointed out that the tendency of the courts strictly to confine [183] the groups of persons who may contest non-conforming charitable bequests may be explained by the fact that the desirability of this statute is open to question. He further pointed out that if certain relatives of a testator were thought to be entitled to a minimal proportion of his estate, there seems little reason why, alone among other possible legatees, charitable institutions should be singled out for restrictive treatment. One may indeed grant that the making of a charitable bequest is perhaps the most usual way of cutting off or disinheriting relatives, but one must also grant that it can be a most meritorious act. It is definitely to be questioned whether an act with so much potentiality for good should be singled out for restriction and curtailment.

[177] *In re* Sonderling's Will, 157 Misc. 231, 283 N. Y. S. 568 (1935).

[178] *In re* Hills, 157 Misc. 109, 283 N. Y. S. 733 (1934).

[179] "Persons Entitled to Challenge a Devise or Bequest Invalid Under a Charitable Statute," *Yale Law Journal*, XLI (1932), 773.

[180] Robb *v.* Washington and Jefferson College, 185 N. Y. 494, 8 N. E. 362 (1906).

[181] Allen *v.* Stevens, 161 N. Y. 122, 55 N. E. 568 (1899), *modified* in Decker *v.* Vreeland, 220 N. Y. 326, 115 N. E. 989 (1917).

[182] "Standing to Contest Wills Violating Charitable Bequest Statutes," *Columbia Law Review*, L (1950), 98.

[183] Cf. *supra*, pp. 165 & 167.

CONCLUSIONS

Two general conclusions first present themselves:

I. The theory of New York law is contrary to the canonical concept of juridical or moral personality, since it insists that the creation of any such entity is the result of its own legislative authority.[1] New York law does not acknowledge the divine right of the Church to utilize the medium of moral personality in the fullest sense,[2] without at least some reference to the State.

II. New York law also differs from canon law with regard to the division of legal personality. The canonical concept of a non-collegiate moral personality has no exact counterpart in New York jurisprudence.[3] The law of this State does not accept the doctrine whereby an aggregate of property is regarded as a separate, distinct artificial entity, with rights and duties of its own. There is need of incorporation [4] in order that any such institution, e.g., a college or a hospital, may receive legal recognition in New York.

In the light of the two general observations that have just been made, a more particular comparison of the two systems of law under consideration will now be undertaken in the remaining conclusions. In each of these the teaching of the canon law will be given first, and then will follow a statement of the jurisprudence of the New York law on the same subject.

1. Once moral personalities in the Church are constituted as such canonically, they are endowed with the capacity for certain rights. Included in these rights is the capacity to acquire and administer property.[5]

Among the rights possessed by New York corporations is the right to take, hold, and dispose of property for its corporate pur-

---

[1] Cf. *supra*, p. 34.

[2] Cf. *supra*, pp. 17-18 & 52.

[3] Cf. *supra*, p. 34.

[4] The term here refers to the establishment of legal personality for an aggregate of physical persons.

[5] Cf. *supra*, p. 7.

poses, subject, however, to statutory limitations.[6] In New York there are certain statutory limitations on this power, which, more in theory than in practice, clash with the rights of the Church, such as the statute which limits the right of religious, charitable, and educational corporations to take property beyond a certain amount,[7] or the statute which requires a religious corporation to have leave of the court before it alienates any of its real property.[8]

2. Moral entities in the Church are endowed with moral personality either by the very operation of law itself,[9] or by a special concession of the proper ecclesiastical authorities.[10]

In New York, ecclesiastical moral personalities as such have no standing before the law.[11] For charitable, educational, and religious purposes, corporations may be created by special act.[12] There are also general incorporation laws for each of these purposes. Charitable corporations may be created under the Membership Corporations Law; [13] educational corporations may be formed under Membership Corporations Law also, or by an act of the Regents; [14] and religious corporations may be organized under the Religious Corporations Law.[15]

3. Moral personalities in the Church are subject to the exclusive control of ecclesiastical authority.[16]

In New York, corporations formed for charitable, educational, or religious purposes are subject in their operations to the supervision of the State.[17] Catholic church corporations, however, are subject by law to ecclesiastical control,[18] and provisions for such

---

[6] Cf. *supra*, p. 35.
[7] Cf. *supra*, pp. 35–36.
[8] Cf. *supra*, pp. 75–78.
[9] Cf. *supra*, pp. 21–23.
[10] Cf. *supra*, pp. 23–28.
[11] Cf. *supra*, p. 52.
[12] Cf. *supra*, pp. 34, 37–38, 43, 54.
[13] Cf. *supra*, p. 36.
[14] Cf. *supra*, pp. 36, 42–43.
[15] Cf. *supra*, pp. 51–56.
[16] Cf. *supra*, p. 18.
[17] Cf. *supra*, p. 52.
[18] Cf. *supra*, pp. 49–50, 52.

control may be written into the by-laws of educational and charitable corporations formed under Catholic auspices.[19]

4. Moral personalities in the Church yield to extinction upon an act of authoritative suppression, or in consequence of the juridical fact that their substratum has ceased to exist for one hundred years.[20]

Membership corporations in New York are dissolved in consequence of certain judicial proceedings, or their members may seek voluntary dissolution.[21] Educational corporations formed under the Regents are not subject to dissolution through the ordinary processes for dissolution of membership corporations, but their dissolution may be declared by the court on petition of their trustees.[22] Religious corporations enjoy a similar exemption, and a special process is provided for their dissolution.[23] Any corporation in New York is liable to dissolution, if it abuses its corporate powers and violates the laws of the State.[24]

5. In canon law a pious cause, in its more extensive connotation,[25] comprises all pious, religious, and charitable works favored by the Church. "Piety" includes every work of religion, every spiritual work of mercy, and every work of physical charity to men which is undertaken for the love of God.[26] Works in aid of men's mundane necessities are not intrinsically pious. They will be pious or simply humanitarian according as the intent of the person who performs the work, or of the donor who makes a gift for the performance of that work, is duly manifest.[27]

In New York law the purposes which enjoy the favor of the "Tilden Act"[28] and of related laws[29] are designated "charitable

[19] Cf. *supra*, pp. 35, 38-39.
[20] Cf. *supra*, pp. 28-32.
[21] Cf. *supra*, pp. 35, 40-42.
[22] Cf. *supra*, pp. 35, 44.
[23] Cf. *supra*, pp. 35, 74-75.
[24] Cf. *supra*, p. 74.
[25] Cf. *supra*, p. 103.
[26] Cf. *supra*, p. 104.
[27] Cf. *supra*, pp. 103-106.
[28] Cf. *supra*, p. 141.
[29] Cf. *supra*, pp. 141-142.

uses." A use is charitable, if it is primarily a "public" use.[30] Religious and educational uses are also recognized as charitable uses.[31]

6. Canonically, private property becomes dedicated to pious causes in consequence of the owner's pious will (*pia voluntas*).[32] The Code of Canon Law upholds the moral obligation to use the goods which an owner has with his pious will dedicated to pious causes in full accord with the purposes and the manner intended by the owner.[33] If the pious will of such an owner is defeated for want of civil formalities, then those who because of this fact obtain such piously dedicated property are obliged in conscience to fulfill the intent of that pious dedication.[34]

In New York law, goods are dedicated to charity when the one who holds them is under legal obligation to use them for charity. Such obligations are created and enforced within the general pattern of the trust devise.[35] When a charitable gift is made apart from all specification of a definite and competent beneficiary, the law of New York raises a charitable trust, though the owner may not have intended such a trust.[36] The same procedure is followed when the owner intended a trust, but named no trustee or no competent one.[37] The law of New York also saves charitable trusts from certain statutory inconveniences.[38]

7. The canon law has general provisions with regard to property given to moral personalities in the Church.[39] Special provisions obtain for pious gifts which projected the founding of moral personalities.[40] Contracts made by moral personalities in the Church for the creation of pious foundations are subject to certain ante-

<hr>

30 Cf. *supra*, pp. 143-144.

31 Cf. *supra*, pp. 144-145.

32 Cf. *supra*, p. 106.

33 Cf. *supra*, p. 107.

34 Cf. *supra*, p. 117.

35 Cf. *supra*, p. 145.

36 Cf. *supra*, pp. 146, 147-148.

37 Cf. *supra*, p. 146.

38 Cf. *supra*, pp. 152-154.

39 Cf. *supra*, pp. 112-113.

40 Cf. *supra*, pp. 113-114.

cedent canonical requirements and to the approval of the ordinaries.[41]

In New York law, corporations receiving charitable gifts for specified purposes or with directions for the management of these gifts are obliged to carry out the donor's purposes and directions, even though there be no trust in the technical sense.[42]

8. Canon law confers broad administrative powers upon the ordinaries for the purpose of obtaining the due execution of pious wills.[43]

In New York, the authority of the State in matters concerning the enforcement of charitable gifts is always exercised through a judicial process. This is true, even though some of the powers involved, including *cy pres*, are really administrative powers.[44]

9. In canon law, the power to relax, to specify, or to modify the works to which a person is obliged under the terms of a pious will may be exercised in some special cases by the ordinary, but is otherwise reserved to the Holy See.[45]

The authority to change the objects specified by a deceased donor for his charitable gift is given by law to the Supreme Court and the Surrogate's Court. This is part of the *cy pres* power.[46]

10. Canon law nowhere prescribes "solemnities" for a pious will, although it does in some cases expressly urge compliance with the civil law in this respect. This directive, however, does not affect the validity of any last will made without such solemnities.[47]

New York law demands "solemnities" which do have an effect on the validity of such gifts.[48]

11. Canon law sets no general limitation on the amount of property which may be given by will. The natural claims, however, of certain relatives ("necessary heirs") on the bounty of the testator are recognized, even against the interests of pious causes.[49]

[41] Cf. *supra*, pp. 114-115.
[42] Cf. *supra*, pp. 148-152.
[43] Cf. *supra*, pp. 116-124.
[44] Cf. *supra*, pp. 154-158.
[45] Cf. *supra*, pp. 124-127.
[46] Cf. *supra*, pp. 155-157.
[47] Cf. *supra*, pp. 131-134.
[48] Cf. *supra*, p. 132.
[49] Cf. *supra*, pp. 134-135.

New York law limits the amount of testimentary gifts for charity, when there are certain privileged survivors.[50] There are also provisions which restrict the general rights in the making of a testament in order that certain privileged survivors may reap the more abundant favors.[51]

[50] Cf. *supra,* pp. 163-168.
[51] Cf. *supra,* pp. 134-135.

BIBLIOGRAPHY

Sources

Acta Apostolicae Sedis, Commentarium Officiale, Romae, 1909-1929; Civitate Vaticana, 1929-

Bouscaren, T. Lincoln, *The Canon Law Digest,* 3 vols. and Supplements through 1953-1955, Milwaukee: Bruce & Co., 1934-1949-1953-1954-1955-1956.

Consolidated Laws of the State of New York, Albany, 1909.

Corpus Juris, 71 vols., Vol. 68, New York: American Law Book Co., 1934.

Corpus Juris Secundum, 95 vols., Vol. 14, Brooklyn: American Law Book Co., 1939.

Denzinger, H.-Umberg, J., *Enchiridion Symbolorum Definitionum et Declarationum de Rebus Fidei et Morum,* editio vigesima sexta, emendata et aucta, Friburgi Brisgoviae: Herder & Co., 1947.

Jaffé, Philippus, *Regesta Pontificum Romanorum ab condita Ecclesia ad annum post Christum natum MCXCVIII,* ed. 2. correctam et auctam auspiciis Gulielmi Wattenbach curaverunt, S. Loewenfeld, F. Kaltenbrunner, P. Ewald, 2 vols., Lipsiae, 1885-1888.

Laws of the State of New York, edited by Jones and Varick, 2 vols., Vol. I, New York, 1789.

Laws of the State of New York passed at the Eighty-sixth Session of the Legislature, Albany, 1863.

McKinney's Consolidated Laws of New York Annotated, 68 Books, Brooklyn: Edward Thompson Company; Book 13, Decedent Estate Law, 1949, with 1956 Cumulative Annual Pocket Part; Book 16, Education Law, 1953, with 1956 Cumulative Annual Pocket Part; Book 22, General Corporations Law, 1943, with 1956 Cumulative Annual Pocket Part; Book 36, Membership Corporations Law, 1943, with 1956 Cumulative Annual Pocket Part; Book 49, Real Property Law, 1945, with 1956 Cumulative Annual Pocket Part; Book 50, Religious Corporations Law, 1952, with 1956 Cumulative Annual Pocket Part; Book 59, Tax Law, 1949, with 1956 Cumulative Annual Pocket Part.

Nichols, Clark-Cahill, James, *Annotated New York Civil Practice Acts,* 16 vols., Vol. I, with 1956 Cumulative Pocket Index, Chicago-Rochester: 1937.

Potthast, Augustus, *Regesta Pontificum Romanorum inde ab anno post Christum natum MCXCVIII ad annum MCCCIV,* 2 vols., Berolini, 1874-1875.

Purdon's Pennsylvania Statutes Annotated, Title 20, Decedents' and Trust Estates, Philadelphia: Biset, 1950, with 1956 Cumulative Annual Pocket Part.

Revised Statutes of the State of New York, 2 vols., Vol. I, Albany, 1829.

West's Annotated California Codes, Probate Code, Vol. 52, St. Paul: West Publ. Co., 1956.

REFERENCE WORKS

Abbo, John A.-Hannan, Jerome D., *The Sacred Canons,* St. Louis: B. Herder Book Co., 1952.

Adler, Philip, *Tax Exemption on Real Estate, an Increasing Menace,* New York, 1922.

Beste, Udalricus, *Introductio in Codicem,* 3. ed., Collegeville: St. John's Abbey Press, 1946.

————, *Introductio in Codicem,* 4. ed., Neapoli: D'Aurea, 1956.

Blat, Albertus, *Commentarium Textus Codicis Iuris Canonici,* 5 vols. in 7, Vol. II, Pars I, 2. ed., Romae: Collegio Angelico, 1921.

Bogert, George, *Handbook of the Law of Trusts,* 2. ed., St. Paul: West Publ. Co., 1942.

Bouscaren, T. Lincoln-Ellis, Adam C., *Canon Law,* Milwaukee: Bruce, 1946.

Brown, Brendan, *The Canonical Juristic Personality with Special Reference to Its Status in the United States of America,* The Catholic University of America Canon Law Studies, n. 39, Washington, D. C.: The Catholic University of America, 1927.

Byrne, Harry, *Investment of Church Funds,* The Catholic University of America Canon Law Studies, n. 309, Washington, D. C.: The Catholic University of America Press, 1951.

Cance, Adrien, *Le Code de Droit Canonique,* 3 vols., Vol. III, 7. ed., Paris: Gabalda, 1946.

Cappello, Felix, *Summa Iuris Canonici,* 3 vols., Vol. II, 4. ed., Romae: Apud Aedes Universitatis Gregorianae, 1945.

————, *Summa Iuris Publici Ecclesiastici,* 5. ed., Romae: Apud Aedes Universitatis Gregorianae, 1943.

————, *Tractatus Canonici-Moralis de Sacramentis,* 3 vols., Vol. III, Romae: Marietti, 1923.

Cobb, Sanford, *The Rise of Religious Liberty in America,* New York, 1901.

Cocchi, Guidus, *Commentarium in Codicem Iuris Canonici,* 8 vols., Vol. VI, 5. ed., Taurinorum Augustae: Marietti, 1937.

Cooley, Thomas, *The Law of Taxation,* 4 vols., Vol. II, 4. ed., Chicago, 1924.

Coronata, Matthaeus Conte a, *Institutiones Iuris Canonici,* 5 vols., Vol. I, 4. ed., 1950, Vol. II, 4. ed., 1951, Romae: Marietti.

Dignan, Patrick, *A History of the Legal Incorporation of Catholic Church Property in the United States,* New York: Kenedy, 1935.

Farley, J., *The Life of John Cardinal McCloskey,* New York, 1918.

Feeney, Thomas, *Restitutio in Integrum,* The Catholic University of America Canon Law Studies, n. 129, Washington, D. C.: The Catholic University of America Press, 1941.

Five Great Encyclicals, New York: Paulist Press, 1939.

Fowler, Robert, *The Law of Charitable Uses, Trusts, and Donations in New York,* New York, 1896.

Gillet, P., *La Personalité Juridique en Droit Ecclésiastique*, Molines: Godenne, 1927.

Goodwine, John, *The Right of the Church to Acquire Temporal Goods*, The Catholic University of America Canon Law Studies, n. 131, Washington, D. C.: The Catholic University of America Press, 1941.

Hannan, Jerome, *The Canon Law of Wills*, The Catholic University of America Canon Law Studies, n. 86, Washington, D. C.: The Catholic University of America, 1934.

Jone, Heribertus, *Commentarium in Codicem Iuris Canonici*, 3 vols., Vol. I, Paderborn: Schöningh, 1950.

Michiels, Gommarus, *Principia Generalia de Personis in Ecclesia*, 1. ed., Lublin: 1932.

————, *Principia Generalia de Personis in Ecclesia*, 2. ed., Parisiis-Tornaci-Romae: Desclée, 1955.

Nicolau, Michael-Salaverri, Joachim, *Sacrae Theologiae Summa*, 4 vols., Vol. I, 3. ed., Matriti: Biblioteca de Auctores Cristianos, 1955.

O'Callaghan, E. B., *Documentary History of New York*, 4 vols., Vol. III, New York, 1849.

O'Toole, Edward J., *Law of Trusts*, Brooklyn, 1933.

Ottaviani, A., *Institutiones Juris Publici Ecclesiastici*, 2 vols., Vol. I, 3. ed., Romae: Typis Polyglottis Vaticanis, 1947.

Prümmer, Dominicus, *Manuale Iuris Canonici*, 5. ed., Friburgi Brisgoviae: B. Herder Book Co., 1927.

Restatement of the Laws of Trusts, 2 vols., Vol. II, St. Paul: American Law Institute, 1935.

Saxe, J., *Charitable Exemption from Taxation in New York State on Real and Personal Property*, New York, 1933.

Scott, Austin, *The Law of Trusts*, 4 vols., Vol. III, Boston: Little, Brown & Co., 1939.

Tobin, C. J., Hannan, W. E., Tolman, L. L., *The Exemption from Taxation of Privately Owned Real Property Used for Religious, Charitable and Educational Purposes in New York State*, Albany, 1934-38.

Torpey, William, *Judicial Doctrines of Religious Rights in America*, Chapel Hill: University of North Carolina Press, 1948.

Van Hove, A., *Commentarium Lovaniense in Codicem Iuris Canonici*, 1 vol. in 5 toms., Tom. I, *Prolegomena*, 2. ed., Mechliniae-Romae: H. Dessain, 1945.

Vermeersch, A.-Creusen, J., *Epitome Iuris Canonici*, 3 vols., Vol. I, 7. ed., 1949; Vol. II, 6. ed., 1940, Mechliniae-Romae: H. Dessain.

Vromant, G., *De Bonis Ecclesiae Temporalibus*, 3. ed., Bruges-Paris: Desclée de Brouwer, 1953.

Wernz, Franciscus, *Ius Decretalium*, 6 vols., Vol. I, 2. ed., 1905; Vol. III, 1901, Romae.

Wernz, F.-Vidal, P., *Ius Canonicum ad Codicis Normam Exactum*, 7 Tomes in 8 vols., Tom. IV, Vol. II, Romae: Apud Aedes Universitatis Gregorianae, 1935.

White, Frank, *New York Corporations*, 2 vols., Vol. I, 12. ed., Albany: Bender, 1947, with Cumulative Supplement for 1956.

Woywod, Stanislaus, *A Practical Commentary on the Code of Canon Law*, revised by Callistus Smith, 2 vols., New York: Jos. F. Wagner, Inc., 1948.

Zollman, Carl, *American Church Law*, St. Paul: West Publ. Co., 1933.

————, *American Civil Church Law*, Columbia University Studies, Vol. 77, New York, 1917.

————, *American Law of Charities*, Milwaukee: Bruce Publ. Co., 1924.

Articles

————, "Constitutionality of Tax Benefits Accorded Religion," *Columbia Law Review*, XLIX (1949), 968-992.

————, "Constitutional Limitations of State Court Review of Hierarchical Church Judicatory Decisions," *Columbia Law Review*, LIV (1954), 435-438.

————, "Constitutional Limitations on State Court Review of Hierarchical Church Judicatory Decisions," *Harvard Law Review*, LXIV (1951), 1360-1361.

————, "Exemption of Property Owned or Used by Religious Organizations," *Minnesota Law Review*, XI (1927), 541-551.

————, "Incorporation of Church Property in the United States," *The Ecclesiastical Review*, XLV (1911), 596-598.

————, "Persons Entitled to Challenge a Devise or Bequest Invalid Under a Charitable Statute," *Yale Law Journal*, XLI (1932), 771-773.

————, "Standing to Contest Wills Violating Charitable Bequest Statutes," *Columbia Law Review*, L (1950), 94-99.

Ciprotti, Pio, "A Proposito delle Associazioni di Azione Cattolica," *Il Diritto Ecclesiastico*, XLVIII (1937), 358-365.

————, "De Formali Decreto Quo Persona Juridica Constituitur," *Apollinaris*, X (1937), 269-272.

Cloppers, William, "Charities—Absolute Gift to Public Charitable Corporation," *Boston University Law Review*, XIX (1940), 655-658.

Couly, A., "Extinction des Personnes Morales," *Le Canoniste Contemporain*, XLIV (1921), 113-127.

D'Angelo, Sosius, "De Quiescentia in Codice Iuris Canonici," *Apollinaris*, I (1928), 501-503.

Ghesquières, Louis, "La Corporacion Paroissiale Aux Etats-Unis," *Ephemerides Iuris Canonici*, VII, nn. 3-4 (1951), 269-287; VIII, n. 1 (1952), 45-69.

Gillet, P., "De Piis Fidelium Voluntatibus," *Collectanea Mechliniensia*, XVI (1927), 80-90.

Huot, Dorius, "Bonorum Temporalium apud Religiones Administratio Ordinaria et Extraordinaria," *Commentarium pro Religiosis et Missionariis,* XXXIII (1954), 60-76, 312-328; XXXIV (1955), 55-64, 175-192, 266-273, 365-373.

Larber, Harry, "Liability of Hospitals for the Negligence of Their Employees," *St. John's Law Review,* XV (1941), 275-283.

Larraona, Arcadius, "De Paupertate Simplici," *Commentarium pro Religiosis,* II, (1921), 8-13.

McNamara, R., "Trusteeism in the Atlantic States, 1785-1863," *Catholic Historical Review,* XXX (1944), 135-154.

Powell, Richard, "Land Capacity of Unincorporated Groups," *Columbia Law Review,* XLIX (1949), 297-319.

Preti, Luigi, "Il Riconoscimento delle Persone Morali in Diritto Canonico," *Archivo di Diritto Ecclesiastico,* II (1940), 319-339.

Taylor, Frederick, "A New Chapter in the New York Law of Charitable Corporations," *Cornell Law Quarterly,* XXV (1940), 382-400.

Vermeersch, A., "De Personae Moralis Extinctione et Resurrectione," *Periodica de Re Morali, Canonica, Liturgica,* XX (1931), 84-88.

Visser, J., "De Solemnitatibus Piarum Voluntatum in Iure Canonico," *Apollinaris,* XX (1947), 59-136.

Zollman, Carl, "Powers of American Religious Corporations," *Michigan Law Review,* XIII (1915), 646-666.

————, "Tax Exemption of American Church Property," *Michigan Law Review,* XIV (1916), 646-657.

————, "The Development of the Law of Charities in the United States," *Columbia Law Review,* XIX (1919), 91-111, 286-309.

PERIODICALS

American Ecclesiastical Review, The, The American Ecclesiastical Review, Philadelphia, 1889-1905; *The Ecclesiastical Review,* Philadelphia, 1905-1943; *The American Ecclesiastical Review,* Washington, D. C., 1944-

Apollinaris, Romae, 1928-

Archivo di Diritto Ecclesiastico, Romae, 1939-1943.

Boston University Law Review, Boston, 1921-

Catholic Historical Review, Washington, D. C., 1915-

Collectanea Mechliniensia, Mechliniae, 1911-

Columbia Law Review, New York, 1901-

Commentarium pro Religiosis, Romae, 1920-1934; *Commentarium pro Religiosis et Missionariis,* Romae, 1935-

Cornell Law Quarterly, Ithaca, 1915-

Ephemerides Iuris Canonici, Romae, 1945-

Harvard Law Review, Cambridge, 1887-

Il Diritto Ecclesiastico, Romae, 1890-

Le Canoniste Contemporain, Paris, 1878-1922; *Le Canoniste,* Paris, 1924-1926.
Michigan Law Review, Ann Arbor, 1902-
Minnesota Law Review, Minneapolis, 1916-
Periodica de Religiosis et Missionariis, Brugis, 1905-1919; *Periodica de Re Canonica et Morali, utilia praesertim Religiosis et Missionariis,* Brugis, 1920-1927; *Periodica de Re Morali, Canonica Liturgica,* Brugis, 1927-1936, Romae, 1937-
St. John's Law Review, Brooklyn, 1926-
Yale Law Journal, New Haven, 1891-

CIVIL LAW CASES CITED

(Page numbers after each case refer to where it may be found in the text.)

Allen *v.* Stevens, 161 N. Y. 122, 52 N. E. 568 (1899), pp. 163, 168.
Amherst College *v.* Ritch, 151 N. Y. 333, 45 N. E. 876, *aff'y* 91 Hun. 509 (1897), p. 160.
Application of Brooklyn Children's Aid Society, 269 App. Div. 789, 55 N. Y. S. 2d 323 (1945), p. 149.
Application of Congregation Beth David Anshey Roman of Romania, 206 Misc. 600, 133 N. Y. S. 2d 589 (1954), p. 78.
Associate Presbyterian Congregation of Hebron *v.* Hanna, 113 App. Div. 12, 98 N. Y. S. 1082 (1906), p. 78.
Ayers *v.* Methodist Episcopal Church, 3 Sandf. 361 (N. Y. Sup. Ct. 1849), p. 160.
Baxter *v.* McDonnell, 155 N. Y. 83, 49 N. E. 667, *reversing* App. Div. 235, 45 N. Y. S. 765 (1898), p. 52.
Bernstein *v.* Beth Israel Hospital, 236 N. Y. 268, 140 N. E. 694 (1923), pp. 100, 102.
Bing *v.* Thunig, 2 N. Y. 2d 656, 143 N. E. 2d 3 (1957), p. 101.
Board of Foreign Missionaries *v.* Board of Assessors, 244 N. Y. 42, 154 N. E. 816 (1926), pp. 92, 93.
Bogardus *v.* Trinity Church, 4 Paige 178 (N. Y. 1833), pp. 57, 58, 60.
Bogardus *v.* Trinity Church, 15 Wend. 111 (N. Y. 1835), p. 58.
Bogardus *v.* Trinity Church, 4 Sandf. Ch. 633 (N. Y. 1846), p. 59.
Boscom *v.* Alberton, 34 N. Y. 584 (1866), p. 140.
Bowen *v.* Irish Presbyterian Congregation, 19 N. Y. Super. Ct. 245 (1860), p. 78.
Boyles *v.* Roberts, 222 Mo. 613, 121 S. W. 805 (1905), p. 83.
Bowman *v.* Domestic and Foreign Missionary Society, 182 N. Y. 494, 75 N. E. 535 (1905), *modifying* 100 App. Div. 29, 90 N. Y. S. 898 (1904), *reversing* 42 Misc. 574, 87 N. Y. S. 621, pp. 142, 143.

In re Logossa, 163 Misc. 628, 297 N. Y. S. 730 (1937), p. 166.

In re Lyon, 280 N. Y. 391, 21 N. E. 2d 265 (1939), p. 161.

In re MacDowell's Will, 217 N. Y. 454, 112 N. E. 177 (1916), pp. 142, 143, 144.

In re Mawhinney, 146 Misc. 30, 261 N. Y. S. 334, *aff'd* 239 App. Div. 874, 264 N. Y. S. 984 (1933), p. 166.

In re Mergentime's Estate, 129 App. Div. 367, 113 N. Y. S. 948 (1908), *aff'd without opinion,* 195 N. Y. 572, 88 N. E. 1125 (1909), p. 94.

In re Merritt's Will, 171 Misc. 812, 14 N. Y. S. 2d 103, *aff'd* 258 App. Div. 188, 16 N. Y. S. 2d 1 (1939), p. 157.

In re Pessano's Estate, 180 Misc. 829, 45 N. Y. S. 2d 877 (1943), p. 71.

In re Plaster's Will, 266 App. Div. 439, 43 N. Y. S. 2d 1, *aff'd* 293 N. Y. 822, 59 N. E. 2d 181 (1943), pp. 166, 167.

In re Robinson, 203 N. Y. 380, 96 N. E. 925 (1911), pp. 143, 144, 145, 148, 157.

In re Rockefeller, 177 App. Div. 791, 165 N. Y. S. 154 (1917), p. 145.

In re Rowland's Will, 225 App. Div. 118, 232 N. Y. S. 127, p. 167.

In re St. Ann's Church, 23 How. Prac. 285, 14 Abb. Prac. 424 (N. Y. 1862), p. 77.

In re Shattuck's Will, 193 N. Y. 446, 86 N. E. 455 (1908), p. 143.

In re Sonderling's Will, 157 Misc. 231, 283 N. Y. S. 568 (1935), pp. 167, 168.

In re Scott, 31 Misc. 85, 64 N. Y. S. 577 (1900), p. 161.

In re Sheifer's Estate, 178 Misc. 340, 34 N. Y. S. 2d 302 (1942), p. 144.

In re Tiffany's Estate, 157 Misc. 873, 285 N. Y. S. 791 (1935), pp. 145, 148, 153.

In re Tone, 186 App. Div. 365, 174 N. Y. S. 391, *aff'y* 103 Misc. 618, 170 N. Y. S. 844 (1919), *aff'd on opinion below,* 226 N. Y. 696, 123 N. E. 892, p. 159.

In re Walter, 150 Misc. 512, 269 N. Y. S. 402 (1934), p. 150.

In re Watson's Estate, 177 Misc. 308, 30 N. Y. S. 2d 577 (1941), pp. 164, 166, 167.

In re Werner's Will, 181 N. Y. S. 534 (1919), p. 144.

In re Winburn, 139 Misc. 5, 247 N. Y. S. 583 (1931), p. 161.

Isham *v.* Tullager, 14 Abb. N. C. 363 (N. Y. 1881), p. 53.

Jackson *v.* Phillips, 14 Allen (Mass.) 539, p. 143.

Joel *v.* Woman's Hospital, 89 Hun. 73, 35 N. Y. S. 37 (N. Y. 1895), p. 99.

Johnston *v.* Hughes, 112 App. Div. 524, 98 N. Y. S. 525 (1906), *reversed on other grounds,* 187 N. Y. 446 (1907), p. 52.

Jones *v.* State, 28 Neb. 495, 44 N. W. 658 (1890), p. 81.

Kedroff *v.* St. Nicholas Cathedral, 344 U. S. 94 (1952), pp. 86, 87.

Kellogg *v.* Church Charity Foundation of Long Island, 203 N. Y. 191, 96 N. E. 406 (1911), p. 99.

Kerr's Appeal, 89 Pa. 97 (1879), p. 83.

Knickerbocker Hospital *v.* Goldstein, 181 Misc. 540, 41 N. Y. S. 2d 32 (1943), p. 152.

Lawyer *v.* Cipperly, 7 Paige 281 (N. Y. 1838), p. 47.

Levy *v.* Levy, 33 N. Y. 87 (1865), pp. 140, 145.

Lock *v.* Mayer, 50 Misc. 442, 100 N. Y. S. 837 (1906), p. 142.

Voorhees *v.* Presbyterian Church of Amsterdam, 17 Barb. Ch. 103 (N. Y. 1853), p. 138.

Wait *v.* Society for Political Study, 68 Misc. 250, 123 N. Y. S. 637 (1910), pp. 144, 162.

Walker Memorial Baptist Church *v.* Saunders, 285 N. Y. 462, 35 N. E. 2d 42 (1941), p. 53.

Walker *v.* Howell, 20 Misc. 236, 45 N. Y. S. 790 (1897), p. 80.

Washington Ave. Baptist Church *v.* Clark, 158 App. Div. 230, 140 N. Y. S. 1089 (1913), reversing 80 Misc. 306, 141 N. Y. S. 1, p. 142.

Watson *v.* Garvin, 54 Mo. 353 (1873), p. 81.

Watson *v.* Jones, 80 U. S. (13 Wall.) 679 (1872), pp. 81, 82, 86.

West Koshkonang Congregation *v.* Ottesen, 80 Wis. 62, 49 N. W. 24 (1891), p. 83.

Wetmore *v.* Parker, 52 N. Y. 450 (1873), p. 149.

Wheaton *v.* Gates, 18 N. Y. 395 (1858), pp. 78, 79.

White *v.* Howard, 46 N. Y. 144, *aff'y* Barb. Ch. 294 (1871), pp. 159, 162.

Williams *v.* Montgomery, 148 N. Y. 519, 43 N. E. 57 (1896), p. 152.

Williams *v.* Williams, 8 N. Y. 548, 4 Seld. 525 (1853), pp. 138, 139, 145.

Wilson *v.* Brooklyn Homeopathic Hospital, 97 App. Div. 37, 89 N. Y. S. 619 (1904), pp. 68, 100.

Wilson *v.* Tabernacle Baptist Church, 28 Misc. 268, 59 N. Y. S. 148 (1899).

Windt *v.* German Reformed Church, 4 Sand. Ch. 471 (N. Y. 1847), pp. 96, 97.

Wright *v.* Trustees of M. E. Church, 1 Hoffm. 263 (N. Y. Ch. Ct. 1839), p. 161.

Wyatt *v.* Benson, 23 Barb. 327 (N. Y. 1857), p. 76.

Yates *v.* Yates, 9 Barb. 324 (N. Y. 1850), p. 138.

ALPHABETICAL INDEX

BIOGRAPHICAL NOTE

Joseph P. Murphy was born on February 21, 1929, in New York City. He received his elementary education in St. Joseph's Parochial School in the same city. He entered the archdiocesan minor seminary, Cathedral College, in 1943, and St. Joseph's Seminary, Dunwoodie, N. Y., in 1948. From the latter he received the degree of Bachelor of Arts. He was ordained to the priesthood on May 14, 1954. In September of the same year he entered the School of Canon Law at the Catholic University of America. He received the Baccalaureate Degree in Canon Law in June, 1955, and the Licentiate Degree in Canon Law in June, 1956.

CANON LAW STUDIES *

375. KELLEHER, REV. FRANCIS T., A.B., J.C.L., Judicial expenses.
376. BANTIGUE, REV. PEDRO N., J.C.L., The Provincial Council of Manila of 1771. (Its text followed by a commentary on *Actio II, De Episcopis*.)
377. BURNS, REV. DENNIS J., J.C.L., Matrimonial indissolubility: contrary conditions.
378. DEUTSCH, REV. BERNARD F., J.C.L., Jurisdiction of pastors in the external forum.
379. DUNNIVAN, REV. JOHN P., A.B., J.C.L., Prejudicial attempts in pending litigation.
380. ERNST, REV. ALBERT C., A.B., J.C.L., Free admission to church for sacred rites.
381. FRATTIN, PETER LOUIS, J.C.L., The matrimonial impediment of impotence: occlusion of the spermatic ducts and vaginismus.
382. HENRY, REV. CHARLES W., O.S.B., A.B., S.T.L., J.C.L., Canonical Relations between bishops and abbots at the beginning of the tenth century.
383. HOFFMAN, REV. LAWRENCE J., A.B., J.C.L., Clergy conference: Canon 131.
384. MARKHAM, REV. JAMES J., A.B., S.T.L., J.C.L., The Sacred Congregation of Seminaries and Universities of Studies.
385. McGRATH, REV. JOHN J., A.B., LL.B., J.C.L., A comparative study of crime and its imputability in ecclesiastical criminal law and in American criminal law.
386. McGUIRE, REV. JAMES D., O.R.S.A., J.C.L., The postulancy.
387. MUNDAY, REV. JAMES E., J.C.L., Ecclesiastical property in Australia and New Zealand.
388. MURPHY, REV. JOSEPH P., A.B., J.C.L., The laws of the State of New York affecting church property.
389. PICKARD, REV. WILLIAM M., J.C.L., Judicial experts: a source of evidence in ecclesiastical trials.
390. RUDDY, REV. JAMES, J.C.L., The Apostolic Constitution *Christus Dominus*: text, translation and commentary, with short annotations on the Motu Proprio *Sacram Communionem*.
391. VANYO, REV. LEO V., A.B., J.C.L., Requisites of intention in the reception of the sacraments.

---

* For a complete list of the available numbers of this series apply to the Catholic University of America Press, 620 Michigan Avenue, N.E., Washington (17), D. C., for a general catalog.